Taking Game Fish

**From
Dry Flies
to
Downrigger
Fishing**

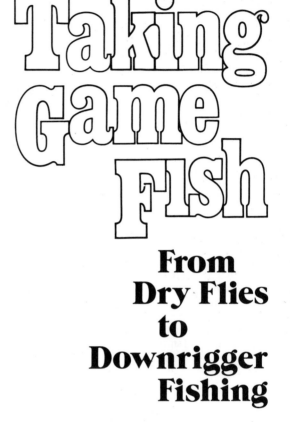

Taking Game Fish

From Dry Flies to Downrigger Fishing

A Freshwater Fishing Anthology Edited by Todd Swainbank
Illustrated by Gordon L. Eggleston

The Crossing Press/Trumansburg, New York 14886

PHOTO CREDITS
Cover photo of J. Michael Kimball by Jill Kimball.
Bill Butler—58, 63, 75; Roger Coyle—269; Gordon Eggleston—108, 109, 115, 146, 150; Niles Eggleston—86; Ron Howard—11, 236, 240; Jill Kimball—181, 188, 216; Mike Kimball—217; Kris Lee—223; Pam Swainbank—130; Todd Swainbank—32, 34, 40; Nelson Wertman—251,265.

Library of Congress Cataloging in Publication Data

Main entry under title:

Taking game fish

1. Fishing. I. Swainbank, Todd
SH441.T34   799.1'2   79-20982
ISBN 0-89594-026-4
ISBN 0-89594-025-6 pbk.

Introduction

Many novice anglers feel that Lady Luck governs success or failure. Nothing could be further from the truth. Though there is an occasional fish caught by luck, most fish are caught by skill. Or, phrased another way, 10 percent of the fishermen catch 90 percent of the fish, because those 10 percent are experts.

This book will make a better fisherman out of you. It is written by 6 expert anglers who convey a tremendous amount of information on tackle and technique for a wide variety of fish.

This information is not limited to any one section of this country. Game fish have similar preferences wherever they are found.

Read the book, practice what is preached and more than likely you'll catch more fish and have more fun doing it.

See you fishin' —

Todd Swainbank

Contents

1/Panfish:
Fishing for Fun

by Ron Howard

Panfish are not glamorous. Most of them weigh less than a pound and very few will pose a serious threat to your tackle. Considered "kids' fish" by most anglers, very few will be found adorning trophy room walls. But panfish are everyone's fish; they are fun to catch, available, aggressive and spunky. They provide enough challenge for the experienced angler and yet are easy enough for a beginner. In contrast to more glamorous species, they don't require specialized tackle or sophisticated techniques for success. In fact, panfish offer a respite from the competitive atmosphere of game fishing and a return to the simple pleasures of just plain fishing.

Panfish is a generic term for many members of the sunfish, perch, temperate bass and catfish families. Some anglers might also include a few minnows, suckers and even the pickerel. Heaviest fishing pressure is on bluegills, pumpkinseeds, crappies, rock bass, yellow perch, white bass, white perch and bullheads, with species like shell-crackers and yellow bass being important in some regions.

The tackle used to take these fish ranges from handlines and cane poles to ultralight fly or spin tackle. The fish are not overly fussy about the type of tackle as long as the bait or lure is in the right place at the right time and presented without excessive disturbance. Using ultralight spinning tackle with tiny

lures or light fly tackle with deer hair bugs or fairly large
nymphs adds to the pleasure of panfishing because the light
tackle lets these relatively small fish put on a good show and aids
in good presentation under clear water conditions. Most panfish
are strong, dogged fighters, quite large for their size; thus they
provide angling fun and thrills that go beyond their actual
weight.

Panfish eat almost anything smaller than they are. In
fact, human swimmers might not be safe if these aggressive fish
reached 10 to 20 pounds. Many of the centrarchids (sunfish) and
and large perch feed heavily on insect larvae, crustaceans, small
mollusks and smaller fish. Others like white bass and crappies
are almost exclusively minnow eaters. Food preferences often
dictate their habitat. Bait fishermen can increase their
effectiveness by studying the feeding preferences of the type of
fish being sought.

Small minnows, worms, insect larvae, small crayfish,
crickets, grasshoppers and similar baits are excellent natural
panfish catchers. Miniature plugs, small spoons or spinners, very
small spinner baits and tiny jigs will all take panfish and small
plastic grub-tailed jigs are effective on many species. Although
standard sized lures will attract strikes, only outsized specimens
(or unlucky ones) will be hooked on them. The smaller lures fit
their mouths better, bringing a greater proportion of productive
strikes. A standard assortment of trout flies, scaled down bass
poppers or hair bugs and sponge rubber crickets or spiders make
a good fly rod assortment for panfish. Tactics for presenting
these baits or lures are similar to those discussed in other
chapters of this book. Still-fishing, either on the bottom or using
a bobber to suspend the bait, is a simple but very effective
approach to catching panfish.

Just as their food preferences are varied, so are their
habitats. Yellow perch prefer different habitats, their choice
being dependent on size and sex. Smaller fish, mostly males, are
found in relatively shallow water, often among weeds. Larger
jack perch, mostly females, are found in much deeper water.
Most members of the sunfish family are found in relatively

shallow weedy areas, but the larger specimens may be located in deeper areas or along dropoffs. Crappies are often in shallow water during the spring but they, like black bass, may suspend in the thermocline during the summer. The temperate basses like white perch and yellow bass are found in deep areas of rivers as well as in lakes or ponds. The lake populations are primarily pelagic—that is, they are usually at middle depths following schools of bait fish. Thus, a bluegill fisherman may hunt for spawning beds in relatively shallow water or search for schooled fish along the edges of weedy dropoffs. Crappie anglers may look for shallow cover or sunken treetops during spawning season, but they concentrate on suspended fish during the summer and winter. White bass fishermen often must chase schooling fish on the surface of large lakes. In other words, tactics must be adjusted to the fishing being done.

Panfish are easy to catch – perfect for teaching youngsters how to fish.

Because they are not usually as skittish as game fish, panfish are an excellent training ground for beginning anglers. For experienced anglers, panfish provide simple fun fishing. They are truly action fish providing sport when other fishing is slow. Fishing for larger specimens can provide sufficient challenge for any angler as well as the satisfaction of a relatively constant flow of strikes. A lost fish or missed strike will more frequently bring a laugh than an expletive. Panfishing is relaxed fishing.

To get outsized specimens of any panfish species, you need special tactics. Tactics suitable for bass, walleyes or other game fish (covered elsewhere in this book) are usually appropriate.

Feel free to experiment, adapting your techniques to local conditions.

Most of these species are very prolific. They grow fast, reproduce early and produce large numbers of young. They prey on smaller fishes, insects and other aquatic life, while forming a forage base for larger predators. Since most fishing pressure is on the larger predatory fishes, heavily fished lakes may become overpopulated with panfish which then become stunted. Game fish often grow well under such conditions, but they are difficult to catch and their reproduction is poor because their young must compete with numerous young panfish for food and space. Removing panfish, therefore, is an excellent management tool, and anglers should feel free to keep as many fish as they wish to use.

A significant part of the fun in panfishing is in the eating. Most panfish are excellent table fare if they are handled with care to retain their quality. For best results, they should be kept alive and/or on ice until they are prepared for consumption. Since much panfishing is done in summer, the ice chest is usually a better choice than a crowded stringer for preserving peak flavor.

Panfish may be pan dressed or filleted in preparation for the table. Their abundance, by the way, makes them an excellent choice for teaching youngsters how to clean fish. Most panfish are cleaned by scaling them and removing the entrails, fins and head. Scaling may be done several ways. The scales come off best if the knife or scaler is moved against the grain of the scales, that is, from tail to head. The scales will come off much less easily if the fish is scaled from head to tail.

Some anglers prefer to skin panfish like yellow perch and bluegills. The fish is cleaned as usual; but rather than scale it, the angler cuts the skin along the back from head to tail and peels the skin off using pliers or a knife blade to grip it. Bullheads and other catfish require skinning. The most frequently used method involves hanging the fish on a mounted spike and pulling the skin off using a pair of pliers.

Fish may be filleted by cutting behind the operculum, then down along the spinal ray on each side of the spine. A thin, flexible knife is slid along the bones, peeling the flesh from the skeleton. The fillets may be skinned by slipping the knife between the skin and flesh and sawing toward the head end of the fillet while keeping the skin very tight. With a little practice, the technique will become a smooth and efficient processing method.

Panfish is generally fried, either in a pan or deepfried with a tempura batter or any favorite coating. But they also can be boiled, steamed, poached or broiled. They can be used in nearly every fish recipe including chowder. Be creative. For example, you may wish to boil the fillets in seasoned water, flake the meat and use it in salads, just as you would tuna.

Some type of panfish can be taken at any time of year, under any water conditions and at any time of day. The best time to fish for them is whenever you can get out during the time of year when the particular fish is most accessible, like May and June for bedding bluefills. Panfish are abundant and willing. Study your local waters to build a repertoire of fishing spots and times. Try panfishing, just for the fun of it!

2/Largemouth Bass Basics

by Bill Butler

It has often been stated that 10% of the fishermen catch 90% of the fish. That may be an exaggerated estimate, but it is a fact that certain anglers always are successful, while others experience mixed results at best. The reason for this is not some new secret lure or technique. Successful bass fishermen or for that matter *all* successful fishermen, are engaged in a never ending learning process; the most important tool a bass angler has is his head. Every fishing trip should be viewed as a new learning experience. The successful bass fisherman learns to apply his accumulated knowledge to the methods he uses.

The largemouth bass, *Micropterus salmoides,* is a product of his environment in each different body of water. What this means is that environmental factors such as amount of cover, depth, water clarity, *etc.* will cause bass to behave differently in one lake than in another. Therefore, the same largemouth that school up in 30 feet of water on a submerged point in a deep clear impoundment like Table Rock in Missouri might be found in 6 to 10 feet of water on weedlines in Oneida Lake in upstate New York. The bass in each body of water relate to the conditions around them. The ability to read these conditions enables the successful fisherman to find the fish on any given lake or river. The ability to analyze the environmental factors around him leads the successful bass angler to correct lure selection and presentation. When he begins to catch fish, he is establishing the pattern for that particular day. Catching the fish is the easy part ... locating them is what separates the very successful angler from the others.

Factors that Influence Success

Many different factors are taken into consideration by the successful bass fisherman. We will examine some of these and discuss how they relate to the largemouth bass population from lake to lake.

Season of the Year. This is a primary factor in determining where the bass should be. Each season will cause the fish to move to a new location on most bodies of water.

Type of Lake. Bass in a deep clear lake will not be found in the same places as they will be on a shallow, weedy body of water.

Size of Lake. Obviously, a larger lake offers more possibilities and choices in searching for Mr. Bass. Small farm ponds often will have one or two primary holding points for the bass population, while a large lake such as Lake Champlain offers never ending possibilities for both the fisherman and the fish.

While discussing types and sizes of lakes, let's list the basic categories that are generally found in the United States:

Deep, clear, natural lakes. Lakes with depths of over 50 feet, predominately rock or gravel bottom, with aquatic vegetation found along shorelines and in coves. Good examples of this type would be the Finger Lakes in upstate New York. These lakes usually have populations of both largemouth and smallmouth bass, as well as other game fish.

Shallow, natural lakes. This type of lake, seldom exceeding 30 feet in depth, has far more aquatic vegetation. The bottom varies from rock to mud and the bottom contour variations are less extreme than on the deeper lakes. A good example of this type is Oneida Lake in upstate New York, and certain portions of Lake Champlain.

Natural, "dishpan" lakes. Extremely shallow, with very heavy vegetation, and a muck bottom with little variation. Lake Toho in Florida is an excellent example of a "dishpan" lake with miles and miles of 4 to 6 foot deep water filled with heavy aquatic vegetation.

Man-made reservoirs. These are common in the South and West. They are generally created by construction of a dam across an existing river or stream, and the surrounding terrain is permanently flooded. Because of this, man-made impoundments offer various types of cover and structure not found in natural lakes. Standing timber, old roads and railroads, and entire fields of bushes and shrubs are covered by water in these impoundments and create fishing conditions unlike any found on natural bodies of water. Most reservoirs have both very shallow and very deep sections. Aquatic vegetation is not as common as on natural lakes.

Other factors to consider when locating bass:

Water Temperature. Bass are cold blooded with their body temperature and metabolism fluctuating with the water temperature. When the water temperature is below 50 degrees, bass are extremely sluggish and do not feed actively. At 55 degrees, bass become more active and when the water temperature reaches 65 to 70 degrees in the spring, bass will be very active. Their preferred temperature range in the summer is 68 to 74 degrees, and they will hold at whatever depth is necessary to be in approximately that range. However, bass will frequent 80 degree and warmer shallows in midsummer at certain times when feeding. The preferred temperature range is not without exceptions, but it is a good base to begin with in understanding how water temperature can affect your fishing success.

Aquatic Vegetation. Lily pads, reeds, bullrushes and various weedlines all are used by bass as protective cover at various times. The type and amount of vegetation where you are fishing will help determine your bait selection and presentation.

Shoreline Type. Some shorelines will attract bass better than others. Fallen trees, boat docks and overhanging bushes will be much more productive under most circumstances than a beach or barren mud bank.

Amount of Sunlight. Since bass don't have eyelids, they are sensitive to bright light. As a result, on extremely sunny days they will seek protection from the sun.

Water Clarity. This should help determine what color lure you choose as well as how close you can fish to whatever cover you have in mind. Extremely clear water means using a lighter test line. It is a fact that on clear bodies of water a fisherman using 6 pound test line will generally have better success than someone in the same boat using 20 pound line.

Food Availability. There is an old saying on the Bass Tournament trail that goes, "Find the food, find the fish." What it means is that the most promising area on a lake will be devoid of bass unless natural forage (such as minnows, crayfish, frogs, insects, *etc.*) is available.

If you find a good looking bay or cove and you see schools of minnows, chances are you will find that bass are in the area at some time during the day. Game fish such as bass follow their food supply. That is why on southern reservoirs, a common practice is to search for schools of shad, which is the primary forage fish for bass. I have also applied this technique to northern bodies of water like Lake Champlain, where I located bass and northern pike chasing giant schools of shiners or yellow perch.

Bottom Structure. This is a key factor to consider when searching for bass. Are there dropoffs or underwater knolls on the lake you are fishing? The underwater contours of the lake along with the time of year are the two most important factors to analyze when bass fishing. Good topographical maps are as important to the modern bass fisherman as anything he can buy in a tackle store. A tournament bass fisherman would not think of seriously fishing without a good map. The best maps are published by the United States Government agencies such as the Army Corps of Engineers or the U.S. Geologic Survey. These maps provide information concerning depth, dropoffs, ridges, sharp rises, points, holes, and other bottom structures where fish love to hang out. By checking the obvious places on the map, you can begin to put together a pattern even on a lake you are visiting for the first time.

Other factors, such as the amount of boat traffic, water quality, bottom composition and time of day all enter into the bass fishing picture as well as the points already discussed.

Cover and Structure

Now that we have looked at the various factors that should be considered when fishing, let's discuss specific types of cover and structure frequented by largemouth bass on both natural lakes and man-made reservoirs. Remember, bass like cover and structure because it harbors food and provides protection.

NATURAL LAKES

Primary and Secondary Dropoffs. The average lake will slope gradually from shore from 0 to 10 feet then quickly drop to 15 or 20 feet. That quick drop to 20 feet is the primary dropoff and is generally the end of the primary food zone as well as most aquatic vegetation. Then, further out, there is an additional dropoff to 30 or 40 feet. This second ledge is the secondary dropoff. In most lakes, largemouth bass are found on the primary dropoff, but not the secondary. Smallmouth bass will hold on the secondary dropoff if it has a hard consistency. The primary food zone is where most of your fishing efforts should be focused.

Shallow, Weedy Bays. This is an ideal spot to find largemouth in the spring. Depending on the consistency of the bottom, bass may spawn in such locations. Once spring is past, bass may move in to feed in the early morning or evening, but during the rest of the day, this type of bay won't be very productive. (See page 20.)

In the spring, these areas should be extensively fished using shallow water or top water baits, as well as plastic worms. Small openings in the middle of visible grass or pads should not be ignored. Bass will often use these spots as ambush points for

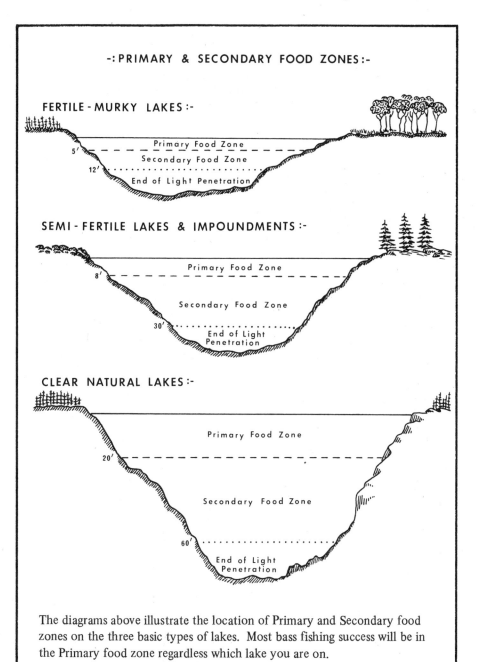

-: PRIMARY & SECONDARY FOOD ZONES :-

FERTILE - MURKY LAKES :-

5'
Primary Food Zone
Secondary Food Zone
12'
End of Light Penetration

SEMI - FERTILE LAKES & IMPOUNDMENTS :-

8'
Primary Food Zone

Secondary Food Zone

30'
End of Light
Penetration

CLEAR NATURAL LAKES :-

Primary Food Zone

20'

Secondary Food Zone

60'
End of Light
Penetration

The diagrams above illustrate the location of Primary and Secondary food zones on the three basic types of lakes. Most bass fishing success will be in the Primary food zone regardless which lake you are on.

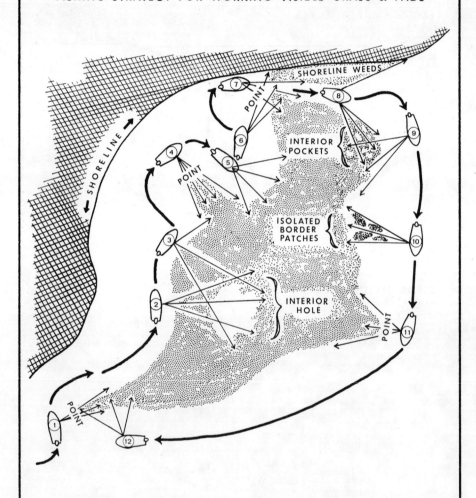

Fish all points, edges and openings in visible grass or pads. This is very good cover for bass, especially during the early season.

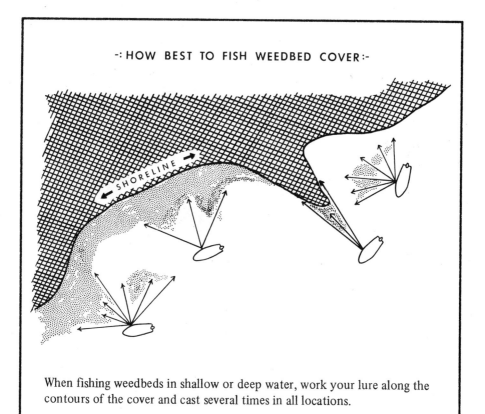

-: HOW BEST TO FISH WEEDBED COVER :-

SHORELINE

When fishing weedbeds in shallow or deep water, work your lure along the contours of the cover and cast several times in all locations.

baitfish. Common types of vegetation in these bays are lily pads, reeds, bullrushes, and milfoil.

Weedbeds in Deeper Water. Weeds growing in deeper water, such as combomba, cabbage weed, or coontail weeds offer excellent bass cover and should always be carefully fished. Combomba and cabbage weeds can grow as deep as 20 feet, while coontail stops at about 8 to 10 feet. These weedbeds should be fished on all sides along with any open pockets in the middle of the bed.

Isolated Deep Hole. Especially on a very shallow lake, a deeper hole will attract bass as a refuge from light, surface noise, or boating disturbances.

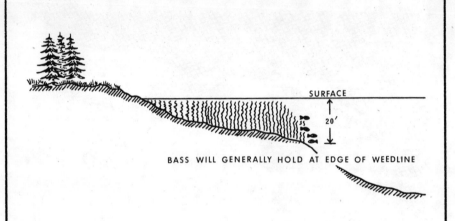

-: FISHING A WEEDLINE :-

SURFACE

20'

BASS WILL GENERALLY HOLD AT EDGE OF WEEDLINE

The weedline is the *outside edge* of the weed growth coming out from the shoreline. Usually associated with the primary dropoff, it is an excellent spot to find bass during most of the warm weather season. The weedline or outside edge will be in 6 to 20 feet of water, depending upon water clarity. The clearer the lake, the deeper the weedline will be.

Submerged Reefs. Underwater rockpiles are well known smallmouth hangouts, but largemouth bass will also frequent these spots, especially if they are no deeper than 30 feet.

Weedlines. The weedline is generally considered the outside edge of the weedgrowth coming out from the shoreline. As stated earlier, this outside edge is often right at or near the primary dropoff and generally is no deeper than 20 feet. However, the outside edge of the weedline provides shelter, protection, and a point of ambush for bass in their search for food. This is a primary area for bass in the summer when the shallows are warmer than the preferred temperature range. On natural lakes, weedlines are key features to look for when searching for bass.

Underwater Saddles or Trenches. These depressions in the bottom are good spots in summertime on natural lakes, especially if some type of cover such as deep weedbeds are nearby to attract baitfish.

Mouths of Creeks and Rivers. In early spring, largemouth will congregate where feeder streams enter the lake, because of the warmer water moving in. This is usually a pre-spawn condition however, and once the lake temperature reaches 65 degrees these areas no longer seem to hold the fish.

Submerged Weedbeds. If you have a depthfinder you can often find weedbeds that do not appear on the surface. These areas generally hold fish because they offer protection, good depth and baitfish.

Fallen Trees or Brush in Water. Usually found along the shoreline or in coves, this type of cover offers excellent

-: UNDERWATER TRENCH OR SADDLE :-

Illustrated above is a typical summer bass pattern around weedbeds. The bottom contours show a deep trench or saddle as well as a submerged knoll. Both are bass hotspots.

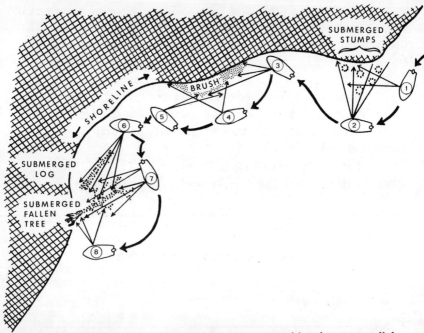

-: FISHING SUBMERGED TREES, STUMPS, LOGS & BRUSH :-

When fishing fallen trees, submerged logs, stumps and brush, cast parallel repeatedly along the cover. Work all sides and angles of the obstacles. If it is a bright day, *always* fish the shady side first because bass will avoid bright sunlight.

protection and usually attracts baitfish. However, if the surrounding water is less than 5 feet deep, this area may only be productive in the spring. However, if the water has sufficient depth, fish will hold there all season. Even if found in shallow water, this spot could produce all summer in the very early morning.

Rubble-rock or Riprap. Usually found along man-made structures such as bridges, marinas or roadways running along

-: STRATEGY FOR FISHING PIERS & DOCKS :-

SIDE VIEW (Sun to front):

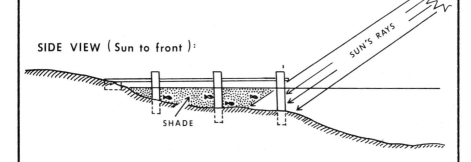

SUN'S RAYS

SHADE

TOP VIEW (Sun to the side):

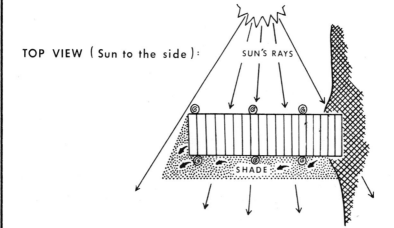

SUN'S RAYS

SHADE

When fishing piers or docks, remember that the bass will hold near the pilings. If it is a bright day, fish on the shaded side first.

water. This is an excellent spring hangout for bass. The rocks tend to heat up and warm the water, providing a great home for crayfish, a favorite in the bass diet. If sufficiently deep water is nearby, bass will use this riprap as a feeding area all season.

Piers, Boat Docks, and Boat Houses. These offer cover, protection, and attract baitfish. They should be fished in the spring, because they generally are in water less than 10 feet deep. (See page 25.)

Underwater Points. These are points extending from the shoreline toward deeper water. Bass move up on a point to feed and can generally be found off the deeper end of certain points all season long, once spawning is completed.

Bridges and Bridge Pilings. Depending on the depth of the surrounding water, bass will use these man-made objects as cover

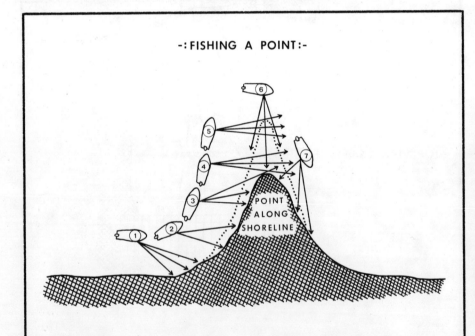

-: FISHING A POINT :-

When fishing a point, a crankbait or jig will be very effective. Saturate the entire area and be sure to remember that the point extends out toward open water.

and protection. This type of cover should be fished vertically, to cover all depths available.

MAN-MADE RESERVOIRS

Man-made reservoirs provide types of structure and cover that do not exist in natural lakes. To find these types of structure, a good map and depthfinder are needed.

Old River or Creek Bed. When the reservoir was constructed, the original river or creek was dammed up and the surrounding area flooded. However, the bed of that original river or creek, with all of its bends, holes, and configurations is still a prime bass area because it is like a deep trench that winds its way throughout the impoundment.

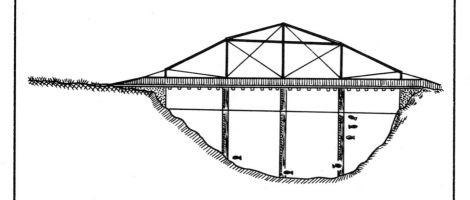

-: BRIDGE PILINGS...GOOD DEEP WATER STRUCTURES :-

Bridge pilings are easily fished with jigs, tail-spinners or plastic worms. This is excellent summer and winter cover when bass are deep.

Where creek beds meet the river bed is a key spot because bass will use these beds as migratory paths.

Stump Fields. Before many of the reservoirs were flooded standing timber was cut to prevent boating problems. However, the remaining underwater stumps and roots are usually very productive, depending on the depth of the water. Any small trees or brush left uncut becomes great bass cover once the area is flooded.

Old Road Beds and Drainage Ditches. Most roads are slightly elevated with ditches on either side. When underwater, these represent good fish-holding structure and should be checked out.

Seasonal Patterns

Beginning with the end of winter, the early spring movement of largemouth bass is from deep water to the warmest available areas. During this period, bass will seek out shallow, weedy bays and coves, boat docks or gradually sloping shorelines.

As the water continues to warm up with the coming of spring, the fish will seek out nesting areas. Largemouth prefer a slightly hard bottom for their nest, but they will use a tangle of roots or vegetation if nothing better is available. Spawning time is generally controlled by weather conditions and water temperature. In northern waters bass generally spawn from early May into June. Obviously, the spawning period is earlier the farther south you travel. For the spawn to begin, the water temperature usually must be at least 65 degrees. Fishing for spawning bass is shallow water fishing—you can often see the fish guarding the nest. Fish caught during this period, in my opinion, should always be released. This will help protect your fishing resource for future years.

After the spawn, summer patterns begin. As the weedlines become established, the largemouth congregate at locations offering cover and access to deep water. They will still migrate to shallow water feeding areas, but pounding the bank in 2 feet of water at midafternoon is now a waste of time.

This is the mistake made by most beginning bass anglers— that lily pad field or fallen tree in 2 feet of water that was so productive in early spring still looks great, and the novice bass fisherman spends hours casting surface plugs or spinnerbaits at this type of cover.

However, in the summer the bass have moved to deeper water where the temperature is in the preferred range, and cover is still available. Weedlines, dropoffs, points, underwater weedbeds, *etc.* now are the haunts you have to seek out if you want to be successful.

In very early morning or at night, the bass will move to the shallows to feed, but then move back to deeper water.

As summer ends, the largemouth will begin to frequent the shallows again as the water cools down. They also seem to sense the approach of winter; an angler can get great catches in fall because the fish are feeding heavily in preparation for the lean months ahead.

As the temperature drops below 40 degrees at night, the bass move out of the shallows and school up in their winter home, usually along dropoffs and points in at least 15 feet of water, if it is available. They can be caught at this time, but they are sluggish and the bait must be worked very slowly.

Basic Bass Lures

PLASTIC WORMS

The plastic worm was first introduced about 25 years ago. It is by far the most popular bass bait, although it is difficult to fish effectively. A keen sense of feel must be developed: the good worm fisherman can feel with his hands exactly what the worm is doing as he crawls it over, around and through various types of cover. The worm can be fished shallow or deep and can be rigged in many different ways. The most popular worm rig is

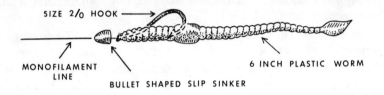

-: TEXAS WORM RIG :-

SIZE 2/0 HOOK

MONOFILAMENT LINE

BULLET SHAPED SLIP SINKER

6 INCH PLASTIC WORM

The Texas Worm Rig is the most commonly used. However, the worm can also be rigged to fit almost any fishing situation.

the Texas style rig where the hook point is turned back into the worm to make it weedless.

The sinker size should be as light as possible, and the hook size should increase or decrease with the size of the worm. Generally accepted hook and worm matchups are as follows:

Worm	Hook
4"	1
6"	1/0 - 2/0
7"	2/0 - 3/0
9"	4/0 - 5/0

Also important when worm fishing is keeping slack out of your line and watching the point where your line enters the water for any telltale taps that you couldn't feel. Many bass caught on worms are caught because the angler saw his line move, even though he didn't feel anything. Set the hook immediately, as it is a fact that a bass can inhale and exhale a worm in less than one second. The rod you use when worm fishing should be stiff enough to allow you to solidly set the hook.

Plastic worms come in a rainbow of colors and many different sizes and styles. The most popular colors on the Pro Bass tournament circuit are purple, black, blue, brown, and strawberry. Are colors important? Yes, colors can make a difference depending on particular fishing conditions. In very clear water, blue is a good choice. Black is good in virtually all conditions. In very muddy water many of the pros use yellowish colors. Purple offers excellent contrast with the surrounding cover.

When you are worm fishing, try to develop your sense of feel and watch your line. The hook should be set immediately when anything is seen or felt. Another thing to remember is *never* work the rod and reel at the same time. Take your rod tip from about 9 o'clock to 11, and then reel in the slack. Repeat this process, crawling the worm along the bottom. This is a good basic retrieve for learning how to fish the plastic worm. However, the worm can also be hopped, jiggled or rapidly crawled. There is no one standard way to fish this bait, which is why it is so much fun.

The most popular sizes are 4, 6, 7, 8, and 9 inch, with 6 inch being a good size to start with. Recently, plastic lizards, which are generally fished the same way, have become very popular.

The worm is a great bait in all seasons of the year and can be rigged so many different ways it can be applied to almost any fishing situation.

SPINNERBAITS

The basic spinnerbait concept is a V-shaped safety-pin type wire frame with one or two spinners on the top wire and a hair, rubber or vinyl skirt around the hook on the bottom wire. Spinnerbaits are easily the second most popular bass bait, behind the plastic worm. There are many different versions and sizes on the market today: the angler can choose baits with large blades, small blades, the new propeller-style buzzing baits, single blades and tandemspins.

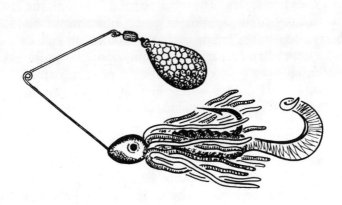

Spinnerbaits are deadly on both largemouth and smallmouth bass. Most anglers dress the hook with a twister type grub or pork rind.

Bill Butler Sr. and Jr. with a stringer of lunker northern largemouth taken by buzzing spinnerbaits around fallen trees in 12 feet of water.

The vinyl or rubber skirted versions are more popular than hair. The most popular sizes are 1/8, 1/4, 3/8, and 1/2 ounce, with 1/4 ounce being a good all-around size. Colors that are popular include chartreuse, white, black and yellow. A general rule for colors is to use a bright lure on a bright day and a dark lure on a dark day.

Some spinnerbait terms are:

Buzzing. This is a very popular method where the bait is retrieved on or just under the surface, and the blades or propellers create a very noticeable wake on the surface. Recently, special spinnerbaits called buzz baits have been developed especially for this style of fishing. Instead of standard blades, they feature a large propeller to churn up the surface.

-: FLUTTER FISHING THE SPINNER BAIT :-

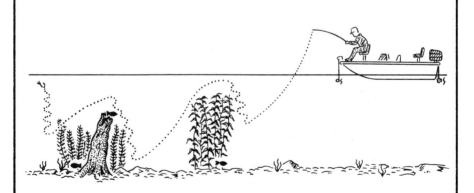

The flutter-fishing method is very effective and should be tried whenever spinnerbaits are used. Let the bait drop vertically and flutter its way toward the bottom.

Bill Butler Jr. with a lunker largemouth taken in heavy cover on a spinnerbait. The fish would not take a standard retrieve, but when the spinnerbait was allowed to drop straight down, or flutter-fished, the bass inhaled it.

Drop-fishing or Flutter Fishing. This is a very good technique to use around fallen trees, docks, bridge pilings, or in open spaces in weeds or pads. The spinnerbait is allowed to free-fall toward the bottom, which will cause the blade or blades to revolve. Most of the pros use a short-armed single spin for this technique. (See page 33.)

Trailer Hook. A good way to make sure you hook your fish is to use a trailer hook. The eye of a second hook is slipped over the first hook giving you double hooking capacity.

Tuning your Spinnerbait. Make sure the upper arm with the blades is directly over top of the hook. The bait should not lean to either side when retrieved. Spinnerbaits can be used all year long, but they are especially effective when the bass are shallow in spring and fall. The standard retrieve is to reel the bait back about 12 inches under the surface, so it is still visible. As discussed earlier, it can also be drop-fished or buzzed on the surface. An added feature of the spinnerbait is that it is a very good bait for fishing in weeds or logs, because the top arm protects the hook. It can actually be crawled over and through fallen trees without getting hung up when the rod is in the hands of a skilled angler.

When casting a spinnerbait at a stump or group of pads, be sure to cast beyond the target and bring the bait back past it. If you cast directly at the target area, the resulting splash may scare off the fish.

Another helpful idea is to use a twister tail on your spinnerbait for added action. Both the plastic twister worms or pork rind strips are excellent for this purpose.

The biggest mistake you can make when using a spinnerbait is to use only one type of retrieve. Experiment with different techniques and you will find that one retrieve will work best on one day whereas the very next day something else will be better.

Also, develop the ability to work that spinnerbait through the thickest cover you can find. Old Ironjaw is in there waiting for you!

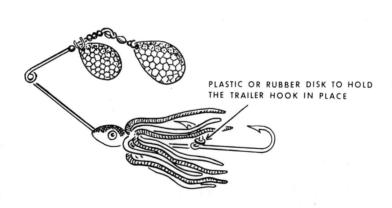

PLASTIC OR RUBBER DISK TO HOLD
THE TRAILER HOOK IN PLACE

A trailer hook provides extra hooking power, especially if the fish are striking short. A small plastic or rubber disk will hold the trailer hook in place.

CRANKBAITS

The growth in popularity experienced in recent years by crankbaits can be traced to a lure called the Big O developed in Tennessee in the early 1970's. This original plug looked like a pregnant minnow, floated at rest and when retrieved would wiggle its way back about 6 feet under the surface. Crankbaits are any plug following this same basic concept. They come in various sizes, shapes, and colors; the depth to which they will dive on retrieve is dependent on the size and angle of slant of the lip on the bait.

Today you can buy crankbaits that swim inches under the surface, or dive to 15 feet. They are made of plastic or balsa wood. The most popular sizes for bass are 1/8, 1/4, 3/8, and 1/2 ounce.

Some of the more popular crankbaits are the Rebel Wee-R, Mann's Deep Pig, Norman's Deep N and Little N, and Bagley's Balsa B's.

Crankbaits can be fished rapidly or just crawled along. The fisherman who is successful with these lures continually varies his retrieve.

Use crankbaits all season long. Choose the appropriate type for the depth you are fishing and go get em!

GRUBS AND LEADHEAD JIGS

The small plastic grub was initially developed as a bait for salt water speckled trout. However the tournament pros consider the grub and jighead combination to be one of the best baits that can be used.

Jigging is similar to worm fishing because you must develop a keen sense of feel and watch your line very closely.

About 90% of the time, bass will hit a grub on the fall. The only indication of the fish will be a very slight movement at the point where the line enters the water. The hook should be immediately set.

Grub fishing is especially effective for vertically jigging bridge pilings or deep structure such as rock piles or sunken

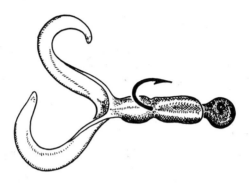

Jigs and dressings come in many shapes and sizes. The flattened slider type head and double tail Super Tail is a popular combination for bass and other game fish.

depressions or points. Jigging is productive all season long if done properly.

The most popular sizes for bassing are 2 to 4 inch grubs on a 1/8 to 1/2 ounce leadhead jig, depending on what depth you are fishing.

The Twister-tail style grub is a very good choice because the tail has quite a bit of extra action. Because these baits are small, 6 to 12 pound line is the best choice. Because of the light line, most of the pros favor open faced spinning reels and a light 5½ to 6 foot spinning rod, rather than heavy bait-casting equipment.

SURFACE BAITS

The old standby topwater plug provides exciting fishing, primarily in shallow water. Slowly worked across the surface, topwater plugs can be literally knocked out of the water by Old Ironjaw. They can be used with bait-casting or spinning gear.

Popular topwater plugs include the Jitterbug, Hula Popper and Zara Spook.

SPOONS

Both standard and weedless spoons are deadly baits for taking largemouth. Jigging spoons over deepwater structure is a popular technique on southern reservoirs, while on natural lakes weedless spoons like the Johnson Silver Minnow are very effective when worked around and through heavy cover, especially weeds and lily pads. A good trick is to add a twister tail or pork rind strip to the hook of a Johnson spoon for added action.

A very productive technique is skittering a spoon over milfoil or pads. This involves a steady retrieve holding the rod tip high, so the spoon skitters over the top of the vegetation.

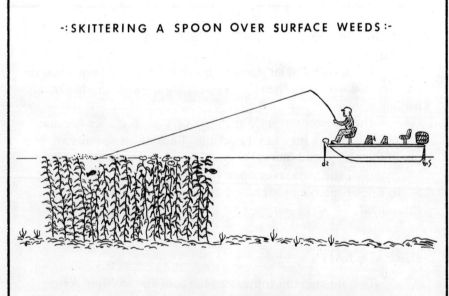

-:SKITTERING A SPOON OVER SURFACE WEEDS:-

By holding your rod tip high, you can retrieve a weedless spoon over the top of heavy vegetation. Skittering offers very exciting fishing as bass explode through the weeds to take the spoon.

"Skittering" a Johnson spoon with pork rind or plastic dressing across lily pads and other vegetation can produce violent strikes from large mouth bass and northern pike.

Rod and Reel Selection

A properly equipped bass fisherman should have a light action rod, plus a stiff rod. The light action rod should be used when fishing with grubs or under tough circumstances when the use of light line and small baits is required.

Bait-casting and spinning tackle each have their advantages. Just be sure to use quality brand-name gear; nothing is more disappointing than losing a big fish because of poorly made discount equipment.

Most bass fishermen use different line sizes depending on the fishing situation. Your light rod should have 4, 6, or 8 pound test, while standard bass tackle usually means using 12 to 20 pound line. If you are fishing in heavy cover, you need strong line to pull that trophy out of there!

Boats and Equipment

Modern bass boats today are equipped with a trolling motor, depth finder and other electronic gear designed with one thing in mind ... *fishing*!

However, even if your idea of a fishing boat is a 10 foot aluminum johnboat, a trolling motor is an extremely valuable tool. It allows you to maneuver silently from spot to spot; and it's a heck of a lot easier than rowing. A portable depthfinder can also be added to any boat so the angler can read bottom structure. This is a real necessity if you plan to fish anywhere other than the shoreline. Learning to read the various signals on the depthfinder takes practice, but eventually the average angler can determine where there are underwater weedbeds, stumps, rock piles, dropoffs and other structures. Therefore, the depth-finder is an invaluable aid to the serious fisherman.

Modern bass boats, equipped with elevated seats, depth finders, electric trolling motor and aerated live-wells are designed with fishing in mind. Pictured below is a well-equipped bass boat fishing a shallow bay in early spring.

Basic Bassing Tips

Keep your lure in the Fish Zone. You should fish parallel rather than perpendicular to fallen trees, logs, weedlines and undercut banks. That way the entire retrieve is around the cover, rather than only the first few feet.

When catching fish, stay snagged. Never unsnag a lure that's hung up if it means spooking fish. Let me give an example. You are working a spinnerbait through fallen trees and in a few minutes you've taken two nice bass. Your next cast gets hung on a branch. Rather than going in with the boat and spooking the remaining fish, put that rod down and continue to fish with your spare until you're satisfied that the area has been thoroughly fished. Then retrieve your snagged lure.

Check your line for frays. Fishing in heavy cover will damage your line and it should be re-tied often in the course of the day.

Keep equipment and lures handy. Valuable fishing time is lost every time you fumble around the boat looking for pliers, spare baits, snap swivels, *etc.*

Fish coves outside-in. Work your way into quiet coves, rather than blasting in with your boat to fish the inside shoreline; fish the outside first and work your way in.

Be quiet and careful in your approach. Although voices don't seem to frighten bass, other noises do—banging oars, dropping tackleboxes or pliers. So try the silent approach for better results.

Fish the shaded side first. Bass have fixed pupils and are extremely sensitive to bright sunlight. Regardless of the type of cover, cast to the shaded side on your first try.

Avoid waves. When a strong wind blows up, especially in shallow water, shut down your fishing and try to find sheltered water.

Find the pattern and then stick with it. You're on a strange lake, and by analyzing the factors we've discussed earlier, you decide that the bass should be on weedlines in 10 to 15 feet of water. You check a couple of these weedlines and find fish.

When you are sure of the pattern, stay with it. Concentrate all of your efforts on similar weedlines until the bass stop hitting. If bass are found on one weedline, pattern fishing tells you they will be found also in others.

Release bass gently and quickly. Hold bass by the bottom jaw, quickly take them off the hook, and if you are going to release it, do so promptly. Never throw a fish back in the lake; release them gently.

This chapter started with an explanation of the various factors to analyze when seeking out the elusive largemouth. We have also discussed types of structure and cover as well as basic bass lures.

Applying this information will definitely improve your bass fishing. However, never forget that each fishing trip should be a learning experience. Many pro anglers keep a diary, recording valuable information such as depth the fish were caught, time of day, water temperature, lures that were productive, *etc.* This information is very useful, even when you are on a different body of water. Often, successful techniques from previous trips can be used again if you learned what was done correctly the first time.

So, apply what you've learned, keep casting, and remember that the ultimate thrill in bass fishing is not just catching fish but being good enough to locate them consistently.

3/Tackle, Tips and Techniques for Smallmouth Bass

by Todd Swainbank

One of the most highly prized game fish found in North America is the smallmouth bass. The bronzeback or brownie, as smallmouth are called by legions of admirers from coast to coast, is truly a triple treat to anglers.

First, smallmouth bass are extremely tasty table fare. This bass' preference for cool, clear and clean water contributes to a firm and sweet tasting flesh. Next, the smallmouth's reputation as a battling and acrobatic sportfish cannot be denied. These fish, when hooked on light tackle, often amaze anglers with their stamina. Sometimes, smaller specimens will fool even experienced anglers into thinking they've hooked a lunker because they fight so hard. Compared to their slower, but heavier cousins, the largemouth bass, bronzebacks are truly longwinded, rock-hard, battle-ready middle weights. Lastly, lunker smallmouths (over 4 pounds), as is true of most large specimens of freshwater game fish, are often extremely wary and offer the serious angler a worthy challenge. An angler who is consistently successful in taking smallmouths on artificial lures is likely to be a very versatile fisherman.

Where Are They Found?

Originally, the range of the smallmouth bass was restricted
to the Lake Ontario and Ohio River drainage areas. Now,
fortunately for anglers everywhere, the range has been greatly
expanded north into southern Canada, south to Alabama, and
through the western states to California.

Life History and Spawning Habits

Smallmouth bass are spring spawners throughout most of
their range. Spawning may be as late as the end of June in
southern Canada and as early as April near the southern limit of
their range in Alabama. The spawning ritual, which we are
fortunate to observe yearly at the back door docks of our tackle
store on Cayuga Inlet in Ithaca, New York, usually takes place
when water temperature reaches about 60 degrees F.

Smallmouth bass and their cousins the largemouth and
spotted bass are members of the sunfish family and the spawning
habits of all these species involves the digging of a shallow nest by
the male bass. The smallmouth usually selects a nest site with a
firm gravel-covered bottom, often very near a protecting bank, log
or boulder in shallow water. The completed nest, which is saucer
shaped and 2-3 feet in diameter, is easily observed by watchful
anglers. Digging is accomplished by vigorous use of mouth, fins
and tail. The male then brings one or more females to the nest
for spawning. The eggs stick to the bottom of the nest and are
closely and aggressively guarded by the male. Eggs hatch a few
days later and the tiny bass, called fry, quickly leave the nest to
begin feeding on their own.

Growth rates depend on many factors such as forage
quality and quantity and the length of high metabolism growing
season. Growth rates in many large mid-southern reservoirs are
better than in colder and often less fertile northern waters.
Average growth rates for typical northern waters might
approximate the following: one year old, 3½ to 4 inches; two

years, 5½ to 6½; three years, 8 to 9 inches; four years, 10 to 11 inches; five years, 12½ to 13½ inches; six years, 13½ to 14 inches; seven years, 15 to 16½ inches.*

As with most fish, very few smallmouth bass fry survive the many hazards of early life to become adults. A true lunker smallmouth of over 20 inches and 4 pounds in weight could be as much as 8 to 10 years old and such a fish would be a trophy throughout most of the smallmouth's geographic range.

The world record** weighed a tremendous 11 pounds, 15 ounces and was caught in one of the most famous smallmouth lakes in the country, Dale Hollow Lake in Kentucky. It was caught July 9, 1955, by David L. Hayes.

Habitats Preferred by Smallmouths

Simply stated the smallmouth bass is an adaptable species that thrives best in rivers and lakes that offer gravel, rock or other firm bottoms and fairly clear, clean and cool water. The bodies of water that I primarily fish for smallmouth bass can basically be divided into two types of lakes.

The first type is termed an *oligotrophic* lake. This refers to the youngest geological stage in the life of a lake and is characterized by relatively small amounts of plant life and a fairly small number of pounds of fish per acre yield. Lakes of this type are usually very large and very deep, with clear, clean water. These lakes are relatively infertile, with clean rocky bottoms. Such lakes very often are populated with many trout and salmon species and are found in the areas of the country that experienced intense glaciation.

Examples are the Finger Lakes, found in the southern tier of New York state. My home lake is Cayuga, 40 miles long with

---

*K. Lagler, *Freshwater Fishery Biology* (Dubuque, Iowa: Wm. Brown Co.), p.51.

**"Fish of the month; The Smallmouth Bass," *Fishing Facts Magazine* (July 1976), p. 100.

an average depth of 175 feet and a maximum depth of 435 feet. Cayuga and nearby Seneca Lake, with a maximum depth of 618 feet, are, with the exception of the Great Lakes, the two deepest lakes east of the Rocky Mountains.

The second kind of lake is a more common type found across the country. These lakes are also large, but fairly shallow and usually discolored. They are characterized by much higher concentrations of plant life and higher yields of pounds of fish per acre. They are *mesotrophic* lakes and contain large numbers and species of warm water game fish such as walleye pike, largemouth bass, yellow perch and northern pike, plus many panfish and rough fish species.

Examples of this type of lake that I regularly fish would be Oneida Lake and the Inland Sea, Lake Champlain, both found in New York State. Oneida is the largest lake completely within the borders of the state and covers over 50,000 acres with maximum depth of only 55 feet. Over half the lake is less than 35 feet deep.

Champlain is more like an ocean, over 130 miles long and up to 12 miles wide, forming about two-thirds of the New York-Vermont border. Although Champlain has some *very* deep stretches (300-400 feet), they are many miles from the areas I fish. (A lake of this size actually exhibits many different environments.) The areas I fish are primarily bays and coves with less than 40 foot depths.

Large lakes offer the angler a number of benefits that smaller water bodies do not. First, during the spring of the year when smallmouths are migrating to spawn, very large schools will concentrate on the prime spawning areas. Finding the spawning grounds on large lakes can take some time and effort, but will reward the angler with potentially tremendous success. Next, big lakes offer a higher potential for *consistently* producing large numbers of lunker sized fish.

Fishing the big lakes regularly seems to improve an angler's skill in other aspects of fishing. Big lakes, such as the ones mentioned can be very dangerous, demanding equipment and nautical skills superior to those needed by anglers who fish small sheltered streams, rivers or lakes.

An angler who fishes big lakes regularly finds it easy to locate fish quickly when fishing a smaller, unknown lake or river because he has been exposed to many different situations. The reverse is not always true for the fisherman who spends most of his time on smaller bodies of water. The fisherman used to small lakes may have considerable difficulty locating fish on lakes of the size that I speak of.

Outfitting for Big Lake Bassin'

The equipment available to the bass fisherman of today is considerably more diverse than what was available ten years ago. The boom in the popularity of bass together with the formation of major sportsmen organizations like the Bass Anglers Sportsman Society (B.A.S.S.) and big money tournaments have encouraged tremendous product expansion, experimentation, research and development geared primarily to the bass fisherman.

The major components of what is considered today to be standard equipment on a boat rigged for serious big lake bass fishing in our part of the country would be somewhat as follows:

Bass Boat. It should be at least 15 feet long with a wide beam; possessing one (or more) adjustable swiveling pedestal fishing seat; rated for at least a 40 H.P. outboard motor. The hull design would probably be semi-vee or trihull with aluminum or fiberglass construction and upright flotation. All required safety equipment would be included.

My boat is a 16½ foot aluminum Sea Nymph Fishing Machine with two aerated live wells, two raised deck pedestal seats, seven foot long rod and tackle locker and steering console. It is rated to 70 H.P. I've owned it for four years, often fishing hard three to four times a week. It fishes up to three people comfortably and handles rough water well.

Outboard Motors. Although foreign imports are showing up more and more, I and all my fishing friends still prefer motors produced by the big four: Johnson, Evinrude, Chrysler and Mercury. I use an electric start 60 H.P. Evinrude with power tilt (to make shallow water less hazardous). Mounted beside that I sometimes have a five H.P. Evinrude motor for trolling and as an emergency spare.

Electric Motor. An electric motor, whether bow or stern mounted, enables silent and easy maneuvering of the boat and once one has been used, most anglers will want to continue using it. The motor should be a variable speed unit which is powerful enough to hold the boat in position against a breeze.

I favor a foot-controlled, bow mounted motor that can be operated easily while I'm fishing. This keeps my hands free for what they do best and enjoy most--catching fish! My motor is a Minnkota 565 with four speeds and a maximum thrust of 18 pounds and low battery amperage draw. For silently maneuvering the boat around fishy looking cover and structure, the importance of this item, especially when used in conjunction with a depth sounder, cannot be emphasized too much.

Depth Sounders. For pinpointing schools of fish, locating underwater structure and aiding navigation, a "sonar" is a must. It should be operable at fairly high boat speed and give bright, clear signals. Placement and mounting technique depends on type of boat material and the manufacturer's operating instructions.

The transducer for my unit is mounted directly into the water off the transom via a homemade aluminum bracket. This produces very good slow to medium speed signals, although it requires periodic cleaning of algae build-ups when the boat is left in the water for long periods.

Most bassmen favor Humminbird or Lowrance units. Mine is a Lowrance LFG 306, mounted on the steering console so I can read it easily while operating the boat. The unit can be reversed so I can read it while sitting on the front pedestal seat operating the electric motor.

Marker Buoys. When a school of fish or a particularly good looking structure is found on the depth sounder, I throw over marker buoys to mark off the area and then begin a systematic fan casting approach to effectively fish the spot.

Buoys are particularly effective to use when needing pinpoint boat control, such as marking sudden drop offs or sunken islands, especially on windy days. The angler can make a trolling or casting pass and easily return to the exact spot where fish were caught. Very often, especially in midsummer on clear lakes, smallmouths will be tightly grouped in small areas in deep water. If these small schools aren't pinpointed accurately by using the depth sounder and marker buoys, a lot of wasted time results.

Markers come in handy when trolling so I can make repeated passes exactly where I took a fish. Throw them to one side of a school of fish so they won't be spooked. My markers are high visibility yellow and have 70 feet of line attached to a six ounce lead weight. Markers can be easily made from empty clorox plastic bottles or something similar.

Topographical Maps. Every angler who fishes big lakes should purchase the "topo" maps available for the lake in question. Maps are valuable navigational aids and provide enough detailed information so an angler can, by using landmarks and a depth sounder, check the more interesting structures and cover in short order.

The cast-for-cash tournament pros wouldn't think of venturing out for tournament practice days without the most detailed maps they can find. Often a skilled angler, used to reading topo maps can, with a surprising degree of accuracy, pinpoint hot spots without ever having been on the lake.

Maps of nearby lakes are occasionally found in tackle stores or outdoor sports stores. The best source of information is Branch of Distribution, U. S. Geological Survey, 1200 S. Eads Street, Arlington, VA 22202 (for areas east of the Mississippi River); and Branch of Distribution, U. S. Geological Survey, Box 25286, Federal Center, Denver, Colorado 80225 (for areas west of the Mississippi River). The price for each map is $1.25.

Large Landing Net. We are very fortunate in the Northeast to have lakes that are populated by a number of large game fish species. Walleyes, northerns, muskies, big trout and salmon inhabit many waters with smallmouth bass. Although

even large bass can be fairly easily landed by using the
paralyzing lower jaw grip or small nets, I prefer to carry one of
the large nets favored by pike anglers. I may go out fishing with
a 20 inch smallmouth bass on my mind, but if a 40 inch pike
decides to pay a visit I want to be prepared to receive him in
proper style. A big net, within easy reach and not buried under a
pile of tackle, is worth anything to the angler that is fighting the
fish of a lifetime, especially if he is alone in the boat.

Pliers. Smallmouth bass are a hardy species and can be
released unharmed even after fairly rough handling. I prefer to
make the release of a fish as easy on both of us as possible. Pliers
speed up the process of unhooking a well hooked fish, especially
in cold weather. I find needlenose pliers work best.

Anchor Mate. This clever invention for anchor line
storage and retrieval is a blessing to a deep water jig fisherman like
me. (Some are even made that automatically retrieve the anchor
by battery power.) Mine is manually operated by a crank
retriever. It saves my back from the strain of handlining an anchor
up from deep water and is a less dangerous method of anchor
retrieval when in rough water. Also on cold days, since the wet
line doesn't have to be handled, it is a most welcome accessory.

For anchors I have an 18 pound typical double prong
Naval type that grabs well on uneven bottoms and on windy days
in deep water. I use a smaller 15 pound mushroom anchor when
maintaining boat position is less critical or when the boat is over
soft bottoms. I have at least 60 feet of nylon cord for use on
each anchor.

Rod Holders. I don't primarily troll for smallmouth bass
but sometimes it can be a very productive technique. The rod
holders preferred by anyone who trolls regularly have to be heavy
duty, secure the rod firmly and attach to the boat tightly. The
best I've used are Down-Easters, both the D10 and double locking
S10 version. They release quickly with a firm upward pull of the
rod when setting the hook on a striking fish and can be tightened
very securely against the gunwales. I wouldn't trust my rod to
dime store quality holders.

Log Book. Even anglers blessed with a good memory should keep a log book to record the important data that might aid them on future trips. Information such as weather conditions, water temperature, locations and lures that produced action, etc. can be valuable in producing a better understanding of the factors governing success on each body of water.

Rainsuit. Nothing ruins a day's fishing like getting soaked in a rain storm. An easily rolled, two-piece flexnet rainsuit can be stored in the boat until needed. It should be big enough to fit over a fully clothed angler.

Tackle to Tackle Smallmouths

With all the numerous improvements each year in rods, reels and lines, it can be difficult to stay abreast of the situation. Suffice it to say that standard equipment for smallmouth tackle leaves considerable room for personal preference. Many bass fishermen have a number of matched rods and reels rigged and ready in the boat to be prepared for any situation. This saves time when different lures and techniques are called for.

The Jig Outfit. About 75% of my smallmouth fishing is done with one rod. A good spinning jig rod should be either a quality glass or graphite and have a straight cork handle without a fixed reel seat. I mount the reel on the rod using black electrician's tape; this makes a secure, comfortable and warm grip.

Many anglers favor short jig rods. I don't. Many anglers favor medium-medium heavy stiff graphite or fast action glass rods. I don't. The rod action I prefer in a jig rod is rarely seen in any rods today, except custom made ones. Action should be light-light medium, slow action. My favorite is a seven foot high modulus glass rod with Lews Single Foot Fugi Speed Guides and internal glass ferrules. A one piece rod would be even better. I primarily fish 1/8 - 1/4 ounce jigs with the rod and have developed excellent sensitivity with it. Sensitivity is a *must* in jigging.

Many high quality light spinning reels are available. An excellent choice for the jig rod is the Zebco Cardinal 3. This reel has a fast 5:1 gear ratio and a smooth running, easily reached drag system.

The least expensive but most important component of a jig outfit is the line. A high visibility line is required so that those often subtle taps can be easily seen and acted upon by a line-watching angler. An invisible line, that can't easily be seen by the angler, is useless in jig fishing. Many times when guiding I've seen clients get strikes that they never knew they had because they either weren't paying attention or simply couldn't see their line clearly. Berkley High VIS Tensiamatic and Stren in 4 to 6 pound test are very well suited for jig fishing.

Multiple Use Outfit. This outfit should be able to handle just about everything an angler faces in smallmouth fishing. A rod and reel combination of this type can be used for fishing larger, more strain producing baits like crankbaits and can handle the heavier jigging spoons such as the Mannolure and Slabspoon. This combination can also be used for trolling baits such as Rapalas and Rebels and other baits that come through the water easily.

Again I favor a seven foot glass rod, now with a medium-fast taper action and fixed reel seat. Mine is a Shakespeare Purist with Carbaloy guides. The reel should be able to handle 8 to 10 pound test line and two spools will be needed if any trolling is to be done. The Zebco Cardinal 4 reel goes well on the type of rod mentioned. Berkley High Vis and Stren both are excellent lines for this multi purpose outfit and are also suitable for light trolling.

The Bait Casting Outfit. Although the casting combination has limited application in the fishing I do, I've used some that were sporty, fast, and enjoyable.

The bait casting outfit should be lightweight and built to handle light lines and small lures. This outfit will probably see most action in tossing small crankbaits around points, cliffs, shoals and other shoreline cover.

The rod should be a light action graphite with a pistol grip and a length between five and six feet. Mine is a Bass Pro Shops Graphite 96 light action 5½ footer. The reel should be one

of the smaller high speed, narrow spool reels available. The
Shimano Bantam and Ambassador 1500C and 4500C are
excellent choices.

A high visibility line isn't required for crankbait fishing
since the strikes are almost always obvious rod tip benders.
Garcia Royal Bonnyl in brown is a good choice in discolored or
neutral colored water. The more invisible lines are well suited to
crankbait fishing.

Lures and How to Choose Them. There are literally
thousands of lures made in this country and overseas. The
investment in lures by avid anglers often exceeds $500, usually
with mixed results. Many anglers also seek out lures with magical
powers that out-produce all others at all times. Unfortunately,
magic lures don't exist. The only *magic* in fishing is in the
fisherman.

A representative selection of smallmouth lures that cover
most situations would include lures in the following six
categories:

1. *Lead Head Jigs* in 1/8 ounce and 1/4 ounce weights
made with size 1 and 1/0 Eagle Claw 575 hooks for use with
three and four inch plastic Mister Twister grubs, Super Tails, etc.

The most productive lures I've found for smallmouth bass are the small
Mister Twister grubs fished on 1/8 ounce and 1/4 ounce jig heads. These
lures are also deadly on walleyes.

Colors for plastic baits should include chartruese, blue, black, brown, purple, yellow and white.

The best shape of the jig is a matter of opinion; they *all* get snagged on the bottom, especially if you are fishing them right. Charlie Brewers Slider Heads, stand up heads and round ball heads are my favorites.

I might add that anyone who fishes a lot of jigs properly, is going to lose a lot of jigs. A mold for pouring your own lead jigs can save a lot of money.

The line is always tied *directly* to the hookeye of the jig. Smallmouth bass don't have the line cutting teeth that pike possess and a simple improved clinch knot is all that's needed.

This group of lures is among the most consistent producers of smallmouths that exists. Of the 500-1,000 smallmouths I catch each year, 75 to 80 percent are caught on jigs.

2. *Small Crankbaits.* Smallmouth bass show a definite preference for small baits. Small crankbaits are extremely effective when bass are in shallow rocky areas and actively

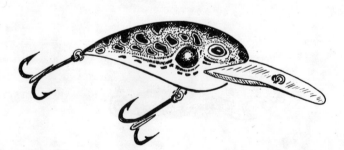

Crankbaits are especially effective for largemouth and smallmouth bass. The depth to which they will dive depends on the length of the lip. Most popular sizes are 1/8 ounce to 5/8 ounce.

feeding. These baits should be either tied directly to the line or used with a small snap that doesn't impede the action of the lure.

Crankbaits that fail to run true through the water can be correctly tuned by adjusting the line eye of the lure with a pair of needle nose pliers. The eye should be aligned straight vertically and placed in the center of the lip or nose of the lure to get proper action.

An excellent small crankbait selection would include lures on the following list:

Natural Ike 1/4 ounce and 1/8 ounce by Lazy Ike
Tiny Deep N 1/8 ounce by Bill Norman
Deep Baby N 1/4 ounce and Relfect N by Norman
Bagleys Honeybee 1/4 ounce by Bagley Baits
Small Mudbugs 1/4 ounce by Arbogast
Deep Piglet 1/8 ounce by Manns Baits
Teeny R 1/8 ounce by Rebel
Shallow R 1/8 ounce by Rebel
Humpback Rattler by Rebel
Floating Rapala size 5, 7, 9, 11
Countdown Rapala size 5, 7, 9
Broken back Rapala size 9

3. *Larger and Deeper Diving Crankbaits.* The larger baits are very effective for fishing deeper waters and for getting down along the edge of a weedline. They also work well when fast retrieved so the lip of the lure bumps and grinds on a rocky bottom. This sends out easily located sounds to nearby fish and prompts them to investigate, especially in discolored water.

A good selection of these baits would include lures on the following list:

Rapala Fat Rap size 5
Rebel Super R
Rebel Deep Wee R
Manns Deep Pig
Bomber Model A
Bomber Water Dog
Original Bomber

Norman Super Scooper
Bagley's Divin' B
Bagley's Killer B II
Medium Size Natural Ike
Medium Size Mud Bugs
Big O Cordell
Deep Big O Cordell
Deep Mini R Rebel

4. *Small Spinnerbaits.* Smaller safety pin style, single hook spinnerbaits can be devastating on bass around shallow shoreline cover and flutter fished around pilings, weedlines and riprap. Because they sink slower than jigs, they can be very effective in discolored water where visibility is shortened.

Most anglers tie these lures directly to the line and dress the hook with a small plastic twister type grub or pork strip.

A good selection of these lures would include ones from the following list:

Mini Rats 1/16 ounce, 1/8 ounce by Bass Pro Shops
Shannon Super Twin 1/4 ounce
Shannon Twin Spin 1/4 ounce
Squirmin' Worm 1/8 ounce, 1/4 ounce by Bass Pro Shops
Stump Jumper 1/8 ounce
Small Hustler Buzz Bug 1/4 ounce
Small Bush Hogs 1/4 ounce

5. *Structure Spoons and Tailspinners.* These lures are especially effective when bass have retreated to deep water dropoffs in midsummer to early fall, or when fishing in rough water or heavy current. They can be cast long distances and jigged back or yoyoed vertically under the boat for suspended fish. Lures should be tied directly with a High Vis line.

A good selection would include lures from the following list:

Mannolure 1/2 ounce by Manns Baits
Swedish Pimple 3/8 ounce, 1/2 ounce
Hopkins Shorty 1/2 ounce

Little George 1/4 ounce, 3/8 ounce by Manns Baits
Bomber Slab Spoon 1/2 ounce

6. *Trolling Lures.* Trolling can be very effective on smallmouths, especially when checking out large areas at specified depths.

Lures can be trolled as they are or weighted with sinkers ahead of them to attain a deeper run.

An angler seriously interested in trolling for bass should purchase a non-stretch monofilament line such as Buck Perry's No Bo and a stiffer rod than the one described as the multipurpose outfit.

A good trolling lure selection would include lures on the following list:

Rapala Floating size 9, 11
Rapala Countdown 9, 11
Rapala Brokenback 11
Rapala DD 90 (discontinued unfortunately)
Rebel D1000 Series Spoon Bill Diver
Rebel 1000 Series Brokenback F
Deep Little N by Norman
Bucks Spoon Plugs, size 500-100
Heddon Clatter Tad
Flatfish Helin
Twin Minnow
Bomber Waterdog

Locating Seasonal Bass Patterns on Different Lake Types

MAY 1 - JUNE 30

This is the favorite time of the year for the bassman. Smallmouths will be found grouped in large numbers in shallow water and are easily caught at this time. Fishing can be fast and furious and multiple lunker potential is excellent.

Spring is a prime time for lunker smallmouths. This one came from the Oneida River.

Pre-season and Early Season Patterns for Oneida and Other Shallow Lakes. Shallow Oneida Lake warms faster than the deep Finger Lakes of New York State. This is an extremely important fact. Spring smallmouth fishing is excellent in lakes similar to Oneida at least two weeks earlier than in the deeper and colder Finger Lakes.

Tributary streams and rivers are at least a few degrees warmer than surrounding waters in early spring. The largest and most suitable tributary to Oneida Lake is the Oneida River located at the western end of the lake. The river offers warmer water, outstanding spawning and feeding habitat, and extensive shoreline cover such as boat docks, boathouses, bridge abuttments and riprap. The extensive riprap areas get tremendous concentrations of fish in May and early June. Oneida Lake is also an outstanding walleye fishery and during the spring this species gets almost all the attention of fishermen. It is a rarity to encounter another bass angler enjoying pre-season, catch and release sport in the river. Consistent large catches of two to four pound fish can be expected and an occasional five pounder is also caught. Although New York State bass season doesn't open until June 16th, a bass man interested in *sport* can find it in and around major lake tributaries in the spring.

We will make three to four trips to Oneida starting around May 1st when water temperature hovers around 50 degrees F. The cold water temperatures make the bass slower and more sluggish than in midsummer. Jigs are by far the most effective lures at this time. As the summer approaches and waters warm, spinnerbaits and crankbaits become effective.

Pre-season and Early Season Patterns for Cayuga Lake and Other Deep Lakes. Though early May finds Cayuga Lake pressured by trout anglers, little pre-season attention is given the battling bronzeback. Although Cayuga has less extensive shoal areas and smaller tributaries than Oneida Lake, similar patterns can be found. Excellent pre-season smallmouth fishing is usually two weeks later than in Oneida Lake due to colder water temperatures.

Tributaries such as Fall Creek, Six Mile Creek, Cayuga Inlet, Taughannock Creek and Salmon Creek all get smallmouth runs with fish seeking gravel spawning grounds. These tributaries can be easily fished from shore and although they contain large numbers of fish, they don't seem to contain the lunkers they did 10 to 15 years ago.

Twelve years ago I caught two smallmouths over six pounds in Fall Creek in May. A fish half that size would be considered large now. Fast action on 10-14 inch fish can easily be had however.

The tributaries mentioned are found on the southern end of the lake. Productive shallow lake shoal areas exist on the north and south ends of the lake.

Cayuga Lake smallmouths, especially lunker specimens, often spawn on the limited shoal areas available. Large schools of bass spread out over the shoals in mid-May and concentrate around good shoreline cover, primarily sunken boulders, docks, pilings and rock cribs.

Jigs cast next to cover and allowed to flutter down often are intercepted by a striking smallmouth. By the end of May and into June small crankbaits (1/8 - 1/4 ounce) fished on light lines (4 - 6 pound test) are very effective. The only time I ever caught two bass on one cast came in June on a small crankbait.

JULY 1 - SEPTEMBER 30

Mid-Season Patterns on Oneida and Other Shallow Lakes. By early July the majority of the smallmouth bass that entered the river have deserted the area for suitable sites in the lake. Water temperature in the river will rise well over 70 degrees F in midsummer and although there are always a few bass in the river, most of them retreat to deeper, cooler waters.

There is one very notable exception to this migration however. The Oneida River has a lock system whereby boaters can travel to Cross Lake and Lake Ontario.

Many spring run bass pass through these locks in May and remain above them throughout the season. Catching a lunker there is rare, but tremendous angling potential exists for fish in the 12 to 16 inch range. The bass above the lock are usually long and lean and jump repeatedly when hooked. (River bass, wherever I've caught them, always seem to outjump their lake counterparts.)

The river water has a brownish tint and small brightly colored crankbaits and small spinnerbaits are devastating on the river bass. The bass above the lock concentrate around the obvious shoreline cover like docks, cribs and rock piles, showing preference for cover that is well shaded from the midday sun.

For the angler searching the main lake, the extensive mid-lake shoal area called Shakleton Shoals is a well known smallmouth spot, offering good deep water rock structure. Trolling with Rapalas and jigging are both productive there.

Submerged rock bars near islands and the island dropoffs are good midsummer smallmouth producers. Occasionally on Oneida in midsummer an oxygen deficiency will exist when many rough fish and panfish can be observed washed up dead on the shore. Often with a depth sounder, an angler can find schools of suspended fish near the surface. If only deep water fishing tactics are used, these fish will be missed. Spinnerbaits and crankbaits work well on shallow suspended fish.

Mid-Season Patterns on Cayuga and Other Deep Lakes. This is traditionally the toughest time of the year on the gin clear Finger Lakes when a number of very difficult situations face the angler.

For a few weeks each year in late June and early July, swarms of alewifes (sawbellies) move into shallow water. Gamefish such as bass gorge themselves on these easily caught forage fish, and with so much food available at this time, catching smallmouths can be extremely difficult, though small silver crankbaits and silver Rapalas *sometimes* work well.

By mid-July the majority of smallmouth bass, especially larger ones, have deserted the quickly warming tributaries and shallow shoals. Shallow water fishing tapers off when temperatures pass 65 degrees F.

Periodic shallow water fish movements occur throughout the summer but are limited usually to the hours around dawn and dusk or during stormy skies and rough water conditions. Night fishing can be productive as smallmouths move into the shallows under the protective cloak of darkness to feed. Spinnerbaits and Rapalas are excellent baits for night fishing, and so are small surface plugs.

Outside edges of weedlines bordering deeper water, fished with the deeper diving crankbaits can yield good catches.

During daylight hours on bright, sunny, calm days, smallmouths will be *very* deep. Occasionally, some are caught by downrigger trout fishermen trolling depths greater than 60 feet.

Deep water structure fishing is the key to success at such times. Underwater points extending into deep water and sharp dropoffs in 20 to 60 foot depths get most of my attention. I often spend considerable time cruising and watching the depth sounder for flashes of suspended fish or a particularly good looking structure.

The heavier spoons and tailspinners can be very effective for these deep water bass. Many bass men never fish deeper than 15 foot depths. In the Finger Lakes to stay on smallmouth bass consistently an angler has to be versatile. The two biggest smallmouth bass I caught in Cayuga last year were in 55 feet of water suspended along an even deeper drop off. Both fish were over 4½ pounds and I lost two more that were probably over five pounds. The Mannolure is my favorite lure for deep muscle jigging. Unlike the plastic twister jigs that require almost no rod action to catch fish, the jigging spoons work best with vigorous rod pumping motions. The development of a sensitive touch is definitely helpful when fishing down that deep.

OCTOBER 1 - NOVEMBER 15

Late Season Patterns on Oneida and Other Shallow Lakes. As lake temperatures drop, smallmouths again group up and approach the shallows for extended feeding forays. Visible shoreline cover becomes productive once again as smallmouths, seemingly sensing the approach of winter, go on their last feeding binge of the season. It was in early October on Lake Champlain that Bill Butler and I caught over 100 smallmouths in six hours on crankbaits along rock cliffs and rubble banks in shallow one to four foot depths. Fall fishing can be *fantastic* and on many lakes solitude is almost guaranteed!

Shallow water migrations occur dramatically in lakes like Oneida and Champlain in the fall. When water temeratures fall to the 55-65 degree F range and if the water is somewhat discolored, smallmouths will spend extended periods feeding around shallow rocky shoals.

Before the water drops below 50 degrees F, a productive technique is to use a small deep diving crankbait and a fast retrieve causing the lure to dig up the bottom and bounce off small rocks. This sends up small mud clouds and the sounds and sights produced draw bass to investigate from quite a distance.

In the fall, smallmouths school in shallow shoal areas. Small Norman crankbaits produced these Champlain bass.

By mid-November smallmouth bass will often move to faster breaking structure in deeper water. The deep edge of green weedlines can also be productive and spinnerbaits and crankbaits retrieved slowly work well. After the water cools to below 50 degrees F, the jig is once again the primary weapon in the bass angler's arsenal. Strikes will become very soft in cold water, much the same as in early spring.

Late Season Patterns on Cayuga Lake and Other Deep Lakes. The fall feeding frenzy takes place on the Finger Lakes also, but because the water is often crystal clear shallow water movements occur usually on dark rainy days when light penetration into the water is at a minimum.

Anglers will do best on bright calm days in the 20 to 40 foot depth range. On darker days, 10 to 20 foot depths will be most productive. In October and November, rainbow trout and smallmouth bass are often found in the same areas and depths; and trolling Rapalas can take outstanding mixed bags. At this time trolling becomes a major part of my fishing game plan. Plastic grub jigs and jigging spoons are also very effective for fishing dropoffs and other deeper structures. Cruising the lake in search of the last green weedbeds can also be a shortcut to finding fish concentrations. In the fall, weeds die off and turn brown, but just as all deciduous tree leaves don't change color at the same time, neither do weed beds. Baitfish and predator fish will often concentrate around the last green, oxygen-producing weedbeds. Bait size yellow perch often school up at this time and perch imitation crankbaits will take fish. Matching artificial lures to the primary forage is sometimes as important to the lake bass fisherman as is matching the hatch to the stream fly angler.

Fall is the most overlooked time of the year for fishing. Pleasure boaters and water skiers disappear when the weather cools. Fair weather anglers desert the lakes for more comfortable pursuits. The veteran angler knows this is the time to grab his tackle, jump in his boat and hightail it down the big blue highway. Solitude and success always await die-hard anglers.

Six of the Best Smallmouth Bass Spots I have Found

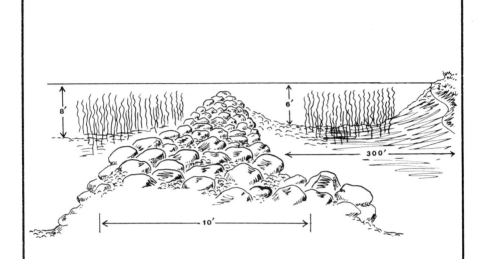

This illustration shows one of the most unique spots I've ever found. It's in Lake Champlain. Because the shoreline markers keep changing, it is becoming harder and harder to find this spot.

How the cobblestone reef emerged so far from shore I'll never know. Maybe millions of years ago a glacier deposited the cobblestone there or maybe some hard working fisherman built up the reef over the years.

Whatever the origin of the reef, we give thanks - it's a lunker hot spot! The reef is about 50 yards long bordered on both sides by extensive tobacco weed beds. A downwind approach casting crankbaits parallel to the reef often produces smallmouths of trophy size. On overcast days the bass will move up on top of the reef to feed and the area will be alive with rising and slashing bass and northern pike. I hope we can find this spot next time we go to Champlain!

A variety of other game fish can be caught from typical bass cover and structures. Anglers interested in identifying potential hot spots for other species should refer to the section on Cover and Structure in Chapter 2, "Largemouth Bass Basics."

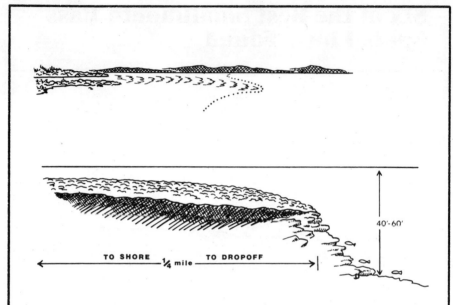

This is an illustration of one of my favorite deepwater structure spots for smallmouth on Cayuga Lake. You'll notice that the main dropoff to deepwater is a long way from shore. This is the something special that makes this spot a smallmouth magnet. Cayuga Lake is *extremely* deep and throughout most of the lake the main dropoffs are close to shore. This spot is one of the few exceptions and smallmouths and other game fish seek out this spot in midsummer under bright skies. On overcast or stormy days in summer or in spring or fall, fish are likely to be scattered over the top of this extensive shoal area on the inside of the dropoff.

I fish there mostly in midsummer. The first cast I ever made there yielded a lunker 4 pounder caught on a Mannolure in about 50 feet of water! The key to success at this time of year is pinpoint boat control and a depth sounder. Bass will tend to school in tight groups along the stair step projecting rock ledges along the dropoff. The heavier jigging spoons or trolling with lead core line or a downrigger will produce the best results.

Occasionally, deep water forage fish like smelt or sawbellies school near this dropoff. Once I was anchored on the spot when this happened; bait was chased right to surface by smallmouths and the action was fast and furious. Such spots often produce mixed bags of bass, trout and pike. I *always* have big fish fever when fishing deep water structure such as this.

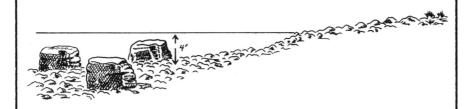

This illustration shows an outstanding early to midseason smallmouth spot
on Cayuga Lake. The rocky rubble provides excellent spawning grounds for
bass and the scattered boulders provide cover. This is the kind of spot I
often guide inexperienced anglers to so they can learn the finer points of jig
and crankbait fishing.

In May and June and on overcast or stormy days in July, this kind of
spot is always good for a few bass. Under bright sunlight, bass will hang
very close to the boulders and a jig allowed to flutter down along the
shadowy side of the boulder often receives a jolting smash.

It was in this spot that I caught the only double of my fishing career:
2 bass on one cast with a small crankbait. This spot is also good at night in
midsummer.

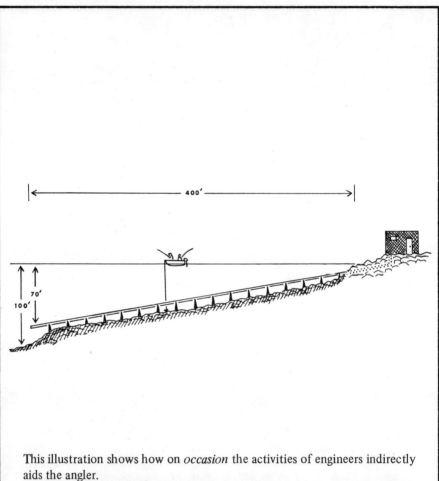

This illustration shows how on *occasion* the activities of engineers indirectly aids the angler.

Pictured is what the intake pipe of a water treatment plant looks like. Game fish began schooling in this area shortly after the completion of the project. The pipe and pipe supports offer cover sanctuary from shallow to very deep water for a variety of game fish.

A depth sounder is needed to pinpoint such structures and a variety of depths can be easily checked along the pipe's length with jigs and jigging spoons. This type of structure is a "tackle graveyard." I once lost 6 jigs on 6 casts there, but the good fishing can make up for lost tackle in a hurry!

This type of spot always seems best for bass in the late summer to fall period. The fish seem to prefer 20 to 40 feet depths.

This illustration shows a classic early season smallmouth spot in the Oneida River. The anglers pictured are fishing the inside of a small island. The bottom composition is gravel and small stones, providing excellent spawning habitat for bass. Overhanging trees provide shade and scattered deadfalls provide cover protection for bedding bass.

The inside of the island is very narrow. A quiet approach and accurate presentation are needed to take fish in this situation.

Although small spinner baits and crankbaits will do well there, we usually fish plastic grub jigs because of the likelihood of getting snagged up. I'd rather lose a half dozen jigs than a half dozen crankbaits. If we get hung up, we simply breakoff and retie without moving in to try to salvage the lure. Moving in on snags in this kind of spot will definitely spook the fish.

There is often a strong current in the spring and boat control can be the critical factor in fishing success. A trick we use sometimes is to make the current work for us by fishing a floating Rapala downstream.

We cast the lure downstream as close to the bank and stickups as possible. The current carries the lure over a likely looking spot. Then we twitch it. The lure will hover over the spot we want to fish until its presence can be tolerated by a bass no longer. This is a great way to force a bedding lunker into trying to destroy the irritating minnow that refuses to swim away.

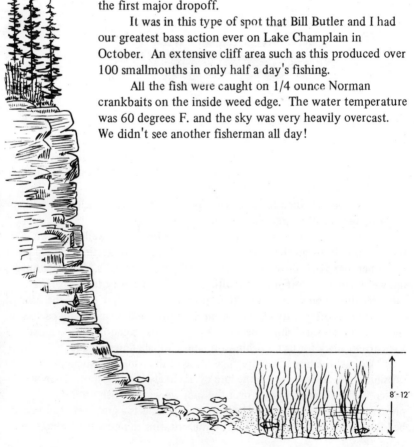

This illustration shows a cliff bank situation common on Lake Champlain and the St. Lawrence River. Boulders and chunk rocks extend well out from the shoreline, providing excellent bottom conditions for smallmouth bass. Notice also that there is a *definite* inside and outside edge to the weedbed.

In spring and fall, bass are likely to be on the inside edge of the weeds all the way to the cliff banks.

In summer, bass are more likely to be located on the outside weed edge in deeper water or scattered well beyond the first major dropoff.

It was in this type of spot that Bill Butler and I had our greatest bass action ever on Lake Champlain in October. An extensive cliff area such as this produced over 100 smallmouths in only half a day's fishing.

All the fish were caught on 1/4 ounce Norman crankbaits on the inside weed edge. The water temperature was 60 degrees F. and the sky was very heavily overcast. We didn't see another fisherman all day!

8'- 12'

4/Fishing for the Wily Walleye

by Todd Swainbank

The walleye pike is the largest member of the perch family. This large, delicious and widely distributed game fish is popular throughout this country and Canada. A shore dinner of freshly caught walleye filets is still the specialty of Canadian fishing guides.

Walleyes were originally found in the Northern states and Canada. By extensive stocking they are now found throughout the U.S. except for a few far West and deep South states. The walleye is easily reared in hatcheries and many hatcheries produce only this species.

The walleye has a reputation as a "feast or famine" specie. During some periods of the year, primarily in the spring, walleyes may appear to be easily caught in large numbers and then suddenly they disappear. Some years will find lakes with fantastic numbers of fish; other years the fishing may seem very poor. This has led many anglers to regard the walleye as a difficult fish to catch. Often the anglers who complain of difficulty in taking walleyes throughout the fishing season simply fail to be versatile in their fishing approach.

As in fishing for any game fish, there is no one best way to do it. Versatility is the key to taking walleyes consistently. Let's take a closer look at the wily walleye and maybe you'll be more likely to catch one--regarded by many as being the best tasting fresh water fish.

Spawning Habits

Walleyes are spring spawners and male fish will seek suitable spawning sites when water temperature warms to the 45-50 degree F range. Males await the larger females on gravel and rubble lake shoals or in tributary streams and rivers. Preferred spawning sites will have current or wave action present. Walleyes are prolific, producing eggs on an average of 25,000-50,000 per pound of body weight.

Spawning takes place at night, in shallow one to five foot depths. Eggs fall to the bottom and are abandoned. Depending on water temperature the eggs hatch three to four weeks later.

Growth Rates

Walleyes thrive best in large rivers and medium to large size lakes. Those found in northern waters grow slower but live longer than fish found in southern rivers and impoundments. A 15-16 inch fish found in a fertile impoundment may be only two years old.* A similar size fish from Canadian waters might be four to five years old. The life expectancy, however, is six to seven years for southern walleyes and 12 to 15 years for slower growing northern fish. The world record walleye which weighed 25 pounds, was caught in Old Hickory Lake, Tennessee by Mabry Harper, August 1, 1960.

Tackle and Tips for Walleyes

Walleyes are school fish, like their cousins the yellow perch. When you find one, your chances of catching others are

---

*A. J. McClane, *1974 New Standard Fishing Encyclopedia,* (New York: Holt, Rhinehart and Winston).

excellent. Their diet consists primarily of other fish. Minnow
imitating lures are very popular for trolling and casting. It seems
I catch most of my walleyes when jigging or crankbaiting for
bass. Walleyes often lie in the deeper water bordering good
smallmouth bass cover and structure. Bait and lure presentations
are best made near the bottom as these fish lie very close to
bottom much of the time.

A medium action spinning rod and fresh water size
spinning reel makes a fine combination for casting and jigging for
walleyes. The same rods and reels mentioned in the chapter on
smallmouth bass will handle walleyes adequately. Although
walleyes can reach large size in many waters and are dogged
fighters, they can be landed easily with light tackle in open water.
A stiffer casting or trolling rod used with a level wind reel is
suggested for those interested in trolling for walleyes.

Trolling

There are two types of trollers: a person who trolls a lake
or river without any idea of what is under the boat or what depth
his lures run at; another who trolls to eliminate unproductive
water in a searching pattern to find fish holding cover or structure
and, hopefully, some fish.

This second type of troller probably uses a depth sounder
of some kind and is keenly aware of depth changes, bottom
contours and changes in bottom composition. He is aware of
daily and seasonal weather and light changes and how his
presentation should vary accordingly. This troller *knows* almost to
to the inch how deep his lures run and he probes whatever depths
are necessary to take whatever species of fish he pursues. He
doesn't depend on luck to find and catch fish, he is versatile.

A troller in search of walleyes may have need of a number
of different type lines to meet the situations faced throughout the

---

A variety of other game fish can be caught from typical bass cover and structures.
Anglers interested in identifying potential hot spots for other species should refer to
the section on Cover and Structure in Chapter 2, "Largemouth Bass Basics."

The top illustration shows a good rig for trolling a floating Rapala for a variety of game fish. A regular 3 way swivel or a branch swivel can be used to keep the lure and weight away from each other. Often the line section with the sinker attached is lighter in strength than the main line to the rod. That way, if the sinker becomes snagged, the lure and swivel might be saved. The floating lure will ride up off the bottom like this.

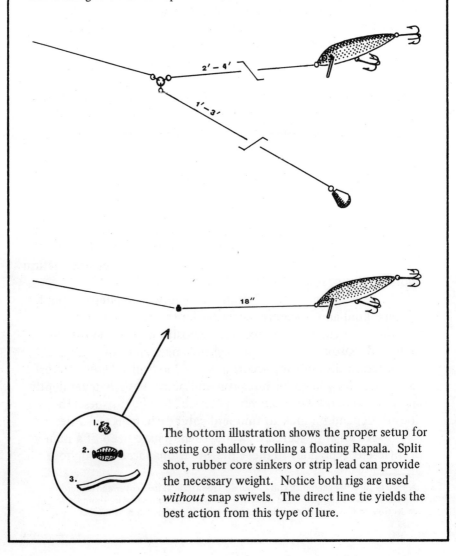

The bottom illustration shows the proper setup for casting or shallow trolling a floating Rapala. Split shot, rubber core sinkers or strip lead can provide the necessary weight. Notice both rigs are used *without* snap swivels. The direct line tie yields the best action from this type of lure.

year. A non-stretch, monofilament line like Buck's No Bo is an excellent all around trolling line. Walleyes often move to deep water in summer, especially in clear lakes. Lead core line and small diameter stainless steel line are very effective trolling lines when deep water depth control is needed. Downriggers also have fishing value for a lot more than just trout and salmon fishing; they can be used effectively for other game fish as well.

Depth and speed control are two of the most important factors governing success or failure in trolling for any species of game fish. The old saying of "Troll as slow as possible for walleyes, then cut it in half" is often true, but high speed trolling can also turn fish on sometimes. So it's best to experiment. Whatever speed you troll, it's a good idea to occasionally pump the rod to suddenly give the lure a burst of speed followed by a pause. This sudden change of pace often prompts a strike.

This lunker walleye was taken in the swift water below a dam off Lake Champlain on a small Norman crankbait.

Stalling the outboard mementarily and then quickly picking up
the pace has the same effect. Incidentally, Rapalas, Rebels and
June Bug spinners with worms are excellent trolling lure choices.

While on the subject of trolling, I might add that very
often in midsummer I see anglers trolling the same depths and
locations that they fish during the spring spawning run. That
sand bar or shallow rock shoal which is red-hot in April or May,
will probably be devoid of walleyes in July and August. It makes
no sense to troll the same spot day after day if it stops producing.
Don't come back empty handed and say, "The fish weren't
biting." Go find the fish and make them bite! Walleyes are
famous for moving great distances in large lakes seeking the large
schools of baitfish needed to support them. Once they have
decimated baitfish populations in one area, they will move to
another. The *consistently* successful walleye angler is a predator
and will move around in search of walleye concentrations in the
areas that baitfish and walleyes are most likely to congregate in.

Underwater points, deep water rock piles, rock ledges, and
deep weed beds are good summer spots. The tailraces below dams
will hold fish throughout the summer if deep,cool water (60-70
degree F) is available. The deep water holes in rivers and the drop
offs near islands are the places to try.

Back Trolling

This method of live bait presentation is very popular in
the Northern states. This system consists of a live bait rig such as
a snell, hook and sliding bullet weight, or walking sinker. The
hole in the weight lets the line run freely through when a fish
takes the bait. A swivel prevents the weight from slipping down
on the hook. The bail on the spinning reel is kept open so no
unnatural sinker drag or line friction is felt by the often subtly
biting walleye.

Back trolling is just that–trolling with your outboard in
reverse gear, usually into the wind. This enables the skipper to
maintain very slow speeds or even hover in place. Anglers' lines

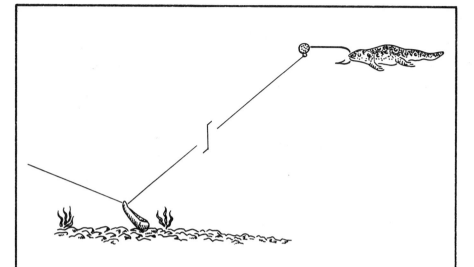

These illustrations show popular Midwestern live bait rigs. The sinker shown is a walking slip sinker type allowing a striking walleye to move off with the bait without feeling the sinker drag.

The floating jig heads keep preferred baits like leeches, minnows and salamanders up off the bottom and easily visible to nearby fish.

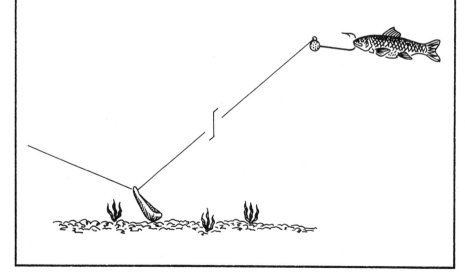

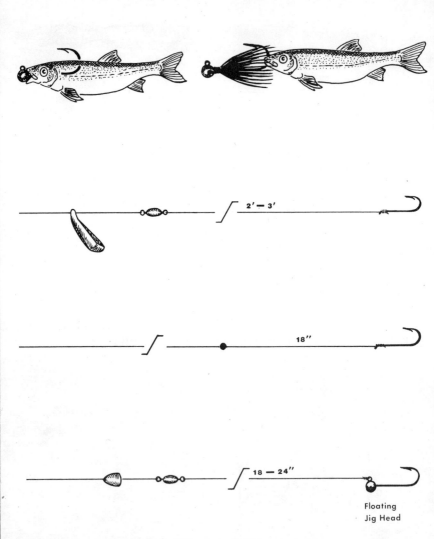

The top illustration shows bait "sweetened" jigs very effective on walleye pike when they don't seem interested in artificial lures. This rig often turns on bass and northern pike too.

Other illustrations show a variety of live bait rigs for bottom bumping or back trolling.

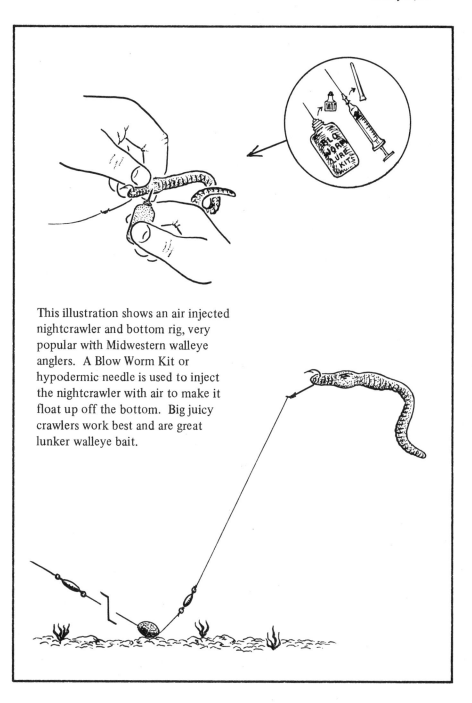

This illustration shows an air injected nightcrawler and bottom rig, very popular with Midwestern walleye anglers. A Blow Worm Kit or hypodermic needle is used to inject the nightcrawler with air to make it float up off the bottom. Big juicy crawlers work best and are great lunker walleye bait.

are thus well ahead of the boat and well away from the propeller. Pinpoint depth and speed control can be maintained using this technique and repeated passes can be made over productive structures quickly.

The live bait presentation can be made with very light lines (4-6 pound test) and tiny hooks without the need of wire leaders. Although walleyes have needle sharp teeth, the teeth are smooth sided and well spaced and I've *never* had one bite through my line. Using light line and fine wire hooks will also improve your catch, as walleyes can be shy of heavy monofilament and they have easily torn mouths. Just check the line often and retie if any nicks develop. Walleyes are dogged fighters, but even lunker sized fish can easily be landed in open water.

Back trolling using air injected nite crawlers or floating jig and worm combinations are very productive on walleyes. Give the fish plenty of time before you strike since walleyes often take bait slowly and deliberately.

Night Fishing for Walleyes

Walleyes are very active night feeders, often moving in schools to shallow shoals, weed beds and sandbars. Trolling a large Rapala can locate fish quickly and then they can be cast to. Mister Twister grubs on 1/8 and 1/4 ounce lead jig heads and the popular bass pattern crank baits are very effective on walleyes, as are bucktail jigs.

Jig fishermen should fish letting the jig flutter and fall over the drop-offs. Walleyes cruise along drop-offs in search of food, ever watchful for a stray crayfish or minnow.

Night fishing can produce fast action, especially on clear lakes in midsummer. During the cool evening hours walleyes will move up from their midday, deep water haunts and spread out to feed actively. Lunker potential is excellent on summer nights. Jigs are outstanding daytime lures too.

So where are the best spots for walleyes? Good waters are common in Manitoba and Ontario. In this country, impoundments such as Dale Hollow, Norris and Center Hill in Tennessee offer excellent lunker potential. In New York, Oneida Lake, Lake Champlain, Black Lake, Sacandaga Reservoir, Conesus Lake, Cross Lake, Lake Erie and the Susquehanna and Chemung Rivers boast good walleye fishing.

 The best walleye lake in the world is no better than the anglers on it. So be versatile, experiment, and maybe you'll find that the walleye isn't so wily after all.

BATTER FRIED BASS OR WALLEYES

 This is *the* recipe for those people that think they hate fish. Bass and walleye filets cook up crisp and crunchy, not unlike fish served in popular fast food fish and chips establishments.

Batter:

2 Cups Bisquick
2 Eggs
1 Cup beer

Beat ingredients with hand beater until batter is smooth. Dip filets in batter and cover each piece completely. Deep fry in *hot* oil, when puffy they are ready to eat, normally in about two minutes. Tastes super!

5/Trophy Northerns and How to Take Them

by Gordon L. Eggleston

Esox lucius! Almost sounds sinister, doesn't it? Well, this great northern pike is sinister—any true pike fisherman will agree *Esox* is a fresh water "Jaws," an incredible predator. To the angler who connects with a mature member of the species, this is a tackle-busting, knuckle-bruiser with power to spare. When these fish get to be 36 to 39 inches long, they are prize adult specimen. The ones measuring 40 inches or more are in a class by themselves, truly trophy fish. Whenever one of these old mossbacks hooks up and makes its first power run, the angler is never sure whether it's the fish or himself who's directing the battle.

This chapter is intended to help you gain knowledge and skill in challenging trophy size northern pike with rod and reel. I will deal primarily with the use of artificial lures through spin or bait casting, using the tactics and insights gained from 25 extended fishing trips to the St. Lawrence River and the rivers of Ontario and Quebec in Canada. Though this information is based on northern lakes and rivers, I feel it will apply also to pike waters elsewhere in the United States and Canada.

The Fish and Its Characteristics

The great northern pike is a very adaptable fish which prefers water temperatures of from 55 to 65 degrees Fahrenheit with lower and upper tolerances in the lower 40's to mid 70's respectively. They are found in both clear and tannic acid darkened waters (primarily between the latitudes of 36 degrees and 52 degrees) and, depending upon the depth of the water thrive at both shallow and intermediate levels, depending upon: 1)abundance of food sources. Like most fish, northern pike are carnivorous. It will readily attack any fish, reptile, bird or animal which it can swallow whole; *e.g.*, fallfish, shiners, suckers, small sturgeon, walleye pike, next size smaller northerns, frogs, mice, muskrats, ducklings, *etc.*; 2) water temperature; 3) oxygen content of water; 4) protective cover; and 5) biological spawning instincts. Spawning takes place during the spring of the year (March through June depending upon latitude). Unlike many fish species which build a bed or nest, the female (hen) deposits her eggs over a shallow, soft bottomed river cove or lakeside bay near an inflowing stream. The male will accompany the hen to fertilize the eggs as they wallow about close to shore. Breeding temperature range is from 45 degrees to 55 degrees F.

Most anglers categorize fish as either shallow or deep water species but cannot reach any agreement on the point where shallow water ends and deep water begins. In my opinion, any specie may be classified as either a shallow and/or intermediate water fish or an intermediate and/or deep water fish. On such a three point scale (shallow, intermediate, deep), rather than the usual two point scale (shallow, deep), the cutoff point for a shallow water specie would be 15 feet, for intermediate range 30 feet, for deep water 150 feet. Below that depth not many fresh water fish are taken. I believe that northern pike are primarily a shallow to intermediate range fish which can be taken down to 30 feet below the surface.

North American northern pike come in two varieties, with white rectangular markings along their olive green sides and with multiple white spots (like the markings on a lake trout) along their bluish green sides. These bluish green fish are sometimes called blue or silver pike. They are far rarer than the olive green variety and they rarely come in trophy size. Of this type taken in the past number of years by our group while fishing Canadian waters, only one was of trophy size, 43¼ inches long, 19 pounds 4 ounces, taken by Niles Eggleston, August 15, 1974, on a pearl-crystal scale Dardevlet from Chibaugamau Preserve, Quebec, Canada.

For years the world record for northern pike taken via rod and reel, was held by Peter Dubuc. The fish was taken from the Sacandaga Reservoir in New York State on September 15, 1940. It measured 52½ inches and weighed 46 pounds 2 ounces. Although it no longer remains as a world record, it still holds as the United States record. The officially recognized world record stands at 52 pounds 3 ounces and was taken in West Germany during September of 1971. Unverified reports, as researched by Keith Gardner,* claim a Finnish record pike of 56 pounds (1905), a Scottish record of just over 70 pounds (early 1900's) and a 55 pounder claimed to have been taken from the waters of Alberta, Canada, in recent years. The official Canadian record-breaking northern pike was taken in Saskatchewan, weighing 42 pounds 12 ounces.

Despite their size and ferocity, northern pike (in their natural habitat) are generally not long-lived fish. However, pike have attained a life span of 75 years (over 100 pounds) in Europe when kept in large aquariums.** In the wild their rate of growth is rapid, and yet a fish 15 to 20 years old is felt to be an exception to the rule. Mature pike of 36 inches or over fight in a totally different manner than do those of immature age and size, often fighting to the point of total exhaustion before being landed. At such times even careful handling and proper reviving technique may not be enough to restore stability and life.

---

*Keith Gardner, "Field Testing the Leader-Free Pike Lure," *Fishing World Magazine,* May/June 1978.
**K. L. Lagler, *Freshwater Fishery Biology,* (Dubuque, Iowa: Wm. C. Brown Co., 1973), p. 38.

Unlike a feeding walleye pike, which tends to either tail-gate or swim in from the side to "chomp down" on its prey (like a dog with a bone), a northern on the take will suck in and crush, or slash into, its prey. Generally a feeding northern will wait in ambush from a position of cover (*e.g.,* weed bed, submerged tree, rock ledge, *etc.*) or will cruise about openly in search of a meal. It will usually attack from below and to the rear of its prey. Often the attack will be from beneath and to the side, but seldom will it be directed head-on. It is amazing how gracefully and swiftly an old mossback can overtake its prey (natural or artificial) once the attack begins. Upon reaching its target the mouth opens as the gill cover and cheeks flare, creating a vacuum which impedes escape of the prey. Generally, upon impact the mouth crushes shut as the head turns in a slashing movement. The prey is often dead upon impact. The prey may be held and crushed as the momentum of the pike's attacking rush subsides before being carried to the bottom or to cover where it will be gradually turned and swallowed head first. Then again, there are times when a pike will attack and continue the run, without pause, while crushing the prey between jaws, tongue and roof of mouth. Once well away from the scene and in deeper water, the pike will turn the prey and swallow it in the usual manner. Should the fish wish to reject its prey, it may either open its mouth and shake its head free or, in some cases involving smaller hard or foreign objects, may discharge it through the flared gills. One look at the massive head and jaws, the three distinctly different sets of teeth (each designed for a specific task)* as well as the streamlined elongated body justifies the pike's reputation as an accomplished killer.

Although typical pike habitat, regardless of size, may include a few northerns in attendance, pike are not considered to be a school fish. I have found that prime feeding areas of perhaps 75 yards in length by 50 yards in width may possess as many as 6 or 8 large adult northerns at one time.

---

*Slashing teeth of upper and lower jaws for killing or crippling prey; holding teeth of upper surface of tongue and of mouth roof for crushing and gripping prey; and screening teeth of inner gills edge to prevent prey's escape unless desired.

Unlike their close relative, the muskellunge (musky),
which may live a lifetime as an inhabitant of a specific area, adult
northerns tend to cover more ground. Much as an African lion
may follow a herd of waterbuck or impala until the urge to dine
prompts an attack, so an adult northern pike moves with a school
of fish until succumbing to the urge to feed. This is why an
angler is wise to linger for 5 to 10 minutes at a spot where fish
(*e.g.*, a school of walleyes) which have been hitting on nearly
every cast suddenly stop abruptly. This should be acknowledged
as a signal to the angler that one of two things has taken place
down below: the school has moved on or a big northern has
moved in. At such times the angler should slip on a pike lure and
wire leader and be ready in his casting for a take by an adult
northern. Certainly pike will frequent a particular area which has
proven generally rich in food sources. However, the angler in

Gordon Eggleston and his nephew Tom display a brace of trophy northerns
taken at the edge of a weedy river cove. The combined weight of the two
fish was 42 pounds 4 ounces.

search of trophy pike must keep in mind that they will range to a large extent.

This observation is based upon research and encounters experienced by our party while fishing the prime Chibaugamau waters in Quebec. For three years, beginning in 1971, we marked each fish caught and released *via* a paper hole-punch (1971 punched tail, 1972 punched dorsal fin and 1973 punched anal fin). Some such fish were recaught and, over this span of time, were found at different locations from when originally taken. Also, two experiences regarding a northern's tendency to roam substantiate this observation:

1) During a 7-day fishing trip a trophy size northern was lost after taking a large fallfish being used as live bait on a monofilament rig. After cutting the mono on the strike, the pike apparently moved upstream from the river site as the following day the rig with dead fallfish was found floating near shore one mile above where it had broken free.

2) Just last year my brother caught a trophy size northern from a weedy lake bay. It still held in its cheek the black jig which was lost on the fish while jigging for walleyes the preceding day, a distance of approximately 1¼ miles. That the jig was lost by another angler was not possible since our party was the only one to portage back into this area to fish.

Fishing for northern pike is much like fishing for any other specie in that the angler should heed and react to his gut feelings about lure selection, the presence of trophy fish and casting/retrieve techniques. Typical haunts frequented by trophy pike might best be presented by a description (and accompanying diagrams) of those river and lake feeding areas which have proven most successful for me over the years. The actual names of the rivers and lakes have been omitted other than to say that, for the most part, they are located within the Chibaugamau Preserve of upper Quebec. Our party has adopted a policy of naming each hot spot (whether for northerns or for walleyes) to assist our pinpointing research and statistics according to exact location. These names will, along with certain statistics gained over a 9 year span, appear with each description.

Identification of Prime Trophy Northern Pike Haunts

1) River Coves. *Example:* High Hopes. *Statistics:* Has produced 72 pike of 30 inches or over by our party. *Description:* Over the years we have come to refer to this small cove as High Hopes and it has never let us down. It has become our Number 1 producer of adult northerns. Any pike fisherman could immediately recognize the spot as possessing all the necessary ingredients which spell success. Located alongside the main inlet stream to the large lake (about 300 yards from its entrance), the cove contains a weed bed which runs outward some 25 yards from the whole of its inner shoreline. All the weeds of this cove are long, slender (1/4 inch width) and a yellowish-green in color; we refer to them as pike weed. They are limp in structure, reaching to and beyond the surface with about 12 inches lying on top of the water during normal water level conditions. The shoreline pike weeds are nearly impenetrable with heavy surface growth, a mass of tiny yellow buds. The thickness suddenly breaks into an intermediate strip of like weeds which offer various pockets and open lanes here and there. Finally, some 75 yards from the inner

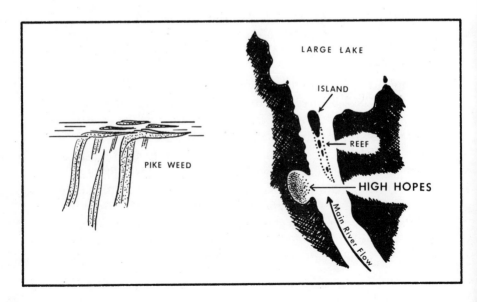

PIKE WEED

LARGE LAKE

ISLAND

REEF

HIGH HOPES

Main River Flow

shoreline, the weeds thin to only a patch here and there across the mouth of the cove. The bottom is silt over coarse gravel and rock. The water is dark in color as the result of the high tannic acid concentration, like all these waters. The depth is approximately 4 feet at the outer edge of the thick weed strip, 6 feet among the intermediate weeds and from 10 to 12 feet at the center of the river. When it comes to pike fishing, High Hopes is my favorite type of setting: moderately shallow water, a sizeable bed of pike weeds and a deeper water flow immediately adjacent affording structure (reef, boulders or bottom rocks, sunken trees or logs, *etc.*) for the fish when not in a feeding mood. Although always fishable due to its sheltered location, ideal conditions prevail when 1) the surface is calm and sky is overcast and 2) when a slight breeze slowly drifts the angler parallel to the inner shoreline. In fishing, the angler should work his way inward gradually on drift. Casts are best made with the grain of the weeds through open lanes and open pockets, using accurate, shortened casts. The thick surface weeds are unfishable except by using weedless spoons rapidly retrieved atop water (skittering or, as we call it, Rubber Ducky). All other weeds are best fished with either a slow or alternate slow and let-back retrieve.

2) **River Weed Beds.** *Example:* Big Ben. *Statistics:* Has produced 27 pike of 30 inches or over by our party. *Description:* Big Ben received its name because of a house sized boulder which lies submerged (reaching just inches beneath the surface under normal water level conditions) nearly at midstream just at the river's bend. The river at this point is about 50 yards wide and of slow current. It is always an especially good spot for walleyes and fallfish; both a favorite diet of pike. Immediately below the boulder at the river bend is a large, thick, underwater tobacco cabbage weed bed at the very edge of the main current which bows such weeds downstream preventing their reaching the water's surface, the tops being about 4 feet underwater. When both lighting and water conditions allow, the angler can see a narrow strip of pike weeds, whose tops float upon the surface. Also, there is a small patch of surfacing pike weeds growing in about 4

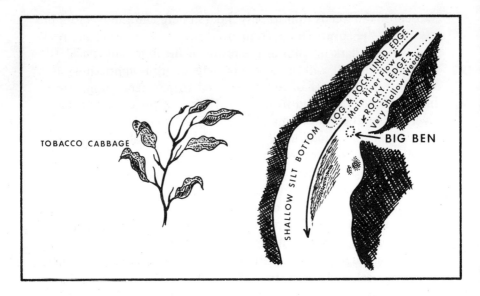

feet of water between the shoreline and the tobacco cabbage weeds.

Water depth where the tobacco cabbage bows to the current is some 15 feet in depth. Although a few large northerns have been taken over the years from along the main stream edge of the rocky ledge above Big Ben, the majority come from both the pike weed patches and tobacco cabbage at the current's edge. While casting to the pike weeds and above the submerged tobacco cabbage produces best results from the shallower inside-current edge, trolling upstream just off the tobacco cabbage edge within the main current gives the depth necessary for best results at this location.

3) River Sandbars and Adjacent Holes. *Example:* Hot Spot No. 2. *Statistics:* Has produced 17 pike of 30 inches or over by our party. *Description:* Hot Spot No. 2 is another river producer of large northerns and walleyes. It also contains fallfish and lake whitefish (northern whitefish) in good numbers and, as previously mentioned, wherever walleyes, fallfish and whitefish are gathered, the setting is right for intruding trophy northerns as well.

On one side of the river hole is a large slant rock which slopes down to the water where its end and upstream side immediately drop off to a depth of 8 feet. The other side of the river contains a long, parallel-to-current sandbar. Under normal conditions a strip of the bar is about 1 foot above water and is separated from the inner shoreline by very shallow water. Immediately to the current side of the strip the bar drops off quickly to a depth of from 8 to 10 feet. The river bottom is mainly sand and, along the bottom paralleling the sandbar dropoff, there is a thick, short-stemmed coontail weedbed. The current flow through this area is slow. Above Hot Spot No. 2 the current winds slowly through a wide spot in the river, flanked on both sides by curly-leafed cabbage weeds which rise to within inches of the surface from a bottom depth of only 3 to 4 feet. The channel through these weeds is edged with tobacco cabbage where the water is about 5 feet deep. The channel is approximately 10 to 12 yards wide and 6 feet deep at its

center. While only small (hammerhandle or snake) pike in large numbers have been taken from the weeds and channel above Hot Spot No. 2, trophy size pike have often come from the hole between sandbar and the slant rock where, at midstream, the water depth is 12 feet. The best way to take these fish is to anchor at the sandbar dropoff and jig the hole and weed bed. Downstream wind trolling and upstream motor trolling of a plug (crankbait) are also good ways of fishing the area although the distance of such trolls is short.

4) Structural River Narrows. *Example:* The Chute. *Statistics:* Has produced 7 pike of 30 inches or over by our party. *Description:* The Chute is the narrowest point in the main lake inlet river. Huge, high boulders on each side force all the river flow to funnel through an opening 8 feet wide. Immediately below, the current swirls over a rocky bottom about 8 feet deep. The force is so great through the opening that rooster tails 3 to 4 feet high roll and splash. However, the approaching flow is slow as it passes over small scattered boulders which rise to 3 to 4 inches from the surface under normal water level conditions. Such boulders are at a depth of about 5 feet with submerged curly-leafed cabbage weeds about their base. The shoreline along one side is very shallow and rocky with curly-leafed cabbage (submerged) and thin-leafed cabbage (submerged) extending out to nearly midstream and bowing to the downstream current. The opposite shoreline forms part of the main current as the water flows over rocks at a depth of about 4 feet. The main channel is about 5 feet deep with a hard bottom. Although not many large northerns have been taken here, we generally stop to cast spoons from the shallow, rocky edge as any pike which we have taken here are adult size and have come from the edge weeds near midstream within from 30 to 40 feet from the chute itself. It is an ideal haunt for feeding northerns as any crippled or weak fish will be carried through the restricted area. It is interesting to note that, once hooked, the northern will avoid running downstream through the chute, preferring to fight it out within the confines of the narrow channel. Walleyes, fallfish and small pike are often taken from the varied pool current just below the chute. However, such fish have always proven to be small in size and quite thin from competing against the current. A structural river narrows need not be a chute alone. Any narrow restriction to a river's flow may work equally well if conditions are right.

5) Lakeside Reefs. *Example:* Bar & Grill. *Statistics:* Has produced 21 pike of 30 inches or over by our party. *Description:* The Bar & Grill is a favorite dining spot frequented by schools of walleyes; consequently the name and consequently a favorite dining spot for big northerns as well. There is no outward appearance which would prompt a passing angler to stop and fish the area. In fact, it is one of those places which is best discovered through the use of a sonar probe unit as its success rests more on what is beneath the water rather than what is visible above or around. Bar & Grill is located about halfway down a big lake. It consists of a long, rocky, underwater bar or reef which extends

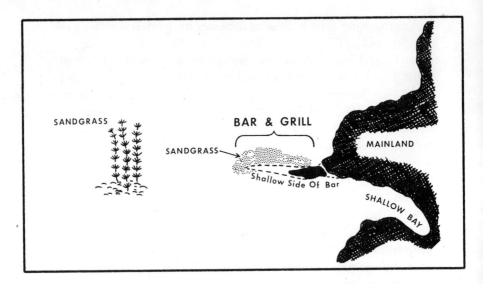

some 75 yards into the lake (at a right angle to the mainland).
The bar is approximately 10 yards wide and slopes very gradually
as it extends. The water depth above the bar is from one foot at
shoreline to 8 feet at its distal end. The lead edge drops abruptly
to the lake bottom at a depth of from 8 to 15 feet. The bottom
appears to be composed of silt and gravel with occasional rock
projections here and there. The only weed cover in the area is a
scattering of sandgrass, low in height, dark in color, crusty in
texture and quite brittle. The major problem faced in fishing the
area, as is often the case in open lake angling, is maintaining
position in rough water conditions. At such times trolling is much
the easier because it prevents slack line from becoming a handicap
to the angler. When starting to fish the Bar & Grill (when water
conditions are favorable for casting) we generally run a troll just
off the bar on the deeper side using a crankbait in order to locate
a school of walleyes. Once such fish are located, we anchor at
casting distance from the reef and work jigs. As previously
mentioned, if the walleyes stop abruptly or if a northern makes his
presence known, we switch to a spoon such as a Dardevlet, as
attached to a 6 inch wire leader, and spend from 5 to 10 minutes
casting the lure before repeating the fish-locating troll.

6) Weedy Lake Bays. *Example:* Battlefield Bay.
Statistics: Has produced 52 pike of 30 inches or over by our
party (9 of which were trophy northerns of 40 inches or longer.)
Description: Battlefield Bay is well named for the many
campaigns which have taken place within its weed beds between
its powerful fighting pike and members of our party. In one year
alone (1971) we landed 15 of 30 inches or better in our 7 day
trip. It is situated about half way down a lake much like the one
we camp on except it has fewer shoreline bays and less varying
structure. Although small in size, this bay is one of the two best
located on the lake. It also ranks as the second best all time
producer of lunker northerns for our party. The bay is about 75
yards deep by 100 yards wide at the mouth, possesses a mixture
of pike weeds, tobacco cabbage
and a few small long-stemmed
pads. Generally the thinner pike
weeds along the lakeside edge
have proven the most productive
over the years. The inner and
middle bay bottom is silt over
sand and the outer bottom is
sand. A tiny stream enters the
bay at its innermost point
providing a small amount of
oxygenated water of cold,
spring-fed temperature. What
does make the bay a hot spot is
not the entrance of the tiny
stream but the favorable
(although shallow) water depth
and temperature, abundant
cover for predator and prey
alike, immediately adjacent deep
lake waters, and, lastly, an
abundance of small bait fish of
various kinds. The inner and
thick mid-bay weeds are in

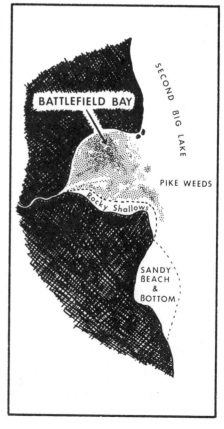

shallow water depth of about 3 feet under normal water level conditions. Depth of the outer weeds is from 4 to 5 feet. From the bay's mouth the sand bottom gradually slopes lakeward some distance before dropping noticeably to a depth of from 12 to 15 feet; well within the lake itself. The bay is best fished in the same manner as explained earlier under Fishing River Coves.

      7) Lake Lagoons. *Example:* Old Folks Home. *Statistics:* Has produced 33 pike of 30 inches or over by our party. Of these 7 were of trophy size with my largest measuring 45-¼ inches and weighing 23 pounds, 9 ounces. *Description:* Old Folks Home received its name in dedication to the numerous old mossbacks that have been encountered (but not all landed) while fishing this massive, weedy-but-shallow location. It is situated at the extreme end of the large lake along the edge of a big bay and is approximately 125 yards long by 60 yards wide. A stream of moderate current enters the end of the lagoon and broadens to flow with a slower current through a long, wide field of pike weed to empty into the bay. For the most part, the bed of pike weed is thick with a few thin-stemmed pads and curly-leafed cabbage at its downstream conclusion. These are followed by a bottom cover of sandgrass along the entire mouth of the lagoon. The water

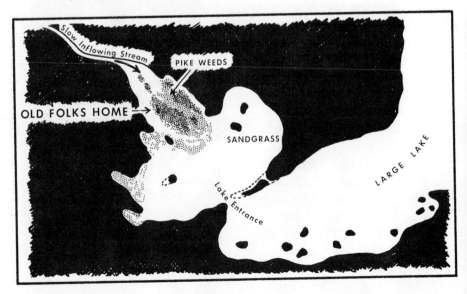

depth over the whole width of the area is approximately 4-½ to 5 feet under normal water level conditions. However, at the entrance to the bay there is a buildup of silt, of which the entire bottom is formed, with a water depth of only from 3-½ to 4 feet. Like all the waters in this part of the country, the lake is dark. The stream offers good oxygen level, cold water temperature and a haven for small bait fish, fish which walleyes and fallfish will seek during the evening hours. Because of the stream channel, length of the lagoon and openness of the bay, wind often prevents the most desirable drift float when fishing the area. I prefer such a float for casting to be downstream through the weed bed rather than working across the width of the weeds. Both immature and adult pike can be found among the weeds of this lagoon. However, after the first drift one is able to tell which will be taken during the outing. Immature pike will generally sense when the big boys are on the prowl. At such times they will make themselves scarce and will seek sanctuary rather than chance feeding. Therefore, if a small pike is taken it usually indicates that either trophy pike are not around or that they are not feeding. However, if a drift or two is made without taking an immature pike it may well mean that an old mossback is ready for the taking. Retrieving spoons in either Rubber Ducky fashion atop the thicker weeds or by working with the grain of weeds, through lanes and pockets, employing a slow-steady or an alternate slow and let-back method have proven to be the most effective techniques for obtaining results. It should also be mentioned that lagoons, such as Old Folks Home are typical spring spawning areas sought by great northern pike. At such times these areas will receive a number of huge pike.

8) **Lake Islands.** *Example:* Jig-A-Boo Island. *Statistics:* Has produced 21 pike of 30 inches or over by our party. *Description:* Jig-A-Boo has become our top island producer of both large walleyes and large northerns. It can always be relied upon to offer various sized walleyes plus adult size pike which move in to dine on the walleyes. The island is tall and quite steep in its incline to the water at one end where a rock formation

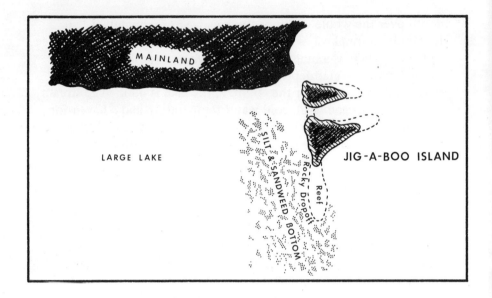

projects outward into the lake to present a reef some 40 yards long by 20 yards wide. Water depth above the reef is from 3 to 4 feet. Along the entire downlake edge of the reef the water depth drops to some 10 to 12 feet where a swath of large, irregular shaped rocks make jigging somewhat difficult, yet rewarding. The bottom beyond this rocky depth is composed of silt from which patches of short-stemmed sandgrass grow in abundance. The water depth here is some 15 to 18 feet. Although we will troll plugs along the island edge (starting from behind the reef and working to the far end) when either action slows or weather hinders working the reef, the most productive spot is the rocky depth alongside the reef and its adjacent lake bottom. The boat is anchored to the reef where jigs are cast beyond the rocky dropoff and are slowly worked back to the boat in the normal jigging manner. As the use of wire leader attached jigs result in poor action, we prefer to risk the chance of a breakoff by a northern by working the lure with a direct tie to the line. If a northern is found to be present we will attach a shallow running crankbait and cast the reef's shallow water or will cast either a spoon or a moderate-level running crankbait to work the dropoff rocks.

The following should serve as a guide to recognizing an island hot spot:

Because each structure and cover (*i.e.,* submerged rock formations, submerged trees, stumps and logs as well as both submerged and surfacing vegetation) are often found near and around certain islands, the angler in quest of northern pike should never overlook such areas.

Structure, cover and adequate water depth are keys to finding baitfish and in consequence predators such as northern pike can be expected to be nearby. Fish in shallow waters vacant of cover are easy prey to bird and animal predators such as gulls, herons, loons, terns, mergansers, fish hawks, otters *etc.* Therefore, water depth possessing cover offers any fish greater security particularly during the daylight hours.

Of course, a sonar unit is an asset to the angler for quickly sorting out unfavorable islands from those which offer all the ingredients necessary for favorable fishing. However, for those who must rely upon observation and experimentation, there is one tip which can be of great assistance. This is to examine an island in light of its side profile.

Those of good height and offering the sharpest incline (ends and/or sides) to the water's surface usually mean deep water

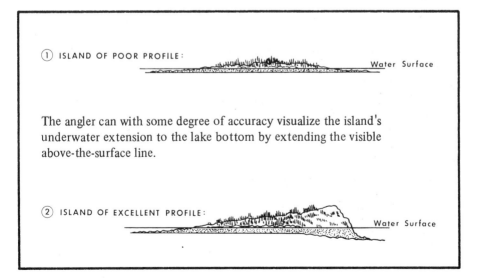

① ISLAND OF POOR PROFILE :   Water Surface

The angler can with some degree of accuracy visualize the island's underwater extension to the lake bottom by extending the visible above-the-surface line.

② ISLAND OF EXCELLENT PROFILE :   Water Surface

and fish. On the other hand, islands low in height with gradually sloping sides and/or ends will generally lack the immediate shoreline depth and structure necessary for success.

9) Lake Outlet Areas. *Example:* Dinner Bucket. *Statistics:* Has produced 7 pike of 30 inches or over by our party. *Description:* Lake outlets are generally of two types, a deep lake basin or a shallow lake flat at the head of an outflowing river channel. Each serves the same function. It forms a funnel through which, and by which, a lake's water level is maintained in constant balance. The outflowing waters create current flow which begins from further within the lake as its water level rises. The Dinner Bucket is an outlet of the second type possessing a wide, shallow flat which funnels into a shallow channel flanked by rocks as the river begins. There is a large boulder island around which the water flows; a narrow, secondary flow on the one side and a wider, deeper main flow on the other. The bottom of the flat is sand silt (patched with sandgrass) and the channel is sand and rock (covered with curly-leafed cabbage which bows to the downstream current). The flat is quite uniform in depth at approximately 5 feet. The main channel is about 6 feet at its

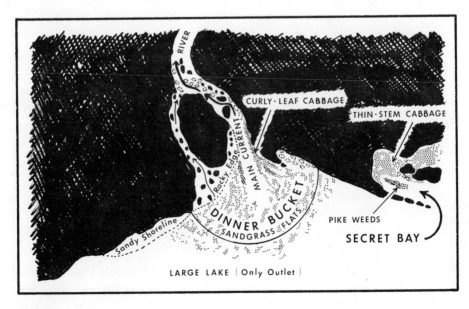

RIVER

CURLY-LEAF CABBAGE

THIN-STEM CABBAGE

MAIN CURRENT

Rocky Edge

DINNER BUCKET

SANDGRASS FLATS

Sandy Shoreline

PIKE WEEDS

SECRET BAY

LARGE LAKE (Only Outlet)

center. The northerns taken during the early morning hours will generally be located along or near the rocky edge of the current rather than from the midstream current. Rather than cruise in search of prey, these pike will wait among the weeds near the rocky edge to strike from ambush. During the early evening hours such pike will generally be found at the flat where walleyes and fallfish move in to feed. I personally feel that, because of the current and lack of good water depth, the fish will spend most of the day in the deeper lake waters. However, during the evening and early morning hours (and possibly at night) they will move into the area to feed. Adjacent bays and deep water structure of within ¼ mile or less of a river outlet should always be investigated, especially during midday when the shallow type outlet area becomes unproductive. As diagramed, Secret Bay is a prime example of a weedy bay which would otherwise not be overly productive were it not for the fact that it is close at hand to the lake's outlet which is abundant in providing food sources. In fact, it has produced 7 northerns of 36 inches or better over the years most of which were taken during the midday hours.

10) Late Fall, Early Winter & Winter Haunts. The information listed below is based on data obtained from people who have fished various New York State waters for northern pike:

Water Fishing

    a) Area: Shoreline docks and pilings. *Method:* Casting from either boat, dock or shore. *Tackle:* Jigs, small (*e.g.,* Little Cleo) to medium (*e.g.,* Dardevlet) spoons or plugs such as a Countdown Rapala or Canadian Wiggler; all except jigs being fished using a 6 inch wire leader.

    b) Area: Shoreline submerged weed beds. *Method:* Casting from either boat, dock or shore or by boat trolling of outer edges at slow speed. *Tackle:* ¾ ounce bucktail jigs (orange and white, yellow and black), Little Cleo (fluorescent and silver), Dardevlet (either silver or pearl scale) or Canadian Wiggler (silver) for casting. The same, except for jigs, if trolling.

c) Area: Sunken shoreline trees, logs, pipelines or other similar structure offering shelter for food source congregation. *Method:* Casting from either boat or shore. *Tackle:* Same as for fishing shoreline docks, pilings or weed beds and jigs in particular as fished without wire leader.

d) Area: Lake inlets offering muddy water discharge where its lead edge meets the lake's clear water. *Method:* Casting or trolling from a boat worked along the dividing water line; working lure slow and at varying depths. *Tackle:* Spoons and crankbaits of either medium or large (up to lengths of 8 inches) size designed to either run at moderate or deep levels.

e) Area: Lead edge of iced-over lake bays where unfrozen waters begin. *Methods:* Slow speed trolling along the lead edge of the ice. *Tackle:* Spoons and crankbaits (plugs) of medium length worked at or near bottom level.

Ice Fishing

a) Area: Either lake bays or river coves which offer complete freezing (of safe to travel thickness) and whose bottom provides weed beds. Such areas should be of sufficient depth as to prevent complete surface-to-bottom freezing, should provide adequate oxygen-to-water content and should be immediately adjacent to a deep water area. *Method:* Use of either hand line or tip-ups. *Tackle:* Live bait (*e.g.*, Missouri Minnows, Golden Shiners, Suckers, *etc.*) or such artificials as a Swedish Pimple, 1/8 or 1/4 ounce jig with either plastic worm or Mr. Twister tail attached, or a jigging lure (*e.g.*, Rapala Jigging Lure).

A variety of other game fish can be caught from typical bass cover and structures. Anglers interested in identifying potential hot spots for other species should refer to the section on Cover and Structure in Chapter 2, "Largemouth Bass Basics."

Favorable Conditions for Action

Although I have taken northerns at all times of day (not at night) regardless of weather conditions, there are definite periods which tend to prompt action, especially in regards to the taking of trophy pike.

Early Morning. Fishing the first two hours of daylight is a prime time for the taking of most fresh water game fish. It certainly is my favorite time of day when fishing for trophy size northern pike. At such times both pike and their prey are most apt to be found near shallow shoreline areas. Especially good early morning locations are weedy lake lagoons and bays, weedy river coves, lake outlets and structural river narrows. Generally speaking, weather conditions (especially winds) are calm from dawn to mid-morning and thus afford the angler with more favorable surface visibility as well as more favorable lure presentations. Moving in under a shroud of slowly rising fog to fish a glassy-surfaced bay of thick pike weed, coupled with the eerie cry of a distant loon in the stillness of early morn, can send a chill of anticipation coursing throughout the frame of any true pike fisherman.

Midday. I cannot say why but it seems that trophy northerns will often feed between the hours of 10 AM and 2 PM during the summer and early autumn months. I have taken a number of adult pike at such times over the years providing the day was not clear and calm. The areas which I prefer between mid-morning and late afternoon are the deeper lake and river areas (if fishable) and certain weedy bays or coves (if choppy or rough waters prevail). It should be mentioned that two anglers fishing a weedy area together, when winds prevent a slow and controlled drift, are wasting both time and energy whenever one does not control the boat or canoe for the other. Therefore, although any angler would rather fish than operate a boat, under rough conditions it is most productive to take turns fishing and holding the boat for each successive drift.

Late Afternoon/Early Evening. When the sun approaches the horizon in its descent, big northerns tend to move into the same areas as during the early morning hours. Casting is much preferred to trolling at such times as the pike tend to cruise the shallower waters in search of a meal. Trophy size walleyes, large mouth bass, brown trout and certain other species of fresh water game fish can be considered as primarily nocturnal feeders, but not northern pike. Therefore, once darkness begins to set in, an angler can forget about northerns.

Days of Overcast Skies with Calm Waters. Schools of walleyes will feed during overcast days in calm or choppy waters and thus will offer the high possibility of there being a feeding northern nearby or within their midst. Consequently, areas frequented by walleyes during the day (particularly deep waters with nearby shoreline cover) are always a wise choice. Also, weedy areas (bays, lagoons and coves) will remain productive longer into the day when overcast and calm as compared to days when the sky clears and the water remains placid. Either casting (surface weed areas) or trolling (deeper water areas) can be expected to provide good results.

Days of Choppy Waters. As previously mentioned, choppy waters can often spell success when it comes to trophy pike fishing as the big boys will often cruise about at near surface and moderate depth waters in search of food. At such times the angler should be observant for sign and location of near-surface feeding pike of trophy size. I have observed a fallfish, of from 10 to 12 inches in length, skipping in bounds of 10 or 12 feet across the surface of a bay during choppy water conditions. Although no surface sign betrayed the northern's presence, it was obvious that the chase was on. Another sign of near-surface pike is the aerial shower of minnows as the school scatters in fright. This may be accompanied by either a surface wake (sometimes exposing bill and/or a section of back) or a surface swirl of the attacking northern. If in range and ready for a presentation, the angler should immediately cast to about 5 or 6 feet (one side or the other) from where the minnows landed in their flight, allowing the lure, preferably a spoon or spinner, to sink for about two seconds while maintaining a taut line, and return with an alternate fast and let-back retrieve. Such antics do not always spell success for the angler. I have been in the presence of numerous trophy pike involved in stirring up the minnows of a weedy bay and yet was unable to coax one to take an artificial. It can be one of the most frustrating situations to be encountered by a pike fisherman. Another visible sign of a pike's presence is either a surface-breaking swirl or a deep, lingering surface boil. However, the angler must remember that such signs do not necessarily mean that the fish is feeding near the surface. While playing trophy northerns I have observed that a quick power turn executed at a depth of 5 or 6 feet will produce a delayed surface boil of great proportion that seems to continue for a few moments. Therefore, one should govern the depth of retrieve according to the type swirl or boil; if it breaks water, retrieve shallow and if it does not break water, retrieve at a moderate (4 or 5 feet) level. Remember that often a trophy northern will follow at a deep or moderate level and will be provoked into an attack as it observes the lure to begin traveling upward (toward the boat) as if attempting to escape to the surface. A strike at the boat, although spectacular, is the least desirable location for hooking a big fish. Yet, it is a common occurance when fishing pike country. The final sign to heed in observing the presence and location of trophy northerns is a movement or parting of surface weeds or submerged brush which breaks the surface. Such vegetation movement is a tipoff of a pike on the prowl.

Rough Water and/or Stormy Weather. Rough weather conditions often result in active feeding by large pike as small bait fish are forced into shallower and more sheltered waters; *e.g.*, bays, lagoons, coves, lake and island shorelines where the waves are beating in over rocks and boulders or island lee-side protection. Within the limits of safety, such times, although not easy and overly enjoyable fishing, can bring great results for the pike fisherman. Again, it may mean that one person handles the boat while the other fishes and that trolling is the preferred method rather than drift or anchored-boat casting.

Concentration of Birds. I have used arctic terns as indicators when fishing for lake trout shortly after ice out in Lac Waconichi, Quebec. As they would group to circle lower and lower we would quickly motor to the spot knowing they had observed a school of bait fish and/or lakers. As the bait was driven to the surface, the terns would drop to about 10 feet from the water and, once the lakers began their feeding frenzy which literally boiled the surface, would swoop to pick up crippled bait fish, sometimes even alighting upon the exposed back of a laker to pick at the cripples. Gulls also have excellent eyesight and are able to spot crippled fish from the air. Occasionally they will congregate and circle over a particular area of water where northerns are feeding. It is not a common occurence, but now and then it will happen and the angler should be aware of the fact.

Outfitting for Trophy Size Northern Pike

Successful northern pike fishing begins with a boat. The angler who attempts to fish for northerns from shore limits his range drastically and, at the same time, limits the chance of landing any trophy size pike hooked. I know of seven trophy size fish including my largest to date, which could not be checked in their first power run of over 100 yards. Had any one of these pike been hooked while fishing from shore it would have been, "Strrrrrrrip-Goodbye!"

I prefer to fish from my "Fish Hawk No. 2;" a 17 foot Grumman square stern aluminum canoe. It is dark green in color, sound-dampened by removable floor mats of one inch thick polyurethane and is powered by a 9½ horse power Evinrude Motor. While a total of 61 northern pike of 10 pounds and over have been taken by myself and others while fishing from this canoe, I readily acknowledge the limitations of fishing and traveling rough waters with such a vehicle. Therefore, I feel that the safest, yet most versatile, way to go is as follows:

A 16 foot aluminum boat (*e.g.*, Starcraft) weighing no more than 300 pounds with either an 18 or 20 horse power motor is my recommendation for maximum boat and motor size. I would recommend a minimum length of 14 feet (wide beam) with a 9½ horse power motor. Such boats should be rigged with a bow-mount anchor rope of 60 feet braided nylon (3/16 inch) rope and accompanying fluke type anchor of from 10 to 15 pounds weight. A foot operated electric motor is a worthwhile accessory for maintaining the correct line of drift while casting. However, when frequent battery recharging is unattainable it is useless. Through the use of such an outfit the angler can safely (within reason) travel and fish large bodies of water and yet be able to portage or line the boat when size and weight become a factor in traversing rapids.

Selection of the proper rod, reel and line is generally governed by personal preference. The rod should possess a stiff backbone (butt stiffness) for setting of the hook within a pike's tightly closed mouth. The reel should possess an easily adjusted and smooth running drag system. The line should be at least 100 yards in length. I have always been a bait casting, rather than spin casting, angler (when I'm not fly fishing for trout). I prefer to carry two casting rods rigged to meet the demands of the particular area being fished at the moment. One is a 5½ foot Fenwick HMG Graphite (GFC554/moderate action) and the other (my favorite) an old 5 foot solid triangular glass Shakespeare with stiff backbone and extra fast 18 inch section of tip (which acts as a shock absorber during times of sudden strike-stress). My reel choice is the Garcia Abu Ambassadeur in models 5600 C or 5000. My line choice is either Squidding (flat braided nylon) or Cortland braided nylon; either line in 15 pounds weight strength. For those wishing to use spinning rod and reel I would suggest that open-faced, rather than closed-face reels, be employed due to the fact that the drag system of most open-faced reels is smoother running than are those of the closed-face models.

As for outfitting the tackle box I would suggest the following:

Lures (Spoons):
1. *Eppinger Dardevlet:* in gold, copper or pearl scale colors.
2. *Marathon* (sometimes called a "Rattle Spoon"): in hammer

   scale finish; either gold or copper in color and of 3 inches
   length.
3. *Aqua Spoon or Flash Bait 166* (Dardevlet imitation but
   lighter in weight; manufactured in Minneapolis, Minn.): in
   either hammer scale finish or plain and in either gold or
   copper.
4. *Weedless Dardevlet* with single weedless trailer hook in copper.
5. *Kush Spoon:* 3½ inches length; with silver belly, red and
   yellow divided back.
6. *Johnson Spoon:* either in silver or black and rigged with
   either a fish belly, Mister Twister tail or plastic worm.
7. *Williams Wobbler:* 6 inch length with gold and silver back and
   belly.

Lures (Plugs):
1. *Cisco Kid:* in orange-dog, yellow or perch colors.
2. *Cisco Kid Junior:* in yellow or perch colors.
3. *Canadian Wiggler:* solid silver color.

4. *Musky Flatfish:* orange/black spots.
5. *Heddon Bomber:* (for trolling) in yellow or perch colors.
6. *Norman 3000-DR:* rainbow trout finish.

Lures (Spinners):
1. *Mepps Spinner/plastic minnow:* large size.
2. *Mepps Giant Killer:* pearl scale blade and yellow tail; for trolling in deep water areas.
3. *Shannon Spinner Bait:* large size in chartreuse or white.
4. *Zorro Spinner Bait:* safety pin large size in chartreuse.
5. *Abu Spinner:* large size in silver blade and red or yellow tail.

Lures (Jigs):
1. *Walleye Jigs:* ¼ and ½ ounce sizes with yellow, white or black hair tails (either bucktail, polar bear or black bear).
2. *Ball-head Jigs:* ¼ and ½ ounce sizes; same colors as walleye jigs.

Essential Tackle Box Fishing Accessories:
1. *Wire Leaders:* I prefer plastic covered, braided wire leaders of from 15 to 18 pounds test in the 6 inch length; leaders with ball bearing swivels and size 10 standard-clip snaps. I have lost very few pike because the leader was too short and have found longer length leaders prevent ease in casting.
2. *Chatillion Scales:* Each of our party carries a pair of Chatillions to either 30 pounds or 60 pounds maximum for weighing all northerns measuring 30 inches or longer. Although not a necessity, such scales take up little room within a tackle box and provide accurate weights for the sake of interest or research.
3. *Long Nose Pliers and Jaw Spreaders* (see Diagram I): These two items are essential safety tools for aiding in the removal of hooks from within the mouth of a pike, whether such fish be of adult or immature size.
4. *Retractable Tape Measure:* Although either a portable measuring board (to the nearest ¼ inch) or attached steel tape to the boat bottom is best for quick, easy and accurate measuring, a retractable metal tape of 6 feet length is a good companion for the Chatillion scales.
5. *Personal Emergency Items:* Any tackle box should possess certain health and safety items for emergency use. The most important among these are bandaids, aspirin, sunburn prevention cream or salve, insect repellent, antacid tablets, a lighter or matches and a small flashlight. Those items which may be damaged or destroyed by water should be stored in a waterproof container or wrap.

The final item to be included in outfitting for trophy northern pike fishing is a large landing net. Each of our party's boats contains a net measuring 36 inches across the opening, a deep heavy duty nylon mesh and a handle with end grip. When the net is not in use, it can be quickly adjusted to half its overall length. An angler works long and hard to hook up with such a fish. Thus, an extra large net might look unnecessary but may well save the angler a trophy northern pike.

DIAGRAM I

Hook Removal Tools for Use
When Dealing with Northern Pike

LONG NOSE GRIP
PLIERS

COIL SPRING JAWS
SPREADER

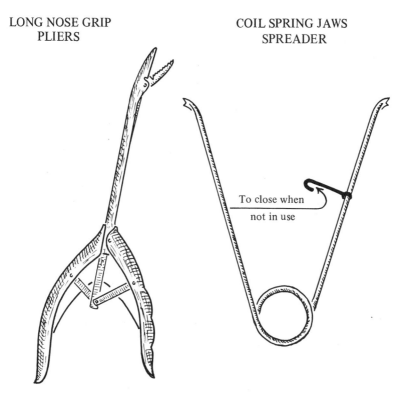

To close when
not in use

    Both of the above, along with a pair of heavy duty rubberized gloves, are highly recommended (for safety reasons) in the removal of hooks from within the mouth of a northern; an adult pike in particular. Any fish possesses certain slime and bacteria which, through portal of entry as caused by a tooth slash or puncture, can produce an infection. Also, as once happened to my brother, a tooth may puncture and break off to cause pain and infection before working its way to the surface at a later date.

Fishing Methods and Techniques

Northerns may be taken by live bait fishing, trolling, spin casting, bait casting and, during winter months, ice fishing. However, for the purpose of this chapter I will hold primarily to my favorite method, bait casting.

Any fishing requires a high degree of concentration on the business at hand for gaining optimum success. Many fine fish have been lost on the strike because of a momentary break (*e.g.,* to slap an insect, to joke with a fishing buddy, to watch a bird while retrieving a lure, *etc.*) in concentration. In both executing and retrieving a cast the angler must 1) properly read sign and structure, 2) select an appropriate choice of lure, 3) present an accurately directed cast to the appropriate location, and 4) work a retrieve which will provoke an attacking response at the correct depth.

In governing the type of retrieve best suited to the location, the angler must recognize the possible food source in relation to its depth as well as the speed (or combination thereof) which will both avoid "fouling up" and will create a lifelike attraction. The following variety of retrieve techniques may be produced through speed of reel handle ratio and/or rod tip raising and lowering during (or between) turning of the handle:

Slow and Steady. I feel too many anglers fail to connect because they tend to retrieve too fast. Immature pike love to chase a fast moving lure but not so for the old mossbacks. The same applies in regards to trolling speed. Casting or trolling, most of the time they like it slow and steady.

Slow with Alternate Rod Lift and Let-Back. This is another producer when either casting or trolling and is executed through an 8 or 10 foot slow-steady retrieve as the rod tip raises, immediately followed by a stop in reeling as the rod tip is lowered. After a slight hesitation the procedure continues.

Slow and Stop. Although not as successful as the slow and steady retrieve, it will cometimes bring results (generally as the lure sinks to the bottom). This technique works well when casting a spoon or a slow sinking or suspending lure.

Fast and Stop. Like the slow and stop retrieve, it is less successful than are certain other retrieves. However, it is a good finish technique toward the completion of a slow and steady retrieve as the lure begins its up-to-the-boat approach. At such times a strike may result either as the lure begins quickening its pace upward or as the lure stops to settle.

Fast and Steady. This sometimes brings results, especially when either working a deep running crankbait along the bottom or or in the "skittering" top water retrieve of a weedless spoon over the top of thick surface weeds. However, it should not be employed in either trolling or retrieving an underwater running spoon or spinnerbait where line twisting is apt to result.

Alternate Fast and Slow. This technique is best employed when using a crankbait, rather than in using a spoon, and may be executed through alternate reeling speed or through alternate reeling while raising and lowering the rod tip (slow reeling while raising the rod tip immediately followed by fast reeling while lowering the rod tip).

At Boat Drop-back. Muskies are notorious for following right up to the boat to strike or reject the lure. Northerns run a close second. The wise angler will always complete a retrieve with this in mind and will hesitate before lifting for the next cast. If a missed strike results as the lure is lifted, it (if using a sinking lure such as a spoon or Canadian Wiggler) should be quickly flipped out from 6 to 8 feet from the boat and allowed to sink on a taut line to a depth of 4 or 5 feet before slowly retrieving. If such lure is a spoon, it often works to let the spoon sink and slowly jig it a few moments (allowing it to hesitate a couple of seconds between each jigging action). In either case, if a follow-up strike is to result, it will generally take place as the lure sinks.

Retrieving a Weeded Lure. In heavily fished waters a weeded-up lure will result only in a rejection by pike and other fish. However, in the unfished areas we fish in Canada, I have taken more than one pike at (or near) the boat while trailing a small amount of weeds attached to the lure. Once I was reaching for a weeded spoon as I lifted it from the water in a fast retrieve only to have a large pike barely miss the spoon (and my hand) by inches. In fact, the largest northern taken by a member of our party was taken by casting an Abu Spinner into thick river weeds. The lure was allowed to sink until hung in the weeds, where it was merely worked by alternate rod pulls and let-backs. In so doing the spinner would flutter back after each pull. Suddenly, the huge northern loomed up to strip the Abu free from the weeds. When landed the trophy pike measured 48 inches and tipped the scales at just over 30 pounds.

Hooking and Playing Trophy Northerns

Contrary to general opinion, a feeding adult northern pike will often follow or attack from a considerable distance. I once observed an old mossback attack a skittered lure from some 20 yards distance. As the spoon splashed its way across one weed patch, there appeared a water raising wake from an adjacent weed patch which closed rapidly, much like a torpedo headed for an unsuspecting ship. Once within about 10 feet of the lure, the pike's bill (upper jaw) broke the surface as the mouth opened and remained so until the strike. It was an awesome sight and but one of numerous observed attacks initiated from a distance. Thus, your presentation may be a bit off and your working a lure may not be the best, yet once a trophy northern hits, there are three essentials for success: proper techniques in hooking, playing and landing of the fish.

Usually when the lure is taken within the mouth, the jaws are crushed shut so rapidly and firmly that the fish is momentarily unaware of what it is holding. Once the big boy either halts or slows in its run, it generally will relax the jaws slightly. At this time I prefer to drive the hook home with 2 or 3 firm and forceful up and to the side thrusts of the rod tip. At such time the angler

Bill Ware with a 48 inch northern of just over 30 pounds which fell victim to an Abu spinner fished over a river weedbed.

---

must be careful to keep a taut line between each hooking thrust. Many times the jaws are so tightly crushed over the lure that the hook barbs do not penetrate the flesh until the jaws relax or open slightly. At this moment the hooks must be driven home immediately lest the pike attempts to throw the lure. Then again, there are times at which the hooks are immediately set due to the force of the strike; *e.g.,* a slashing or turning strike where the hooks either catch in a gill; or are driven into the corner of the mouth, the soft inner tissue or the outer lip tissue.

　　The two most risky times involving a strike are when a trophy northern strikes at the boat and when such a fish hits from a distance and immediately continues the attack run directly toward the boat. In the first instance, I prefer to let the rod tip absorb the force and weight of the fish by easing the tip down in the direction of the pike's run, even if it means lowering the tip beneath the surface. At the same time, the arms extend and the body leans forward to ease the stress upon the shortened line. Totally different is the situation involving an on-rushing northern. Here the line must be rapidly reeled in to pick up the resulting slack. At such time the rod tip and arms should be kept high in readiness to absorb the force and weight stress of the pike's possible turning away maneuver (if and when he sees either the boat or angler), which generally is not observed but will be felt once the slack line is removed. As slack line is taken up (where it enters or cuts the surface) the angler should observe the direction of such travelling line. Then, at the first pressure, the rod tip and arms should absorb the force by lowering to the direction of the run in order to prevent a breakoff. As with an at-the-boat strike, the body and arms follow through by extending in the direction of the fish until it slows in its run. At such time the hooks are set in the previously mentioned manner.

After a trophy pike is hooked there remain the essential skills of playing and landing the fish before the hurrahs of success can be carried across the waters. First and foremost, enjoy the ensuing thrill of battle, for battle it will be. The angler must remember not to attempt a match of brute strength. Certainly such a fish is strong and you, as angler, are stronger. Nevertheless, the connecting links (the rod, line, leader and hooks) are of lesser mettle.

PLAYING TIPS

Some tips in playing an old mossback which I would suggest, mostly as learned from experience over the years, are as follows:

Get away from cover and obstacles. Nine times out of ten a large northern hooked while fishing within a weed bed will immediately attempt, either by slowly cruising deep along the bottom or in a weed and water slicing full speed run, to move out of the weeds in trade for the sanctuary of deep water. This is his first major mistake in the battle; a mistake which the wise angler will capitalize on. The angler's partner should begin to paddle the boat at a quiet, steady pace as soon as possible. The angler should merely attempt to follow the pike, while maintaining only a holding pressure with the reel drag setting, and not attempt to gain ground on the fish. Once outside the weed bed the boat should continue toward the deepest, obstacle free water in sight until well (100 yards if possible) away from the weed bed's outside edge. At this point the northern will generally have slowed to rest either along or near the bottom. The boat (with motor up) should be positioned broadside to the pike and with the fish between the boat and the weed bed as it is worked slowly up toward the surface. Once the old boy surfaces (much like a submarine) and gets a good look at the boat and/or angler he will realize his dilemma. Once again the angler must be ready to bend to the will of his opponent as the pike (generally) turns to run for the cover of the weed bed or other obstacles (*e.g.,* submerged logs, trees, shoreline rock ledges, *etc.*) from which it began the attack.

Adjust drag tension if needed during the contest. Naturally, proper reel drag tension should have been checked before ever making the first cast of the day. Even the dropping or jarring of a rod during downlake motoring can result in the drag mechanism becoming accidentally altered. Still, there are times during the playing of a large fish when a readjustment may be called for, *e.g.,* more tension to prevent a fish from reaching cover, or less tension to prevent a lightly hooked fish from tearing free. Therefore, the angler should check at first sight of the fish to see how well it is hooked and, if need be, make an appropriate reel drag adjustment. The same applies to raising a fish or slowing its run. However, as far as possible such readjustments should not be attempted during a power surge. One of the main reasons why I outfit my rods with Abu Ambassadeur series 5000 reels is because of the smoothness of the stardrag and the ease of adjustment while playing a large fish.

If need be, during a power run the spool can be lightly thumbed to exert more pressure than is being produced by the drag. As my brother once commented, "They should outlaw Ambassadeur reels 'cause all a guy has to do is hook the fish, hold on and hope he doesn't die of a heart attack once he sees how big the fish is."

Recognize buildup signs of an approaching power surge. Because of a trophy size northern's weight, force and directional thrust, a critical point in the battle develops each time the fish prepares to make another escape run. Such an escape generally follows a few moments rest during the latter stages of the battle; occasionally occuring at a depth, but more often than not within sight of the angler near or at the surface. The tip-off to these power surges is easily recognized even when the fish is out of sight. There is a gradually increasing buildup of momentum by the fish as it swaggers from head to tail. This swaggering is transmitted through line and rod to be felt and timed to its crescendo when (with body, arms and rod) the angler gives to absorb the resulting thrust. The power surge, or thrust, may be directed either downward (in a sounding maneuver), upward (in a surface-breaking, head shaking display of wide mouth and flared gills fury), or straight ahead (sometimes ending in either a surface-breaking glide or wallow). Regardless of the direction taken, as the surge ends the angler once again eases upward to the normal holding position.

Keep a sulking pike on the move. Now and again an angler will hook up with a large northern that decides to remain on the bottom where it will sulk rather than rise to the occasion and fight. To stimulate such a fish into action whereby it will begin to tire, the angler may choose one of two methods. He may hit the rod butt against a firm object (*e.g.,* boat seat) while maintaining rod angle and line tension. Three or four such hits will generally result in either head shaking or a cruising action (or both) by the northern. The second method of stimulation is to strum the line with one hand while maintaining rod angle and line tension with the other.

Be prepared to meet sudden under-the-boat runs. Often a pike will either strike at the boat or will be brought toward the boat. At such a time the fish may make a sudden power surge down and under the boat. Whenever this angle of run is executed by an adult northern, I prefer to maintain a better stress free angle by immediately lowering the rod straight down into the water to within about one foot of the reel, taking care that it is held well away from the boat's side. As the run slows in pace I work the rod around the end of the boat (with rod still in the water) in order to prevent the keel and/or the motor (if it is still down) from cutting the line. Once around the end of the boat I quickly reel in line while raising the rod to its normal holding position, thus maintaining proper line tension. Sometimes an under-the-boat run is unavoidable. However, throughout the battle it is imperative that there is clear communication between angler and partner. One might say that the angler becomes the captain of the ship and his partner the first mate. In playing trophy pike, the angler's partner should never undertake an action without the expressed direction or wish of the angler; *e.g.,* continuing to fish, grabbing the line to assist, attempting to net the fish before the angler or fish is ready, *etc.* Otherwise, should the fish be lost due to the improper or impulsive action of the partner, a lifelong friendship can be destroyed.

Keep weeds free from rod guides. Many times, while fighting a trophy northern in a pike weed patch, the fish will make a cross-grain, arced run which will result in the line cutting or pulling such weeds loose. In the process the weeds will drape over the line and will build up as line is retrieved. If left unattended these weeds will clog the rod tip guide or knot to prevent line from continuing on its way to the reel. When this happens the fish is provided with an opportunity to gain freedom by throwing the hook on a slack line. To counter this possibility, the partner should move to a position whereby he can strip the weeds back down the line toward the fish using the thumb and forefinger. Under no circumstances should he grasp the line with either hand during the process.

Prevent pressuring a surface run. A pressured northern engaged in a surface run can be expected to clear the water to some degree in an attempt to shake free. Many times the line and reel drag alone is enough to trigger such a response. This is why most pike fishermen prefer that a trophy pike do its fighting deep rather than to be allowed near the surface during the early part of the struggle. At any rate, the chance of losing such a fish doubles when he breaks free of the water in a head shaking frenzy. The only good thing about an adult pike's surface display is that he seldom will clear the water in a full bodied leap. However, on those occurrences when he does so, it is a sight that provides a lasting impression.

Prepare for the landing. Once the tide of battle has turned in favor of the angler, a decision regarding how best to land the lunker should be made. There are four methods (netting, beaching, gaffing, or eye socketing) from which to choose depending upon what the angler intends to do with his catch. If intending to boat the fish the angler's partner should organize the boat; *e.g.,* move or close tackle boxes and move rods with attached lures to prevent either being knocked overboard, becoming broken or becoming caught in fish or fishermen. The net should then be rigged, checked for any attached items (*e.g.,* lures, jaw spreaders, Chatillion scales, *etc.*), wetted in preparation for the landing and held free of the water until ready to receive the catch. If beaching is to be employed the partner should don a pair of rubberized gloves before rowing or paddling ashore in preparation for a quick hand landing of the fish once at the beach. If eye socketing is to be employed, the job should be executed using bare hands from a mid-ship position. Hopefully gaffing will not be employed. However, if such is the case, it too should take place at mid-ship. The movement should be in an up-and-over thrust.

Execute a proper landing of the fish. *If by gaff hook,* forget it. This method will kill the fish and may even ruin the skin for mounting, if such is desired.

If by eye socketing, the angler should plan to keep the fish rather than to release it as the method will severly injure it and generally results in death. The method is employed only after the fish is completely played out and is executed by running a hand gently down the back to the head where the thumb and middle finger gently seek the upper eye socket ridgebone. Immediately the thumb and middle finger grip inward and up in a quick, firm and deep grasp. This causes instant paralysis due to nerve pressure. However, once it has been lifted aboard and the grasp has been released, the fishermen should be prepared for much thrashing about.

If by beaching, the fish should be well played out before heading ashore. This method is excellent where the angler wishes to either keep or release the fish and where the trophy pike is too large for easy netting. Such landing should be made at a shallow, non-obstructed shoreline area (preferably a sand beach). Upon beaching the boat, the partner (wearing rubberized gloves) should immediately wade out to about knee depth to grasp the fish with both hands from behind the gill covers; one hand from behind the neck and the other from ahead of the belly). The fish can thus be either slid ashore or lifted and carried ashore. An adult pike should never be dragged ashore by the line.

If by net, the fish should be well played out before any attempt is made. By far, netting is the most desirable method of landing a fish which is intended to be released. Once the angler feels that the trophy size northern is ready for the net he should so advise his partner (netman). Stationed at mid-ship, the netman slowly lowers the net mouth into the water at about an 80 degree angle of entry about two feet ahead and slightly to the side of the pike's head. If the pike attempts to run, the net is quickly lifted from the water. At such a time a jab or desperation scoop by the netman can be disastrous. If and when the fish is ready the net is directed sideward and forward into the path of the pike. At the same time the angler eases pressure allowing the northern to move forward into the net. Extreme care must be executed where a set of hooks are exposed in order to prevent such hooks from becoming snagged in the net as it enters. The follow-through is forward and a turning of the frame to a face-up position as it nears the tail of the fish. If the pike attempts a power run within the net, the netman eases back in such direction to absorb the stress. The fish should be lifted aboard by grasping the handle next to the frame with one hand while the other hand grasps the frame at the distal end. One note in passing: never attempt to land a fish by lifting the line or leader. Such action can either result in a breakoff or an accidental hooking of the fisherman.

Handling and Releasing

As previously mentioned, adult northern pike will fight to near exhaustion and, therefore, require care in handling and releasing in order to survive the ordeal. Evidence of the extent to which a large northern will go in battle is shown through observing its fin coloration upon being landed. The crimson tail and fins are the result of the tremendous exertion which causes the capilaries within these appendages to rupture.

The following are some suggestions for the handling and releasing of adult pike which will help in the preservation of their lives:

1) Avoid letting the fish thrash about (either within the boat or upon a shoreline area) before its release.

2) Avoid allowing the fish to be dropped whereby scales may be removed or bruising may result.

3) Avoid damaging the eyes or gills while removing hooks or while photographing prior to its release. A broken or ruptured gill is a very serious injury to a fish as the gills are its breathing apparatus. I have taken two or three pike which have survived a broken gill, as evidenced by its healing scar tissue, but generally such injury will result in the fish's death.

4) When removing hooks, weighing, measuring and photographing a trophy northern it should be allowed to rest and breathe within the net, as supported within the water, between

phases. An out of the water delay of a few minutes while performing these acts before releasing will only complicate the reviving technique necessary for survival after its release.

5) Extreme care, both in regard to the angler's safety and in regards to the pike's well-being, should be exercised during the hook removal process. A lure hooked in the gills is often best removed from behind the gill; pulling the lure through the gills, unsnapping the lure, resnapping the leader clasp and pulling the leader back out through the mouth. Where there is difficulty in removing the hook from tough inner or outer tissue it is often best to cut the hook free rather than to rip it free. Long nose grip pliers are essential for removal of a hook deeply embedded in the gullet or back of the mouth. Often a live bait fisherman who takes a pike, which is to be released, will snip the leader with a pair of wire cutters because the baited hook is out of sight within the esophagus.

6) The proper method of reviving a northern pike during its release is to gently support it just beneath the surface in calm waters (*e.g.,* the lee side of a boat, protected shoreline waters, *etc.*). The support is executed by holding the fish at the neck (thumb and middle finger just within each gill cover) and at the belly with the palm of the other hand. Work the belly hand forward with slight pressure one time to expel any accumulated air. Then, with a gentle alternating forward and backward movement of the fish through the water, oxygenated water is allowed to pass through the gills. This allows for ease in its breathing. After a few moments, check the pike's stability by releasing its support. If there seems to be difficulty in its remaining upright the process is repeated. However, if the fish remains in good balance and the gills, fins and tail are actively functioning, stimulate its desire to escape by replacing the hands only to run them back to gently squeeze the body at the base of the tail. No healthy fish can tolerate this act and will attempt to flee.

Hook Removal from an Angler

Probably the least obvious cause for concern in regards to angling safety, especially when involved with removing hooks from the mouth of a northern pike, are the hooks themselves. Particularly dangerous are those lures possessing more than one set of hooks. A slip of the hand while such a fish thrashes about can result in a hooked fisherman as well. We have experienced one incident in which one of our party became hooked by a thrashing pike. It was an especially painful experience as both were attached to the same lure. The assistance of the angler's partner was necessitated first to subdue and unhook the pike and then to remove the hook from the angler.

If and when emergency treatment is called for in the removal of a hook from a fisherman, there are two methods from which to choose. The more painful of the two calls for the hook to be cut in two at its shank bend (about ½ inch from the point of penetration). It is then forced until the point and barb reappear through the skin where it is pulled on out.

The second method (see Diagram II) is the newest and best recommended technique which, surprisingly, is nearly painless. It generally requires assistance and is accomplished as follows:

1) Cut a 10 inch length of line or monofilament.

2) Run the 10 inch line section behind the curve of the imbedded hook so as to form a loop around the hook bend.

3) Grasp the looped line and, with a finger of the opposite hand.

4) Push the hook eye down against the skin with firm pressure.

5) Give the loop line a quick, firmly grasped yank while the hook eye is held against the skin.

Through this technique the hook's barb is allowed to follow the entry channel back out without catching the skin. It works like a charm and is a technique every fisherman should be acquainted with.

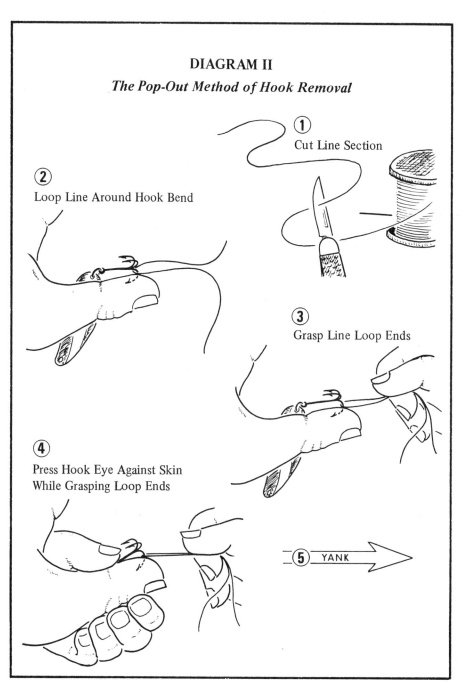

DIAGRAM II

The Pop-Out Method of Hook Removal

① Cut Line Section

② Loop Line Around Hook Bend

③ Grasp Line Loop Ends

④ Press Hook Eye Against Skin While Grasping Loop Ends

⑤ YANK

New York State Areas Possessing Trophy Northerns

Although the serious pike fisherman in search of truly trophy size northern pike will consider the various areas of Quebec, Ontario, Alberta, Saskatchewan and Manitoba in Canada, as well as the states of Wisconsin, Minnesota, and Michigan here in the United States, there are certain hot spots to be considered in New York State as well. Some of the prime areas of note in New York are as follows:

Sacandaga Reservoir. Although not the producer it was in the 1940's and 1950's, trophy pike can still be taken from various locations within this reservoir.

Cayuga Lake. The weedy, northern end of this member of the Finger Lakes is an excellent producer of northerns within the 10 to 24 pound class as well as shoreline areas near the southern end (*e.g.,* the power plant discharge area).

Seneca Lake. Both the Seneca River and, in particular, the Dresden Bay area within the lake yield many trophy size pike each year.

Lake Champlain. This lake offers excellent potential for the taking of very large northerns; the northern and southern ends in particular.

St. Lawrence River. Northern pike of excellent size may be found all along the United States (as well as Canadian) side of the river. Over the years the Clayton and Alexandria Bay areas have proven especially productive.

Ballston Lake. This is an example of a very small lake which has produced some northerns of trophy size over the past few years.

Oneida Lake. This lake is generally considered best for large pike during the spring with the various weedy bays as well as the Oneida River producing best.

Owasco Lake. This lake has produced numerous adult pike of excellent size over the years. The prime time for taking such trophy size fish is during the spring when high water conditions creates flooding of the swamp and marsh areas located along the lake inlet.

POOR MAN'S LOBSTER

Great northern pike, like its cousins the pickerel and the muskellunge, are noted for being a bony fish. Therefore, despite its fine texture and taste, it is often not used for eating. However, there is little chance of missing the forked bones found within a large adult northern and there is meat enough to feed the multitude. One of my favorite recipes for serving such fish is Poor Man's Lobster, which is prepared in the following manner:

1) Cut the loin strips from each side of the backbone
2) Place 2 quarts of water in a large boiler and add 1½ tablespoons salt.
3) Bring salted water to a boil while placing the pike loins in a large piece of cheesecloth and tie off to form a mesh bag of fish.
4) Add the mesh bag of fish to the boiling water and cover.
5) Allow to cook for 5 minutes after water resumes boiling.
6) Melt 8 ounces of either butter or margarine; if using margarine, add ½ teaspoon imitation butter flavoring after the margarine has melted and stir a few seconds.
7) Remove the mesh bag of fish from boiling water and allow to drain while placing melted butter or margarine into individual cups.
8) Remove fish from cheesecloth and serve in equal portions.

To eat, the meat is flaked apart and each is dipped in melted butter/margarine to be eaten. The taste is very much like that of butter-dipped lobster and will be relished by anyone who enjoys seafood.

6/Garpin' for Carp

by Todd Swainbank

Fishing for any species is what the angler makes it. Pity the poor carp whose introduction into this country is regarded as a fisheries management fiasco. Derisively called "Bugle-mouth Bass," shot with arrows, speared, stoned, blamed for fouling waterways and eating game fish eggs, caught and often thrown on the bank to rot, carp get no respect! Since we're stuck with them anyway, let's take a closer look at these powerful, widely distributed and much maligned fish. With many of our natural waterways succumbing to years of pollution and degradation, anglers may well reverse their negative feeling about "rough fish" species and gladly pursue these hardier breeds.

Life History and Growth Rates
(According to McClanes New Standard Fishing Encyclopedia)*

Carp were brought to this country from Germany in 1876 and because of their wide adaptability, tremendous reproductive potential and tolerance of many bottom types, have established themselves in virtually every major waterway.

---

*A. J. McClane, *1974 New Standard Fishing Encyclopedia*, (New York: Holt, Rhinehart and Winston), p. 197.

These fish spawn between April and July depending on latitude. When water temperatures warm to 60-65 degrees F., shallow water migrations occur, especially in weedy areas. Tremendous splashing and thrashing accompanies spawning and often overly inspired breeders beach themselves.

Eggs are broadcast over wide areas and stick in masses to plants and bottom debris. The eggs are then deserted and hatch in about a week. Since carp are very prolific, an average of 150,000 eggs per pound of body weight is not unusual. A twenty pound fish may deposit as many as 2 million eggs.

Carp gain an average of 1 pound of weight each year, with gains of 3 pounds yearly in exceptionally fertile waters. It is this rapid growth potential that attracted underdeveloped countries to the carp as a cheap food source. The fast growth results from one of the most efficient food to flesh conversions in the animal kingdom. The omnivorous carp expends very little energy when moving slowly over the bottom, sucking up just about anything tasty with their vacuum cleaner type mouths.

The rod and reel record for this country is a mammouth 55 pounds, 5 ounces for a carp caught in Clearwater Lake, Minnesota. The heaviest carp on record is an 83 pound, 8 ounce lunker netted in South Africa.

Carp are long lived (20 to 25 years in the wild), tolerant of high and low temperatures, able to utilize atmospheric oxygen (and so are the last to die in polluted waters) and above all, smart.

What Would a Good Public Relations Campaign Say About Carp?

Carp have reputations for eating game fish eggs. According According to a 5 year study conducted by the N.Y.S. Department of Conservation in which over 600 stomach analyses were done, not a single fish egg was found. Compared to the egg eating, nest raiding pirate, the popular blue gill sunfish, the carp might pick

up an egg on occasion because they are wide ranging bottom
feeders, but it would be a rare occurrence.

Carp are very powerful fighters. Their thick bodies and
broad tails enable them to fight long and hard, even if not as
spectacularly as some more popular species. When hooked in
shallow mud flat areas they will streak with surprising speed and
power for deep water in a staight line high speed surge.

Carp are among the "smartest" fish in fresh water.
Different species of game fish were put in separate ponds, then
each fish was caught using a variety of techniques. Researchers
wanted to learn how long it took to catch the same fish twice
using the same technique. When the results were in, it took
longer to fool the same carp twice than any other test species.

Carp are highly esteemed for both food and sport in
Europe and Asia. In Europe many fishing tournaments are geared

Lunker carp are powerful
battlers. This big one was
caught in Stewart Park in
Ithaca, New York.

toward "rough fish" and light action rods up to 10 feet long are used to provide maximum sport. Everywhere carp are found they can easily be caught using a wide array of tackle and can almost always be caught from shore.

Carp are tasty if prepared properly. It is important to skin them and trim off the dark flesh. They are excellent when smoked and the roe is edible and often sold in canned form. The flesh is an important ingredient in making gefilte fish.

Now does that sound like a fish that should be thrown on the bank to rot?

How to Go Garpin' for Carp

We usually go garpin' for carp in late May. Big carp are spawning then and can be found in shallow canals, rivers and bays. No garpin' for carp excursion is complete without a chilled 12 pack of beer, munchies, a radio and a comfortable seat, in addition to rod and reel.

Night crawlers and canned corn are excellent baits; I've even caught carp on flies, jigs and crankbaits. The ultimate carp bait is however the cornmeal doughball!

Boil water in a small pot, add Karo Syrup and cornmeal, remove from heat and stir. The perfect doughball will have the consistency of Playdough and can actually be bounce tested. If a rolled doughball is thrown at a wall and it bounces off without breaking apart, it is perfect and will stay on the hook for many casts.

A medium action spinning rod and open faced spinning reel filled with 8-10 pound test monofilament line is fine for garpin' for carp. No sinkers should be used if they can be avoided. Carp are very cautious feeders and if sinkers have to be used they should be slip sinkers, so no excess weight is detected as the carp moves off with the bait.

Cover a single baitholder type hook between size 4 and size 8 with a pear shaped doughball and fling it out gently. Put your rod in a "Y" crotched stick, turn on the radio, open a beer and relax. But be ready! When carp are in shallow the action can be unbelievably fast. If action is slow try chumming with canned corn or doughball bits. Baiting areas with stale bread and cakes can keep carp in the same spot for weeks.

Garpin' for Carp Glossary of Terms

Inspired garping carpers have come up with their own vocabulary to describe common events when carp fishing.

Express bite: When a carp picks up your doughball, and streaks off at full speed, you have just had an "express bite." More rods are pulled off the bank and into the water by carp than probably any other fish.

Taking it straight out: When a carp picks up your doughball, let him run all the slack out of your line, and just before your rod tip starts bouncing, set the hook as hard as your tackle allows. "Cross his eyes" as Texas bass anglers say. The carp when hooked will streak off and if your timing is right and your reel drag is set right you can pull yourself right to your feet ready for further combat.

Reverse bite: There is no guarantee that a biting carp will move away from you with the bait, he might move directly toward you. You will notice slack line building up every few seconds. Reel in the slack gently but don't over reel or the carp will feel the rod pressure and drop the bait; then set the hook.

A 50-pounder: When a large carp is hooked (over 20 pounds) start yelling, "It's a 50-pounder!" This brings people running in a hurry and may also cause traffic jams.

Song and dance bite: Wise old carp sometimes take their sweet time about streaking off with the doughball. They take it out an inch at a time, drop it, pick it up and drop it, again and again.

Patience garping carpers, these fish are often 50-pounders. Wait until they take it straight out.

If you give garpin' for carp a try you might be pleasantly surprized, and please, if you don't plan on eating them, don't throw them on the bank.

7/Fishing the Dry Fly for Fun and Challenge

by Gordon L. Eggleston

Having devoted some 27 years to physical education and recreation, I find that those who excel in a particular sport are those who put in their time. So it is in fly fishing. We all begin the sport as novices and may or may not become dedicated, depending on our experiences and degree of success. Should the love affair bloom, the angler will undoubtedly become obsessed with the constant call of the stream, devoting as much time as possible in mastering the challenge of taking trout and/or salmon with the fly rod. Such a fly fisherman is the purist who, "forsaking all others," gives up heart and soul to this lady of streamside happiness. Through off-season study and preparation, as well as diligent in-season presentation, the purist becomes highly knowledgeable in all aspects relative to the salmonoid species and how best to bring such fish to hand. However, the majority of fly fishermen found on the stream fall into an in between categories, neither novice nor purist. Periodically succumbing to impulse prompted by time, weather conditions or season, such anglers beat a hasty path to the nearest stream and briefly flail away.

Fly fishing offers the angler four major channels of approach: fishing the streamer and/or bucktail, the nymph, the wet fly and the dry fly. It is common knowledge that the majority of a trout or salmon's diet (estimated at 90%) is satisfied through feeding on below-the-surface aquatic life and that underwater is the way to go for best results in taking truly trophy size fish: namely by fishing nymphs, wets, streamers/bucktails, assorted live bait and either spin or bait casting of artificial lures. Nevertheless, of the four fly fishing approaches previously mentioned, the dry fly in its imitation of surface floating lifeform definitely offers the angler the most fun and, at the same time, the most challenge.

As this chapter is devoted to the various aspects concerning fishing the dry fly, it is well to begin with the fly itself.

What is a dry fly?

To most anglers unfamiliar with the use of a fly rod, the first thing that registers when mention is made of the dry fly is that it is a tiny winged imitation of the mayfly. However, to the knowledgeable fly fisherman it means far more. The mayfly forms the basis of the dry fly but not the whole.

Because the mayfly forms the basis of the dry fly it deserves a closer look. To comprehend the mayfly and its imitation more fully, one needs to understand its life cycle (Diagram I) and the various stages involving its adult (dun) phase which are of prime importance to the dry fly fisherman.

The cycle begins with a hatch which generally occurs above the water at varying heights. A hatch may occur at any time of day, but major hatches are most often observed during the late afternoon and evening hours and thus tend to trigger a feeding frenzy among trout in the area. Dry flies to match the hatch in color, shape and size may be selected by the angler from among the following styles:

1) **Divided or Fan Wing flies,** often referred to as Traditional Dry Flies, are tied with hackle, feather or synthetic material wings.

DIAGRAM I
The Mayfly Cycle

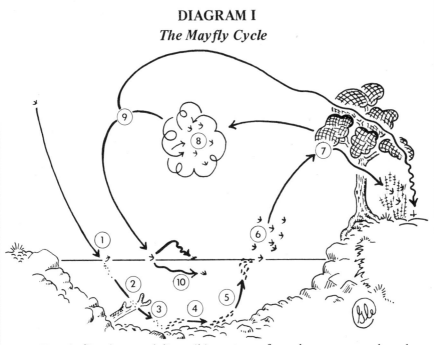

1. Female flies down and dips tail in water surface where eggs are released and washed free by the water.
2. Eggs sink to bottom and adhere to underwater grasses, stones and other underwater obstacles.
3. Eggs hatch (about 30 days) into small larvae (nymph stage).
4. After a time the larvae shucks its shell and another casing replaces it.
5. After from 1 to 2 years the nymph swims to the surface film and floats while working free of its nymphal case.
6. It flutters its wings to dry them and takes off (dun stage): a hatch.
7. It flies to the shoreline to light on grasses, bushes or trees to rest and mature.
8. After about 24 hours it flys back above the water (males first to dance in a swarm with females following) where mating takes place (spinner stage).
9. The male slowly flies off to die, generally on land, while the female flies to the water surface to begin the cycle anew with its egg laying process before itself dying . . . generally on the water (spent spinner stage).
10. While laying its eggs the fly may become washed or drawn beneath the surface and drown (wet fly).

2) **Thorax flies** are tied with forked tail and with both wings and hackle tied one third the way down the hook shank from the hook's eye.

3) **Midges** are the tiniest of insect hatches and are tied in sizes 20 through 28 in keeping with the Traditional Dry Fly patterns. Because of their minute size the angler generally will watch the line as an indicator of a trout's rise and take of the fly.

4) **No Hackle or Comparadun flies** are tied with wings in absence of hackle legs to allow the fly to ride in rather than atop the surface film. Such wings are tied in flared fashion using deer body hair (Comparaduns) or may be tied in semi-upright position using cut feather wings (No Hackle flies).

5) **Wulff flies** were originated by and named after noted fly angler and author Lee Wulff. Such flies are tied the same as Divided Wing dries except with hair wings instead of feather wings.

6) **Spent Wing Spinners** are tied with the wings extended to the sides in imitation of the dying stage of the mayfly. Such flies should be fished in a dead float manner.

The next step is to realize that the insect world far surpasses either fish or animal in both numbers and species and more than the mayfly may find itself riding atop the current of a trout stream or atop the placid water of a lake or pond. When there seems to be an absence of a mayfly hatch, the dry fly enthusiast may resort to a searching pattern. Such flies may be selectedfrom among the following styles:

1) **Attractor flies** representing no specific insect, but tied in color and/or materials designed to draw the trout's attention and prompt a rise.

2) **Variant flies** imitating surface insect life in general, tied without wings while using hackle to represent both legs and wings. Such flies are generally fished with rod twitches to skate the fly on the surface rather than fishing a dead float.

3) **Parachute flies** imitating a general insect, tied with hackle wrapped around the base of an upright wing (generally hair material wings) rather than wrapped in the conventional manner

around the body. The floating ability of this fly is excellent when fished in fast, turbulent waters with the body floating within rather than atop the surface film.

4) **Bivisibles**, full body hackle flies without wings, suggesting rather than defining a floating insect. Such flies are excellent floaters for fast, turbulent water conditions.

5) **Spider flies** tied with long, stiff hackle from thorax to head to imitate water spiders, fished in rod twitches or skittering action across the surface rather than on a dead float.

6) **No Wing Midges**, the same as Variants except tied in sizes 20 through 28. Although not as enjoyable to fish as the larger flies which are easier to observe in their float, midges are effective in taking trout from early spring through late fall. Because of their size, such flies must be fished using a fine tippet of 7X (one pound maximum stress) at the end of a well balanced tapered leader.

The next dry fly in line is the Downwing Fly which is tied in imitation of stone flies, dragon flies, damsel flies and the caddis flies. Such insects possess slender bodies with their wings extending rearward atop the body rather than upright as are those of the mayfly. Common wing material used by the fly tying craftsman is either animal hair or shaped feather material. The legs are imitated through the use of wrapped hackle around the thorax extending forward to the head.

The Caddis, a hardy specie of insect and a food source of trout, has gained popularity among fly fishermen in recent years thanks to the study and writings of Larry Solomon and Eric Leiser.* The two prime designs in the imitation of these flies are as follows:

1) **The Tent Wing Caddis:** This design is tied with extended tent shaped feather wings which are attached atop

---

*Larry Solomon and Eric Leiser: Co-authors of the book, *The Caddis and the Angler.* This book is devoted exclusively to the caddis fly which is felt to make up 50% of the trout's diet from larva stage through its adult stage. This book deals with this species of fly in regards to its entomology and behavior, step by step tying instructions for tying its imitation and new fishing techniques for its presentation. Leiser, president of The River Gate fly fishing store in Cold Springs, New York, is a nationally renowned fly tying craftsman, angler, lecturer and author.

clipped hackle just behind the head. The underside hackle are unclipped to represent legs. Such design allows the fly to float in the surface film rather than atop the surface as is the case with the Fluttering Caddis. In so doing the Tent Wing Caddis merely offers the trout a silhouette representing the natural.

   2) The Fluttering Caddis: This design is tied with extended hair wings from thorax to slightly beyond a slender dubbed body and with a wrapped hackle collar. Of the two designs this is undoubtedly the most popular among most dry fly enthusiasts.

   Terrestrials make up the last major insect for discussion. These are land born insects which often become trapped in the surface of trout or salmon inhabited waters. Examples of these insects are ants, bees, beetles, grass hoppers, leaf hoppers, jassids, crickets, *etc.* Also, although not insects, such trout edibles as inchworms, caterpillars and the like are also considered terrestrials as far as fly tying is concerned. Terrestrial imitations provide an excellent choice by the fly fisherman during those times, especially throughout the summer months, when aquatic hatches are slack. Hair Body Flies are those terrestrial imitations of such full body insects as bees and moths. These flies are named for their tightly wrapped and clipped deer hair bodies. Due to their size, they offer excellent visibility to the angler and, because of the hollow nature of deer body hair, the fly rides high atop turbulent water. The two most popular flies of this design are the Irrestible and the Rat Faced McDougal.

   Hair Body Poppers should be mentioned here. Experienced fishermen have come to understand that the largest trout are nocturnal feeders, going after frogs, mice and large moths. Hair Body Poppers are made in imitation of these prey. They are tied for the most part on large hooks (sizes 1/0, 2 and 4) and, similar to Hair Body Flies, the deer body hair is cropped around the hook shank and trimmed to the desired shape. Because of their size and weight, these flies are not easy to cast and the lack of visibility at night only adds to the difficulty.

   For a change of pace, some dry fly enthusiasts will briefly abandon the trout stream in search of bass and/or panfish with the fly rod. At such times success is increased when swimming a Hair Body Popper over an underwater weed bed or above a submerged stump lot.

Certainly the serious angler can ill afford to acquire a variety of flies in various sizes from each category or style. The least expensive alternative is first to enroll in a fly tying course taught by either a master fly tier or by team-teaching specialists and then to obtain materials with which to tie your own. At the present time a course in fly tying ranges from $15 to $30. If you start from scratch in obtaining the primary quality tying tools and materials necessary to tie 400 flies in sizes 18, 16, 14 and 12, the cost will be approximately $100 at present prices. Before the reader succumbs to shock, please realize that most Orvis tied dries retail at from $1.10 to $1.20 each, a total of from $440 to $480 for 400 flies. Therefore, not only will tying your own flies add to the fun and challenge of the streamside contest, it will result in substantial savings.

It is easy to see that dry fly fishing presents the angler with major decisions before even reaching the stream: namely the wide range of flies from which to choose and their varied purposes as well as whether or not such imitations should be purchased or self produced.

Who is the well-equipped fly fisherman?

Few fly fishermen venture forth equipped only with dries for trout. Most will stock a few wets, nymphs and bucktails in case they are needed. However, for the purpose of this chapter let us hold to the basic necessities of the dry fly angler.

Proper wearing apparel is as important for the enjoyment of of fishing as the tackle being used or the beauty of the area being fished. The guiding principle can be summed up in two words, warm and dry. An inadequately dressed angler facing inclement weather may have trout feeding in abundance all about him but find the experience pure hell. Therefore, wearing apparel should be selected with extreme care. Just as an angler selects flies to match the hatch, so should his clothes, from head to toe, be selected to match the day's conditions. Also, just as the wise angler will carry an extra of each fly pattern in case of emergency, so should he provide for the unexpected by having a complete change of clothes stored at all times within a clean, dry area of his vehicle.

The dry fly angler's tackle begins with his casting apparatus: rod, reel, line and leader. For best results all four components must be matched one to the other as well as to the type of fishing desired. Certainly the novice will begin with one basic rod, reel and line rather than invest in a combination of separate outfits. If small or medium trout stream fishing is the beginner's prime interest, I would suggest a good quality tubular glass rod of from 7½ to 8 feet in length which will handle either a 5 or 6 weight tapered floating line. The reel should be a light single action make of good quality which, once mounted and filled with fly line and backing, will allow the rod to balance when supported by the index finger at the front of the rod's cork grip. Last, a tapered leader matched to the size flies to be cast* should be attached to the tapered end of the fly line. I prefer the use of a leader link to make this connection.

There are numerous tackle accessories available on the market, such as a landing net, wading staff and creel. For the most part these are non-essential items unless the angler wishes to keep rather than release his fish or intends to wade and cross streams of forceful current.

The remaining basic needs of the dry fly angler will nestle nicely within a fishing vest. Therefore, serious thought should be directed to securing the most functional vest possible. Qualities to be looked for in such a vest are 1) wearing comfort when stocked with tackle accessories and miscellaneous items, 2) design for ease in accessibility of stored items and 3) durability of material and construction. The main problem to be avoided when stocking a

---

*As a general rule, the smaller the fly the finer the leader tippet required to properly execute the cast and to work the fly. (See Specifications for Tapered Leaders, pg. 155.)

vest is overstocking to the point where organization for ease of
accessibility suffers and to where weight and a lack of balance
become a burden. The well stocked vest should include the
following necessities:

1) **Fly Boxes and Flies.** The number of boxes carried
should be kept to a minimum, constructed of light but durable
material, possessing multiple compartments offering an easy view
of the flies when the box is closed and in sizes to fit the lower
outside vest pockets with ease. Compartment mixing of various
fly types should be avoided and at least one duplicate of each
pattern should always be included. In case conditions call for
versatility, the angler is wise to carry a box of assorted weighted
nymphs and a fly book of assorted bucktails and wet flies. Such
emergency flies should be stored in the lower inside vest pockets.

2) **Fleece Patch.** Most fishing vests are manufactured
with either a velcro or permanently attached fleece pad near the
shoulder. This should be used to hold a fly which has been fished
before its return to the proper storage compartment. In so doing
the fly is allowed to air dry first and thus prevents the possibility
of becoming ruined, or ruining other flies, by rust. Along the same
line it should be mentioned that it is a good habit to open all fly
compartments at the end of the day's fishing and check to be sure
that water or moisture has not entered a box during the outing. If
such is the case appropriate measures should be taken to dry both
box and flies.

3) **Fly Floatant and Line Dressing.** Fly floatants come in
many makes and forms. There are liquids containing silicone,
aerosol sprays, mucilin pastes and various creams. Any will serve
well to clean and float a dry, either before or after taking a fish.
Because a floatant of one form or another is a necessary part of
any dry fly angler's needs since through the course of a season it is
used extensively, the angler may look to less costly substitutes.
Personally, I go with a mixture of paraffin (shaved) and gasoline
carried in a small wide-mouthed hour glass shaped bottle. It cleans
and floats a fly well, does not appear to discolor the fly, does not
offend the trout and is extremely inexpensive. Line dressing or
cleaner should as far as possible, be applied to the fly line with a

clean flannel pad or soft cloth patch while the line is dry for best results. It generally is obtained in paste form within a small tin container and is applied sparingly by passing the floating line (not leader) through the coated pad or patch. Any excess dressing should be removed. As a quality fly line is expensive, it should be cared for. Dirt and the variety of stream pollutants encountered over the course of a day's fishing not only will prevent a high riding line (necessary to prevent putting down a trout) but if neglected will seriously affect the longevity of even a fine quality line. I prefer to carry both fly floatant and line dressing in one of my vest's small upper pockets. Just a tip: it is wise to carry a small jar of fly cream floatant in case the liquid floatant should spill or leak away.

4) Clippers and Surgical Hemostat. A pair of fingernail clippers (or small snip scissors) attached to a small pin-on-reel with retractable nylon cord for easy accessibility is a must for any fly fisherman, as each time a fly is changed, tippet material must be cut or trimmed. Such a reel is generally pinned at chest or shoulder level for easy access. Surgical hemostats (I prefer the curved-nose over the straight in the 4½ inch length) are far more than a frill. Far too many trout die from the ill treatment received by anglers in their attempt to remove the fly hook from their relatively small mouths. A dentist will attend his patients in as humane a means as possible—the angler should extend the same courtesy to his patient (the trout). The extraction is both simple and painless when performed using the slender grip of a hemostat and the trout swims free to return again another day. I prefer to carry mine within a lower vest pocket but attached to a 12 inch elastic cord hung from the upper front of the vest.

5) Wader or Boot Repair Kit. The wise angler is one who is prepared to meet streamside emergencies successfully. This may well mean repairing a puncture or small tear of boot or wader during the day's fishing. I prefer to carry the Marathon A-1 Wader Repair Kit as it is contained within a small size box containing a buffer, rubber patch material and cement. It is quickly applied and holds equally well on synthetic or natural rubber.

6) **Tapered Leaders and Tippet Material.** One or two spools of tippet material to match the leader(s) should be allowed a permanent place within the vest. I carry mine in the pocket opposite my fly floatant and line dressing. As the leader tippet shortens to 10 or 12 inches through frequent fly changes, I add a 10 or 12 inch replacement section of new material using a Double Surgeon's Knot (see Diagram II).

7) **Leader Sink.** This liquid or paste is necessary to put the leader below the surface where it is out of sight of a trout. For best results such material should be applied with either fingers or brush when the leader is dry and then allowed to air dry before being fished. Nevertheless, streamside application may be called for in some instances. It may also be required to sink a nymph, wet fly or streamer.

8) **Flashlight.** A small C-battery or penlite operated flashlight is another emergency accessory which should be tucked away within the fishing vest. Some of my greatest success has occurred during the last hour of daylight when, without such a light to change fly patterns, I would otherwise have missed out on all the fun. To the night fly angler it serves the same purpose as well as aiding the walk in and out.

9) **Polaroid Sunglasses.** You can pretty well tell a good fisherman when you see one—he is the angler wearing a pair of polaroids while working the water. Through the use of such glasses the angler can see what is going on beneath the surface: structure and obstacles, fish and (for the dry fly angler) the fly as it drifts in or atop the surface film.

10) **Insect Repellent.** Any true outdoorsman knows that a small plastic bottle of good quality insect repellent speaks for itself. Successful fishing requires a high degree of concentration on the business at hand. Distractions, such as biting insects, break this concentration, often resulting in the miss of a good fish, not to mention causing a noticeable decrease in fishing enjoyment.

11) **Rain Gear.** Most fly fishing vests possess a large pocket along the width of the lower back. It is a difficult pocket to reach while fishing unless the angler is a contortionist.

DIAGRAM II

Knots Most Commonly Utilized by Fishermen

Like the spin caster, a fly fisherman is constantly faced with working with monofilament. Therefore, it is important to know how to tie the most effective knot for the material or item requiring attachment. There are two major characteristics of monofilament which are totally different from that of nylon; namely 1) mono tends to crimp easily and 2) it tends to slip on itself under stress. Consequently, certain knots which may be satisfactory with nylon are best avoided with monofilament. While on the subject of monofilament there are two further points of importance which the angler should keep in mind. 1) To prevent mono from crimping in completing slip type knots, one should liquid heat the material at the site of the knot by holding the loose knot in the mouth a minute or so immediately prior to tightening and 2) to use either nail clippers or fine scissors to trim or cut the mono rather than to do so with the teeth which can result in the teeth becoming chipped.

The following knots are those most often employed by the majority of anglers today in meeting their varied fishing needs:

KNOT	DIAGRAM	MAJOR USE
1. NAME NOT KNOWN		To fasten line to lure, snap or leader loop. One of my own personal favorite slip type knots.
2. CLINCH KNOT	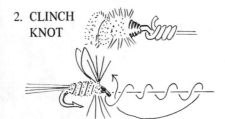	To fasten hook to leader or fly to tippet. It has a tendency to slip when in water. Therefore, care should be taken to assure it is thoroughly tightened before it is trimmed and trimming should avoid being close.

DIAGRAM II (continued)

KNOT	DIAGRAM	MAJOR USE

3. IMPROVED CLINCH

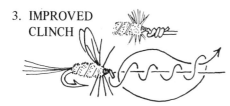

For the same purpose as the Clinch Knot except its chance of slipping is not so great. Thus, it is more commonly used by fly fishermen for attaching flies to a tippet.

4. DOUBLE SURGEON

To join leader material together in making a hand tied tapered leader.

5. BARREL KNOT

For the same purpose as a Double Surgeon except more difficult and time consuming to tie and a bit weaker in stress strength.

6. NEEDLE KNOT

To fasten leader butt to fly line. A needle is used to make a hole in end of line and through its wall through which the butt is passed. The hollow tube separating line from leader loops is removed once knot is ready to be tightened.

7. REVERSE CLINCH

To make a snell hook or to secure a single hook to monofilament line. It is used extensively by bait fishermen; especially by those using fish egg sacs and worm fishermen.

8. LEADER LINK

Line   Leader Butt

A no-knot plastic device for fastening leader butt to fly line. A square knot at end of each material holds them in place.

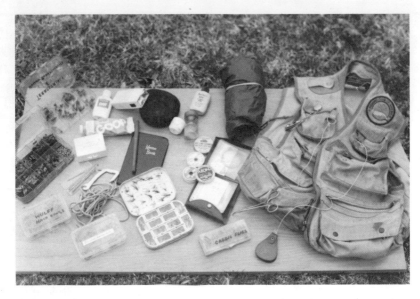

The author's fly vest and its contents. When stocked and ready for a day on the stream, the combined weight is just under 6 pounds.

Therefore, it is impractical to store items of frequent need here. It is, however, ideal for carrying along a rain parka or such optional items as a bag lunch and/or camera (which should be encased in a waterproof plastic or rubberized bag).

12) **Needle Threader.** One of the most useful devices for any fly fisherman, especially useful for changing to tiny midges or when threading a leader tippet through the eye of a fly hook during fading light conditions.

What is involved in reading the water?

The prime requirement for reading the water is the ability to understand the fish. For the dry fly angler this means a working knowledge of the various trout and salmon.

Each trout differs as an individual. Like people, each trout is also to a degree the product of its environment. Lake inhabiting fish vary greatly in shape and color from the same type found in streams because of diet and water conditions. Certainly, hatchery released trout vary noticeably from native born trout in appearance, intelligence and stamina. They are as different from one another as is a plow horse from a wild mustang.

Both salmon and trout have their own preferences of habitat. The prime factors affecting such preference are water temperature, oxygen and feed. Some anglers feel water temperature is the prime essential while others differ in opinion, saying oxygen levels are more important. Then there are those who argue that food supply is paramount in locating the desired fish. What we have here is theory and wherever two or more persons are together and theory arises, argument ensues. Certainly all three are essentials in locating fish. However, regardless of the various research which has been conducted, particularly in regards to water temperature and oxygen, no two resulting charts offer the same conclusion. Undoubtedly such results are accurate for the area surveyed. Yet, certain fish will often become acclimated to the area of country in which they find themselves. If I wished to stir up a dispute among the fishing fraternity, all I would need do is to include a temperature range chart per species suggesting high and low tolerance and preferred water temperatures for each. Such information, according to the particular section of country to be fished, is best secured from a local fisherman who is experienced in thermocline fishing of the area rather than from a temperature chart produced from research carried out on fish some 1000 miles or more away.

Two other factors affecting preference of trout/salmon habitat which deserve mention include spawning drives and unpolluted, yet not necessarily clear, waters. It has been my experience that spawning trout and salmon are easily located in headwaters but extremely difficult to entice (particularly with dry flies) into a take. Yet, spawning results in localizing numbers of trophy size fish due to the natural urge of reproduction during either early spring (*e.g.*, rainbow trout) or late fall (*e.g.*, landlocked salmon).

Perhaps I am misjudging many of my fellow anglers, but it is my opinion that the high majority of fishermen who frequent a favorite stream (or section thereof) all too often make two major mistakes of observation and evaluation. Mentally armed with a gained knowledge of what the trout feeds on, when and where its prime feeding takes place (generally early morning and late afternoon or evening), its habits and how to recognize its movements, the wise angler will take such time as is required to observe and evaluate the situation at hand.

Let us first examine the essentials involved with streamside observation. Ask yourself questions like these:

Are there any fish to be seen and, if so, can they be identified?

Are there any rises and, if so, where and how many?

If aquatic insect life is present, what is its size, shape and color?

If terrestrial insect life is present what is its size, color and specie?

What are the weather conditions as they may affect fly presentation?

What are the water conditions as they may affect fly selection (dry, wet, nymph or streamer) and presentation?

What structure or obstacles are present that affect fly presentation?

Just as some see without observing, others are prone to observe without evaluating. The final link between success and failure lies in the angler's ability to convert such observations and evaluations to appropriate action with the tackle at hand.

Does the absence of both trout and bait fish in a particularly good looking location mean it is really sterile or is there a trophy size fish dominating the spot but is presently lurking in the sanctuary of cover? *or* Which, among the identified trout, will be singled out for prime consideration by the angler in his presentations?

Do the observed trout appear to be feeding and, if so, is their interest centered on surface, bottom or in between food sources? Also, how many trout appear to be on the take, in what precise locations or feeding lanes are such fish and will such lies allow for working the run or pool in the conventional progression from tail to head?

What fly appears to best match an observed natural? Then again, if there is no apparent activity (insect and/or fish) what searching pattern dry might best produce results or will versatility require going under with a wet, nymph or streamer?

From what streamside location should the presentation begin and where, as well as how, should it be directed considering such weather conditions as the direction and force of the wind, the position of the sun (which controls the casting of shadows), and the rain (which can obscure an angler's movements or presence)?

What type fly (dry, wet, nymph or streamer) will best be suited to the present water conditions (current speed, water level, clear or roily in color) as well as how might such selection be best presented and worked?

What type of presentation, and from what location, will best avoid a snagup while affording the most productive float possible in relation to stream structure and streamside obstructions? Also, how will both primary and secondary currents affect the float?

And last but not least, how will a hooked fish be played and where will it best be landed in light of existing stream structure and streamside obstructions?

As one can see there are many considerations to be taken into account in order to place the odds in the angler's favor. Miscalculation in regard to any one consideration can easily spell defeat. However, any observation and evaluation is better than none. The angler who ignores everything in his anxiety to wade in and begin flailing away without a logical plan of attack has little chance of success.

In observing the water, there are three more points to bring up which are important to the angler. First of all, most anglers tend to play a game of fish-and-forget. By this I mean the angler fails, either during or upon completion of fishing each likely looking spot, to log within his mind observed underwater obstacles, tricky currents, trout lies and feeding stations and surrounding casting hazards. Often success hinges upon but one opportunity to place the fly accurately into a natural and, hopefully, a good float. A presentation may go amiss due to improper reading of the area upon the angler's first time fishing the location. However, there is no excuse for repeating the mistake when returning at a future date.

The angler should also keep in mind a stream's physical change. A simple pocket fishing log can be a very useful source of information regarding number and size of fish taken on various flies at various locations over the course of both past and present years. Structure is an all important factor in regard to

The cautious angler will use whatever cover is available in approaching a likely spot.

productivity and spring flooding can, and often does alter a favorite spot. Such flooding may wash out boulders, trees and man-made structures—it may even alter the course of the stream bed entirely. This can also occur during the summer with sudden flash flooding. Once the waters have receded to fishable conditions, the angler faces the task of re-reading the stream in light of those physical changes which have taken place.

Thirdly, the angler should understand certain aspects of a trout's feeding pattern. As with humans and all other life forms, a trout likes to eat. At times it will feast and gorge itself during a feeding frenzy. Then again it will merely snack on a passing tidbit. Sometimes it will take anything that comes along in wild abandon, and there are other times when it will be finicky. As previously mentioned, a trout enjoys an early morning breakfast and a late evening dinner (with the big boys preferring a night on the town). Lunch may occur at any point in between depending upon weather and water conditions in relation to the availability of preferred food sources. I have found that trout generally feed during a day's first and last hours of light. They generally feed from a particular location or feeding lane at the head or tail of a pool, in shallow riffs or other away-from-cover areas. However, when the water is at low level and is clear and the light is bright, the trout usually become extremely wary and prefer to feed, whenever possible, near the security of cover. Such cover may present itself as an undercut bank, a sunken log, the shadows cast by overhanging streamside foliage, a boulder and the like. At those times when the water takes on color, such as during spring runoff or a sudden summer rainstorm, a trout will often cruise about in search of food, safe in the knowledge that such color provides an overall sanctuary. Nocturnal feeders normally will position near the tail of a pool where a current begins to flatten out. As such fish, usually loners of trophy size, are wary despite the cover of darkness, the angler should know the pool well in respect to current, obstructions and the best location for presentation. Also, the approach for presentation should be made without the use of a light (if at all possible) and as silently as possible because both light and sound can easily put such fish down. Here the angler must read the water by sound rather than by sight. The take of a fly by these fish will result in a sucking "slurp" sound. At midday the trophy size trout (which for dry fly fishing I consider to be those of 12 inches or better in stream fishing) will usually seek the sanctuary of major stream obstructions (deep undercut banks, tree roots, rock shelves, brush and driftwood entrapments, *etc.*) while the more gullible smaller trout may be found feeding at various more exposed locations: in the shade, at the edge of current flow, at the edge of cover or behind a boulder or shelter table to name a few.

Confidence...Essential link between success and failure

"Think positive!" This is a common remark to any athlete. It is also strong advice to you as an angler. A negative or indecisive approach to the task at hand will usually end in like results.

Confidence is initiated by a knowledge of weather and water conditions. The dry fly enthusiast knows the importance of clear water to a trout for the visibility of surface floating insects. He also knows that air and water temperature play an important part in affecting insect hatches. Furthermore, he knows that a prime time to hit the stream is immediately preceding or during a rain following a dry spell when trout often will begin a feeding frenzy on insects trapped by the rising water and washed into the current's flow.

Confidence will be reinforced at streamside through correct reading of the water as to where the fish are (or have been observed to be) feeding and where an approach and presentation will afford the best float possible without either putting the trout down or resulting in a rejection. Most areas are fishable providing the angler is willing to observe, evaluate and adjust to the challenge with patience and confident determination.

Next, the proper rod, reel, line and tapered leader come into play in building confidence. Of course such tools should have been determined before ever leaving home. Certainly different conditions call for different tackle. However, no-one can carry three or four balanced outfits afield: namely a midge or flea rod of 4 or 5 feet for tiny feeder streams and ultra brushy areas, a 7 to 7½ foot wand for small stream and small fly fishing, or an 8 to 9 foot piece for laying out larger flies in open water and/or windy fishing conditions. Surely most streams offer a variety of different type areas and the successful fly fisherman is the one who is best able to make do with the tackle at hand. Of course, the leader is an all too often overlooked article of importance. It is the weakest link between fish and fisherman and and should therefore receive special attention from start to finish of an outing. (See pages 158, 159 and accompanying specifications charts.)

Undoubtedly, one of the most important foundations upon which confidence hinges is proper fly selection. The novice dry fly fisherman should become familiar with an aquatic fly emergence chart for the intended fishing area. He should also know the terrestrials frequenting the area. These will vary by locale, season, air temperature, water temperature, time of day, *etc.* Insects of various kinds begin to appear in early spring and may, in certain spring fed feeder streams, continue well into late fall or early winter. Diagram III is provided as a general dry fly reference in respect to those flies, their presence and size (according to hook size imitation) which are good producers when fishing the waters of upstate New York and, in particular, the Finger Lakes region.

Few fly fishermen know as much about aquatic born insects as Swischer, Richards, Marinaro, Schwiebert, Nastasi and Caucci. It is my opinion that few need know each insect by its Latin name. However, all serious fly fishermen must be able to identify the signs of feeding trout and be able to match such feeding with an appropriate imitation. This requires an ability to note color, size and shape of emerging insects as well as an ability

DIAGRAM III

Suggested Dry Flies for Eastern Trout Streams

DRY FLY	Suggested Fly Sizes to Fish per Month					
	APRIL	MAY	JUNE	JULY	AUG.	SEPT.
*Adams	*14-16-18	*14-16-18	*14-16-18	*16-18	*16-18	*18
*Hendrickson	14-16	*14-16	14-16			
*Quill Gordon	12-14	*12-14	14-16			
*Black Gnat	*16-18	*16-18	16-18			
*Royal Coachman	*14-16	*14-16				
*Brown Bivisible	12-14-16	*12-14-16	*14-16	16		
Gold Ribbed Hare's Ear		14-16	14-16			
*March Brown		12-14	*12-14			
*Gray Fox Variant		12-14-16	*14-16	14-16		
White Miller		14-16	14-16	14-16		
Blue Dun		14-16				
Pink Lady		12-14				
*Gray Comparadun			*14-16	*14-16	*16	
*Light Cahill			*10-12-14-16	*14-16		
*Flying Ant			14-16-18	*16-18	16-18	16-18
*Humpy (Goofus Bug)			12-14-16	*14-16	14-16	14-16
*Green Drake			*10-12-14	14-16		
*Red Fox Caddis			*14-16	*16-18	*16-18	16-18
*Woodchuck Caddis			14-16	*16-18	*16-18	16-18
*Flick Dun Variant			16-18	16-18	*18	*18
*Gray Wulff			*12-14	*14	14-16	14-16
*Cream Variant			*12-14-16	*14-16		
Jassids				18	18	18
*Letort Hopper				12-14	10-12	
Letort Cricket				12-14	12-14	
Rat Faced McDougal				12-14	12-14	

*Indicates those flies which have proven most successful for me in New York's Finger Lakes area and my prime success month or months for each fly.

to determine what is taking place beneath the surface in regard to the feeding cycle.

To simplify matters for the novice all dry flies may be grouped into the following six color categories as an aid in fly selection. As experience increases, a working knowledge of an observed natural and its imitation, by name, will soon follow.

COLOR CATEGORY	COMMON EASTERN DRY FLY EXAMPLES
Attractor	Royal Coachman, Royal Wulff, Pink Lady, Gold Ribbed Hare's Ear
Gray	Gray Comparadun, Dark Hendrickson, Blue Dun, Quill Gordon, March Brown, Adams
Brown	Brown Bivisible, Light Shad Caddis, Brown Ant, Thorax Brown Drake
Cream	Light Cahill, Ginger Caddis, Cream Variant, Green Leaf Hopper, Green Drake, Sulfur Dun
Black	Black Gnat, Flying Ant, Beetle (Humpy), Coachman, Jassid, Black Wulff, Letort Cricket
White	White Miller, White Wulff, White Irresistible, Rat Faced McDougal

SPECIFICATIONS FOR TAPERED LEADERS

Basically a properly tapered leader performs the following three functions:

1) It acts as an invisible (or nearly so) connection between the visible fly and the visible line when correctly treated to allow sinking.

2) It allows for a gradual deceleration of the fly to its soft landing at the end of the cast.

3) It allows the fly to react to the current's flow in a natural (lifelike) manner.

Like many fly fishermen I feel that a hand tied knotted leader unfolds more evenly and delicately than a manufactured knotless leader. I tie my own leaders with Orvis leader monofilament and have found their specification charts (see pages 158, 159) ideal for obtaining the proper hinge ratio of taper for leaders of 7½, 9 and 12 feet. However, rather than using the Barrel Knot, as commonly utilized in tying such leaders, I prefer to use the Double Surgeon Knot due to its strength and simplicity. (See pages 144 and 145.)

Just as progress advances knowledge in techniques, rod-reel-line materials, fly tying materials, designs, *etc.*, so are new leader material advancements being made. In its day cat gut was a major advancement in leader material. Yet it was not uniform, lacked in loop turnover qualities and was short lived. Then came monofilament and changed the whole complexion of dry fly fishing. There was, and still is for that matter, controversy concerning stiff versus limp mono. In recent years we have become accustomed to, and pretty well satisfied with, what I call standard monofilament such as Orvis, Maxima (produced in Germany), Berkley, Mason, *etc.* Yet, only recently two super mono products are receiving very creditable comments from those who have tried them. The main quality of these leaders is their increased stress strength as compared to standard mono of the same diameter. One of these super monos, Nylorfi, is manufactured in France. It is a limp mono while the other, Aeon, is a stiff mono which is slightly greater in strength. The only problem is that Aeon, in particular, should be soaked in water for a minute or so just prior to knot tying to prevent the knot from slipping while standard mono only requires mouth-heating a few seconds before knot tightening in order to prevent crimping. In order to demonstrate the difference between standard and the super monofilament leader materials in regard to diameter-to stress strength, the chart on the facing page is provided.

While the length of a leader is determined by seasonal water conditions and rod length, the tippet size is determined by hook size and seasonal water conditions which affect its visibility to trout. The Orvis table on the facing page is provided as an aid in determining what tippet size best matches the various hook sizes to be fished along with my suggested fly per hook size.

		Breaking Strength and Diameter Comparisons of Standard and Super Mono			
		SUPER MONO Stress Strength in Pounds		**STANDARD MONO** Stress Strength in Pounds	
SIZE	DIAMETER	NYLORFI	AEON	ORVIS	MAXIMA
0X	.012"	- - -	10.0	6.5	10.0
1X	.010"	9.4	9.0	5.5	8.0
2X	.009"	8.1	7.0	4.5	6.0
3X	.008"	5.9	6.0	3.8	5.0
4X	.007"	4.8	5.0	3.1	4.0
5X	.006"	3.9	4.0	2.0	3.0
6X	.005"	2.4	3.0	1.4	2.0
7X	.004"	1.7	2.0	1.1	1.0
8X	.003"	1.1	- - - -	.75	- - - -

		Proper Fly Sizes for Selected Leader Diameters		
TIPPET SIZE	DIAMETER	STRENGTH	BALANCING HOOK SIZE	SUGGESTED USE
0X	.012"	6.5 lbs.	2-1/0	large streamers
1X	.010"	5.5 lbs.	4-6-8	trout streamers
2X	.009"	4.5 lbs.	6-8-10	nymphs & streamers
3X	.008"	3.8 lbs.	10-12-14	hair body drys, wets nymphs
4X	.007"	3.1 lbs.	12-14-16	drys & wets
5X	.006"	2.0 lbs.	14-16-18	drys
6X	.005"	1.4 lbs.	16-18-20-22	drys
7X	.004"	1.1 lbs.	18-20-22-28	midges
8X	.003"	.7 lbs.	20-22-28	midges

The three primary tapered leader lengths to meet the normal trout and salmon conditions are 7½, 9 and 12 feet. I recommend the 7½ for early season and rod lengths of 7½ feet or under, 9 for early and midseason conditions for rod lengths of from 8 to 9 feet, and 12 for late season and low water conditions when using rods 8 feet or longer. Orvis specifications for section lengths and diameters of proper ratio for tying these three leaders are as follows. (Although 0X, 1X and 2X tippet leaders do not apply to those leaders normally considered as being designed for most dry fly fishing, they are included for sake of versatility):

Specifications: 7½ Foot Tapered Leader

0X		1X		2X		3X		4X	
Length	Dia.	Length	Dia.	Length	Dia.	Length	Dia.	Length	Dia.
24"	.019"	24"	.019"	24"	.019"	24"	.019"	24"	.019"
16"	.017"	16"	.017"	16"	.017"	16"	.017"	16"	.017"
14"	.015"	14"	.015"	14"	.015"	14"	.015"	14"	.015"
9"	.013"	9"	.013"	9"	.013"	6"	.013"	6"	.013"
9"	.012"	9"	.011"	9"	.011"	6"	.011"	6"	.011"
18"	.011"	18"	.010"	18"	.009"	6"	.009"	6"	.009"
						18"	.008"	18"	.007"

Specifications: 9 Foot Tapered Leader

0X		1X		2X		3X		4X		5X	
L.	Dia.	L.	Dia.	L.	Dia.	L.	Dia.	L.	Dia.	L.	Dia.
36"	.021"	36"	.021"	36"	.021"	36"	.021"	36"	.021"	28"	.021"
16"	.019"	16"	.019"	16"	.019"	16"	.019"	16"	.019"	14"	.019"
12"	.017"	12"	.017"	12"	.017"	12"	.017"	12"	.017"	12"	.017"
8"	.015"	8"	.015"	8"	.015"	6"	.015"	6"	.015"	10"	.015"
8"	.013"	8"	.013"	8"	.013"	6"	.013"	6"	.013"	6"	.013"
8"	.012"	8"	.012"	8"	.012"	6"	.011"	6"	.011"	6"	.011"
20"	.011"	20"	.010"	20"	.009"	6"	.009"	6"	.009"	6"	.009"
						20"	.008"	20"	.007"	6"	.007"
										20"	.006"

Specifications: 12 Foot Tapered Leader							
4X		5X		6X		7X	
Length	Dia.	Length	Dia.	Length	Dia.	Length	Dia.
36"	.021"	36"	.021"	36"	.021"	28"	.021"
24"	.019"	24"	.019"	24"	.019"	18"	.019"
16"	.017"	16"	.017"	16"	.017"	16"	.017"
12"	.015"	12"	.015"	12"	.015"	14"	.015"
7"	.013"	7"	.013"	7"	.013"	12"	.013"
7"	.011"	7"	.011"	7"	.011"	7"	.011"
7"	.009"	7"	.009"	7"	.009"	7"	.009"
7"	.008"	7"	.008"	7"	.007"	7"	.007"
28"	.007"	28"	.006"	28"	.005"	7"	.005"
						28"	.004"

Two of the world's most renowned fly fishermen of the present era have been Lee Wulff and the late Joe Brooks. Not only have these two masters proven their ability with rod and reel but also with pen and lectures on the subject. Both have expressed their personal preference as to favorite dry flies when fishing eastern trout waters. In Wulff's article entitled, *The Essential Fly Box,* * he states, "I can still come up with a fairly short list of basic flies—flies without which I would feel naked on the stream." Likewise Brooks, in his book *Trout Fishing,* ** divulges the basic dry flies he uses for eastern trout fishing. I too have what I refer to as my Survival Kit of dries to bolster confidence.

Dry Fly Survival Kits of Wulff, Brooks and the Author:

Lee Wulff
Adams (sizes 12-20)
Royal Wulff (as an attractor or explorer in sizes 10-14)
Light Cahill (sizes 18 & 20)

---

*Lee Wulff, "The Essential Fly Box," *Fly Fisherman Magazine,* (Winter 1977).
**Joseph Brooks, *Trout Fishing,* (New York: Harper & Row) 1972.

Pale Watery Dun (sizes 18 & 20)
Letort Hopper (sizes 8 & 10)
Flying Ant (sizes 12 & 14)
Beetle (in various sizes)
Skaters (for low water conditions in size 16)

Joe Brooks

Adams (sizes 12 & 16)
Black Gnat (sizes 14 & 16)
Light Cahill (sizes 16 & 18)
Royal Coachman (size 12)
Blue Dun (sizes 16 & 18)
Red Variant (size 16)
Tups Indispensable (sizes 12 & 14)
Dark Hendrickson (sizes 12 & 16)
Jassid (sizes 18 & 20)
Blue Wing Olive (sizes 20 & 24)
Flying Ant (sizes 18 & 20)
Letort Hopper (size 12)

The Author

Adams (sizes 14-16; if only allowed one fly this would be it)
Light Cahill (sizes 14 & 16)
Brown Bivisible (sizes 14 & 16; for riffs and bounding waters)
Dark Hendrickson (size 16)
Cream Variant (size 16)
Flying Ant (size 16)
Red Fox (Light Shad) Caddis (sizes 14 & 16)
Black Beetle or Humpy (size 14)
Gray Comparadun (sizes 14 & 16)
Letort Hopper (size 10)

What are the proper casts?

Weather and water conditions, reading the water, proper
tackle and a knowledge of trout food sources all require
observation and evaluation. However, proficiency in technique in
presentation consists of two parts, the cast and the float.

A cast begins with one or more false casts depending
upon the length of cast needed to reach the desired spot where
the fly is supposed to begin its float. Line is stripped from the
reel during each false cast until such distance is reached, but
should be kept to an absolute minimum to prevent increasing the
possibility of 1) movement discovery by the trout, 2) arm fatigue
and 3) casting errors (hooking obstructions, hooking line or
leader, wind knots, loss of accuracy or ending the cast in a
"whoopse" or collapse of the line). Also, a false cast is
frequently used by a dry fly angler to air-dry a fly (on a short
line) after it has either been treated with floatant, after it has
taken a dunking during a float, or after a missed strike.

The pickup (see Diagram IV) preceding the next cast at
completion of any float is performed by either a lift to backcast
or half roll and lift to backcast except in a Roll Cast where it is
merely flipped back upstream. Regardless of the type cast or
pickup employed, timing and smoothness are all important
factors. One should never be in such a hurry to present the fly
that he rushes through the mechanics involved with any aspect of
the cast.

There are some ten or more different casts from which to
choose depending upon the circumstances. Of these, I feel that
there are five basic casts with which the novice should become
proficient. They are the Basic Overhand Cast (Diagram V), Roll
Cast (Diagram VI), Backhand Cast (Diagram VII), Galway or
Reverse Cast (Diagram VIII) and S-Cast (Diagram IX). With the
mastery of these casts, as well as the Downstream Drift, the dry
fly fisherman should feel confident in meeting most challenges
involved with the presentation.

Before moving into the basic casts, there are some
elementary mechanics which should be mentioned. First, the grip

DIAGRAM IV
The Pickup

A. *Lift to Backcast:*

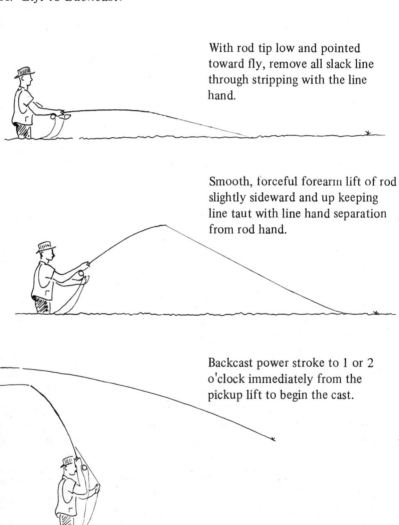

With rod tip low and pointed toward fly, remove all slack line through stripping with the line hand.

Smooth, forceful forearm lift of rod slightly sideward and up keeping line taut with line hand separation from rod hand.

Backcast power stroke to 1 or 2 o'clock immediately from the pickup lift to begin the cast.

DIAGRAM IV (continued)
The Pickup

B. Half Roll & Lift to Backcast:

Rod tip is slowly raised to about 1 or 2 o'clock position as fly and line drift downstream (as in preparation for Roll Cast) until line hangs from rod tip just behind shoulder to contact water surface beside or just in front of the angler.

The rod is then abruptly whipped smoothly forward to force the line to roll or loop toward the fly, keeping line taut with line hand throughout.

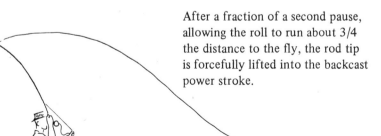

After a fraction of a second pause, allowing the roll to run about 3/4 the distance to the fly, the rod tip is forcefully lifted into the backcast power stroke.

should be above and ahead of the reel with either thumb or forefinger on top of the cork grip. I prefer the thumb on grip so the index and second fingers are ready to hook the line when either skittering or line stripping is desired during the float. However, one's choice here is a personal matter based upon comfort, balance and ease in rod maneuverability.

Secondly, the line pickup begins from a low rod tip position (pointed at the floating fly) while all slack is stripped in with the line hand. Once all slack has been removed from the water the pickup is immediately executed through a smooth forceful forearm lift of the rod (slightly sideward and up) directly into the backcast while maintaining a taut line with the opposite hand (much like ripping apart a piece of cloth).

Next, in executing the backcast and forward cast (or shooting cast) in an obstructed area, or where wind is a factor, it is best to power the rod so the tip stops at an imaginary 1 o'clock position (on backcast) and 11 o'clock position (on forward cast) in order to provide both line speed and a tight loop. Where a gentle (delicate) cast is called for, over placid waters and open areas unaffected by wind, a larger loop may be cast by power strokes from the 2 o'clock to 10 o'clock positions. The power strokes should never be executed lower than these two positions (a common error by the beginner). By dropping the tip lower than 2 o'clock on the backcast there is a tendency to permit line slack which will collapse the forward cast or to increase the chance of hanging the hook up on low obstacles. By dropping the the tip lower than 10 o'clock on the forward cast the tendency is to either increase the chance of hooking oneself, leader, line or rod, or to allow the line to slap the water and thus put down the fish. While casting one should attempt to maintain a locked or firm wrist whereby the rod becomes merely an extension of the forearm. The forearm, rather than the upper arm, should do most of the work. Casting with the wrist instead of the forearm is a common fault in many fly fishermen and an especially difficult alteration in casting technique to be made by the bait or spin caster who turns to the fly rod for his fishing.

In the follow through at completion of the forward power stroke, as the loop straightens in descent to the water, the angler should slowly follow the angle of line descent downward with the rod tip until it is at about eye or chin level. In so doing the chance of line slap is prevented, accuracy is increased, the rod is immediately positioned for setting the hook on an early take and the rod is in a position to mend the line. Also, the line is prevented from slacking whereby fly drag or other unnatural fly movement may result.

Correct reading of the water has led to proper fly selection, approach and positioning for the cast and execution of an appropriate cast. Yet, there are still certain essentials to master in fly presentation during the float. Such essentials are 1) visual concentration on both line (in respect to current and obstructions) and fly (in respect to a rising trout), 2) the method of working the fly in a natural manner, 3) mending of the line, and 4) the method of line retrieve.

Visual Concentration. Most dry fly fishermen have little trouble following the fly during a drift on either placid waters or in slow to moderate currents, especially when floating a size 16 or larger fly or a fly sporting white wings. However, size 18 or smaller dries (even with white wings) create a visual problem for most anglers as do flies of larger sizes riding atop turbulent waters. In these situations one must concentrate upon alterations in the line float (*e.g.,* line hesitation or stop, sudden line slacking, sudden line tension, *etc.*) and upon signs indicating a take near the fly (*e.g.,* surface bulge, surface ring, surface splash, surface swirl or the the sub-surface flash of a fish). Any one of these indications of a take should trigger an immediate hooking response on the part of the angler. Such hooking response in any phase of fly fishing should always be executed through a gentle rod lift rather than by a rod-yanking action. Remember that the trout generally heads downward immediately following the take. If the rod is jerked upward in the opposite direction, the sudden stress upon the tippet will nearly always result in a breakoff of even a fairly small fish. Because of the fine point and barb of a dry fly hook, there

DIAGRAM V
Basic Overhand Cast

(Used for long or short casts where no obstructions hinder backcasts.)

Execute the line pickup with smooth force sideward and up using forearm and locked wrist.

Power rod smoothly but forcefully through the backcast while line hand keeps line taut in a cloth-ripping motion between the two hands. Pause in the timing to allow rear loop to form.

As soon as the turning line nearly straightens (during pause) to cause pulling at the rod, smoothly and forcefully execute a straight over-shoulder forward cast from a 1 to a 2 o'clock position.

Immediately release line hand grip allowing rod energy to shoot stored loop or loops forward through rod guides while holding rod tip pointed at the intended target of the cast.

As leader turns over at completion of forward cast, slowly lower rod tip to eye or chin level while reaching for line with line hand mid-way between rod hand and stripping (first) guide. As the fly lands, the line hand strips slack

rearward past rod hand. The The rod hand index finger hooks line and holds it against cork handle grip in preparation for the retrieve.

DIAGRAM VI
Roll Cast

(Used while fishing upstream where obstructions behind prevent backcasts and a short cast is desired. It is especially effective as a bread-and-butter cast on windy days.)

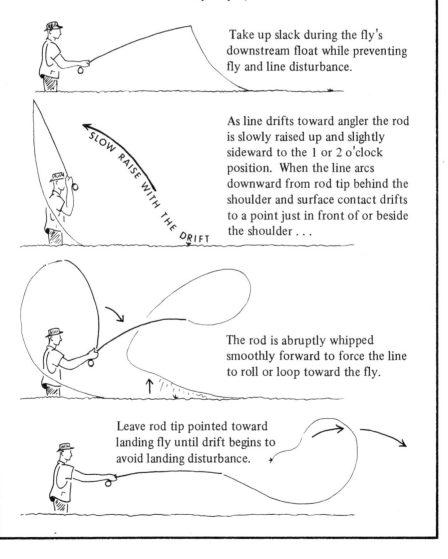

Take up slack during the fly's downstream float while preventing fly and line disturbance.

As line drifts toward angler the rod is slowly raised up and slightly sideward to the 1 or 2 o'clock position. When the line arcs downward from rod tip behind the shoulder and surface contact drifts to a point just in front of or beside the shoulder . . .

The rod is abruptly whipped smoothly forward to force the line to roll or loop toward the fly.

Leave rod tip pointed toward landing fly until drift begins to avoid landing disturbance.

DIAGRAM VII
Backhand Cast

(Used when fishing upstream where obstacles prevent a backcast either behind or from the side.)

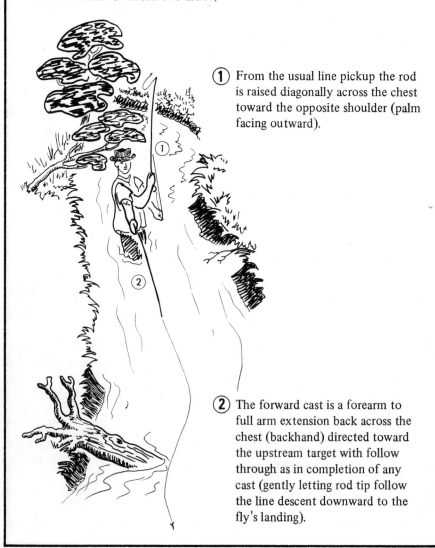

① From the usual line pickup the rod is raised diagonally across the chest toward the opposite shoulder (palm facing outward).

② The forward cast is a forearm to full arm extension back across the chest (backhand) directed toward the upstream target with follow through as in completion of any cast (gently letting rod tip follow the line descent downward to the fly's landing).

DIAGRAM VIII
Galway (Reverse) Cast

(Used where obstructions hinder a backcast but side casting lanes are open.)

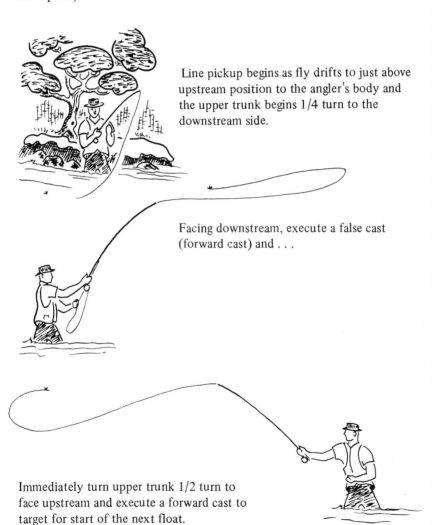

Line pickup begins as fly drifts to just above upstream position to the angler's body and the upper trunk begins 1/4 turn to the downstream side.

Facing downstream, execute a false cast (forward cast) and . . .

Immediately turn upper trunk 1/2 turn to face upstream and execute a forward cast to target for start of the next float.

DIAGRAM IX
S-Cast

(Used to prevent fly and line drag when fishing into a current; probably one of the most essential casts in stream dry fly fishing.)

At the completion of the forward power thrust in the cast, the rod tip is jiggled from side to side while slowly lowering the rod follow through. Thus, the line is caused to fall in a series of reverse curves to the water's surface. This allows the fly to float a greater distance (while the current works out the curves) before fly drag becomes a factor to be dealt with through either mending the line or line pickup for the next cast.

DIAGRAM X

Mending the Line

(An essential technique used while fishing across a current to prevent drag during a dry fly float.)

① Diagonal upstream cast with presentation so the line curves upstream in main current from the fly's float in the current's opposite edge.

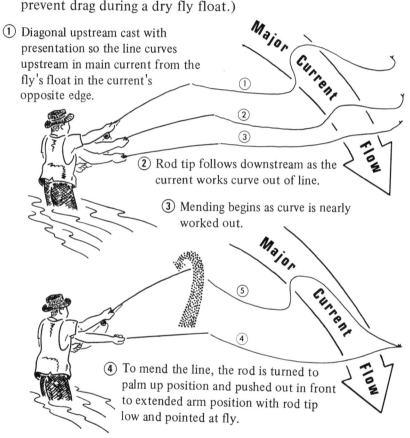

② Rod tip follows downstream as the current works curve out of line.

③ Mending begins as curve is nearly worked out.

④ To mend the line, the rod is turned to palm up position and pushed out in front to extended arm position with rod tip low and pointed at fly.

⑤ A slight flip and half roll rotation of the wrist is immediately executed up and outward in the upstream direction. Thus, the line is picked up off the water's surface and half barrel rolled upstream to land in another upstream curve from the fly which remains in its dead float. This procedure may be required 2 or 3 times during the full course of a good float before making the next cast. Where fly floats *in* main current with line in near less current the line is mended downstream.

is no need to apply rod force in order to penetrate lip or mouth tissue of the fish.

An angler's attempt to set the hook too soon should be mentioned as well. Many fine fish have been missed because the fisherman saw a trout slowly rising for a take of his fly and attempted to set the hook only to lift the fly before the fish had made contact. At such times it is hard to force oneself to wait until either the take is felt or until the trout is observed to arc downward from the surface before lifting the rod to set the hook.

At all times during the float the angler must, through peripheral vision, be aware of the line and leader's position in relation to the fly, current flow and approaching obstructions. The angler must respond in an automatic manner to alter its position if necessary and thus guarantee the longest, most lifelike float possible. This may require mending the line, retrieving slack line, swimming the fly, playing out additional line (in case of a downstream float) or even terminating the float through a line pickup.

Working the Fly. There are but a few methods of working the dry fly. The main technique is to allow the fly to ride atop or within the surface film in a dead float imparting no action to the fly other than allowing the currents (air and water) to swim it in a natural manner, maintaining a slack and drag free leader. Such a float is best employed in working either a mayfly or a caddis imitation.

A second method of working the fly is skittering. This method works best when fishing spider dries and is accomplished by casting diagonally up and across stream, diagonally down and across stream, to placid off current areas or just at the end of a section of riffs. The fly is caused to skip and dart along through either quick stripping of the line, rod twitches and jiggling, or by raising the rod and pulling back its tip.

A third method of working the fly, best used in fishing either placid or slow current waters, is accomplished by periodic lifting and lowering of the rod tip. In so doing, the angler must move the fly only enough to allow it to travel but an inch or two without causing leader and line drag or the fly to submerge and sink. The fly should be allowed to rest between each swim until all surface disturbance signs have disappeared. It is also extremely important that neither line nor leader cause any surface disturbance that may be noticed by the trout while the fly is moved. The best guarantee of this is to treat the leader to allow its sinking beneath the surface and to work a well greased line causing its highest possible floatation.

Another method of note in working a dry fly is called dapping. This is a prime technique used by those fishing a dry with a midge (ultra short) rod of 5 feet or under on small feeder streams where obstructions prevent the angler from casting. By working the short rod into position beyond bankside obstructions, the fly is lowered on a short section of leader to the water's surface where it is twitched up and down so as to imitate an insect flitting to and fro from air to water over a small section of surface area.

The last method of working a fly is the downstream drift. This technique is generally reserved as a last resort in fishing a spot where obstructions along both sides of a stream (and occasionally overhead) prevent more favorable alternatives in presentation. As the angler's approach must be made downstream, the chance of putting down a feeding trout is greatly increased as such fish will be facing upstream. Therefore, the angler should avoid wading any further into the stream than is absolutely necessary and should keep as low a profile as possible throughout both approach and presentation. Wallowing about a stream is one of the quickest ways of turning off a trout. Stirring up a cloud of mud, disturbing stones and rocks as well as waving of arms and body in an attempt to maintain balance while slipping on algae covered rocks and countering the force of a strong current will only result in sending fish reeling for cover long before the fly is sent on its downstream float. In executing the downstream drift I prefer to begin by stripping the leader and 3 to 4 feet of line beyond the rod tip. If at all possible I drop the fly into the edge flow of current, rather than into its main force, and play out line while jiggling the rod tip from side to side causing slight S-curves to fall on the water where the current assists in carrying both fly and line downstream without the fly becoming submerged. If and when a fish rises to take the fly, I find that setting the hook with an up and to the side lift of the rod (rather than directly upward) tends to prevent pulling the fly away from the fish. At the end of the drift I generally will direct the fly into the strong current to sink it, redirect the sunken fly to the edge current flow, and proceed to work it back upstream wet using slow up and down rod tip lifts, allowing it to swim and drift during its return, while taking up slack line periodically.

Line Retrieve. While the line retrieve plays less part in giving action to the dry fly as it does in working a nymph, wet or streamer, it is important in preventing excess slack line during the float. The line retrieves for this purpose are the Strip Retrieve (see Diagram XI) and the Figure 8 (see Diagram XII).

The Strip Retrieve is the prime method of taking up slack when fishing an upstream cast on moderate and turbulent waters. It may be performed either in quick, short retrieves with the line hand grasping and stripping from behind the closed line-supported index finger of the rod hand or, as diagramed (see XI) in either long jerks or a slow drawing action. The stripping hand may either store each stripped length of line in a loop over the hand or allow it to fall into a stripping basket or to the water. Where there is a chance of the line floating into obstructions by the current if allowed to fall free, it is wise either to store the line in loops over the hand or to use a stripping basket.

The Figure 8 Retrieve is best utilized in fishing placid waters and those of slow current as well as in returning the fly from a downstream drift where obstructions prevent stripping while using the alternate rod lift and lower technique as previously mentioned. It is more difficult to learn than is the Strip Retrieve but is a slower and more gentle means of working the fly once mastered. Like the Strip Retrieve, the line may be either allowed to fall free to the water or to be stored in small hand loops throughout the retrieve.

DIAGRAM XI
The Strip Retrieve

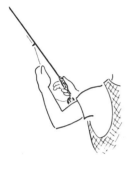

As the line hand grasps the fly line just below the rod stripping guide, the index finger and second finger of the rod hand extend to hook the line at the first joint as it is drawn past with the line hand.

The two line-hooking fingers close loosely against the rod handle as the line hand completes the stripping action.

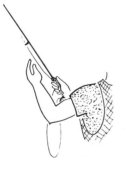

The fly line is held against the handle until the line hand regrasps the fly line once again just below the stripping guide. The sequence is repeated until either a fish takes or until ready for the pickup to execute the next cast.

DIAGRAM XII
The Figure 8 Retrieve

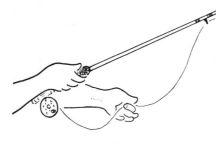

The line (just ahead of the rod hand) is held between thumb and index finger of the line hand (index finger turned inward against the thumb and all other fingers kept free of the line).

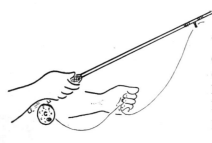

The line hand is rotated inward, closing the three extended fingers over the line in turn ending with the little finger, thus forming a small hand loop which is brought into the palm where it is held while . . .

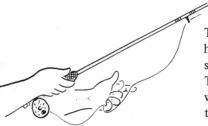

The index finger is withdrawn to hook the line and bring another small loop to the palm for storage. The three fingers are then withdrawn to be rotated once again to bring in another small loop.

This coordinated wrist, thumb and index finger and the last three fingers manipulation is repeated throughout the retrieve.

Where do we go from here?

The dry fly trout fisherman has countless streams, ponds and lakes at his disposal throughout the United States and Canada. All too often anglers overlook the exceptionally good fishing at hand in their own back yard and tend to follow the age old axiom, "the grass is greener on the other side of the fence." We hear of the Delaware, Beaverkill and Schoharie of New York, the Letort, Brodheads and Yellow Breeches of Pennsylvania, the Yellowstone of Wyoming and Montana, the Miramichi of New Brunswick, the Battenkill of Vermont, the Campbell River of British Columbia, the Au Sable of Michigan, the Snake and its tributaries of Idaho . . . and on it goes. However, such waters oft times provide for ultra selective trout (or in some cases, salmon) due, in part, to the multitude of visiting anglers who have come to traffic these and other renowned waters.

What about the lesser known streams? Some of my favorite New York State streams offer the fly enthusiast both quality and quantity fishing. Many are heavily stocked public streams and are only fished with any degree of regularity during the first few weeks of the season. Yet, don't think for a minute that these streams offer merely easy-to-catch hatchery stock. For example, this past spring near Oneonta, New York, the Hartwick Rod & Gun Club stocked the Otego Creek and found a dead brown trout measuring some 32 inches in length. Over the years of fishing this stream I have personally come in contact with two browns of well over 20 inches. Here in the Ithaca area is another fine stream of little reputation called the Six Mile Creek which produced a brown of just over nine pounds a few years ago. It is well stocked and also yields natural reproduction fish—another example of a small stream which has consistently produced numerous trout of 18 inches and up. Even tiny unnamed spring fed feeder streams of from 4 to 5 feet in width can produce surprising results. Such a stream is located near Cooperstown, New York, on Eggleston Hill where I was born and brought up. I know of two browns taken from this willow flanked tributary that measured 18 inches, and just last year my 12 year old son landed a 14 inch brookie there as well. All the trout of this stream are native born fish as stocking was discontinued in the early 1940's. I have found similar streams elsewhere which, because of their smallness and difficulty in fishing, have offered myself and but a very few other anglers many happy returns over the years.

Perhaps by now you are getting the picture, namely your fish are where you find them and this often goes well beyond fishing those waters which have acquired fame over the years as the result of publicity.

So the logical question arises, "How can one find out where these local hot spots and secret gems are located?" It is really simpler than one might think. First, secure topographical maps of the area. In this way not only the major waters but their feeder streams can be pinpointed. The angler is also afforded the various stream names and the most practical access routes to each. Next, the angler should make it known that he or she enjoys the out-of-doors and especially trout fishing. Fishermen, like hunters, possess a special camaraderie and the word has a way of quickly spreading. If one moves to a new community a little patience and an ear to the ground will generally pay off. Conversations with neighbors, fellow workers and local tackle store owners or personnel is a good starting point. Through such sources the angler may gain valuable information regarding not only local hot spots but appropriate tackle, prime times to fish such waters, public and private areas, special local regulations, *etc.* For the visitor who has neither the time to be patient nor time to explore on his own it is wise to seek competent advice. Such advice can be gained by asking for directions to a local tackle store, a local fly tier or a local Trout Unlimited member, any one of whom may be more than happy to answer questions. Another means of locating fishing waters is to ask if there is a local fishing guide in the area. Such information is best secured while visiting a local tackle store. The cost of a day's outing with a reputable guide on unfamiliar waters often pays off handsomely for an outsider with limited time and ready cash. In planning an out of state fishing trip, one should allow time to do essential homework. This consists of writing for state or provincial conservation department fishing guides and literature which are generally offered free of charge and contain helpful information such as maps, rules and regulations, fees, species common to various waters, guide service, *etc.* Last, in locating local hot spots and ferreting out secret gems of your own, investigate for yourself. This is where the topographical map pays off. It generally takes time but can well be worth the effort.

Where do we go from here? Let's go fishing!

SALMON CASSEROLE

Salmon is considered a delicacy perhaps because it is expensive. It requires special preparation to warrant its reputation. My favorite recipe for landlocks is a casserole:

1) Clean and fillet (being sure to skin each fillet) the salmon while it is still fresh. (Remember that all trout and salmon possess more oils than do other species of fish and thus will spoil sooner than most others.)
2) Cut each fillet into 3 or 4 inch lengths.
3) Dip each section in flour and place in a casserole dish greased with butter.
4) Dice 1 onion and 1 stalk of celery.
5) Sprinkle with ½ teaspoon salt, pepper, basil, plus the diced onion and celery.
6) Mix 1 cup of milk with 1 can Cream of Mushroom soup and pour over the fillets.
7) Cover and place in 400 degree preheated oven and bake for 30 minutes.
8) Remove from heat, stir gently (breaking up fillet sections).
9) Let stand uncovered for 5 minutes.
10) Scatter with sprigs of fresh parsley and serve.

8/Nymph Fishing to Non-Surface Feeding Trout

by J. Michael Kimball

The nature of nymph fishing to non-rising trout on the stream bottom is entirely different than nymph fishing to visible feeders on the surface. Tackle, technique, and philosophy arc at opposing ends of the fishing spectrum. The specific information needed and even the angler's attitude will require refocusing. Nymph fishing to non-surface feeders has its own group of converts who thrive on its unique challenges.

One of the major distinctions is the size of the fish. Non-rising fish, customarily invisible to the angler, include not only resident stream fish, but also resident lake fish returning to their spawning beds. These spawners offer the fisherman an opportunity to cast over formidable fish--far larger than their stream bred relatives. The fisherman must know the spawner's habitat as well as his behavior.

Tackle

RODS

There are unique tackle considerations for non-rising fish dependent primarily on stream conditions and also on whether the angling is focused on spawners or resident fish in holding position. Both breeders and holders are oriented to the stream

This over 12 pound steelhead (rainbow) was taken by the author on a stonefly nymph in New York State.

bottom rather than the surface. Since neither fish is actively feeding they will frequently not move any significant distance to capture food. Consequently, it is imperative for the angler to reach the bottom with his nymph. A rod of at least 8 feet is recommended and an even longer rod in the 8-½ to 10-foot category may be more serviceable. The value of the longer rod lies in the angler's need to continually mend the line in order to keep the fly on the stream bed. Further, longer, heavier rods facilitate the use of heavy lines and weighted flies, often so necessary for this type of nymph fishing. Casting weighted lines and flies can be an unsatisfying ordeal to some when contrasted with the delicate casting so often associated with rising fish. However, for many, this lack of finesse is a fair trade for the capture of these outsized fish.

LINES

Most major line companies now produce a "High Density" sinking tip line to facilitate the line and fly in getting to the bottom at the quickest possible rate. I like to use a sinking tip line where the first 10 to 30 feet of the line sinks and the remainder floats. For most conditions, the ten-foot sinking tip is preferable. The longer floating portions of this line permit easier mending and optimum line control.

For extremely deep, fast waters like Montana's Missouri, it is sometimes advantageous to use a lead core shooting head. Sunset Line and Twine Company makes a lead shooting head called "the cannonball," which gets to the bottom exceptionally well. In very still waters, where mending the line is less critical for maintaining a drag-free float, a straight "High Density" sinking line is my choice. Cortland Line Company's No. 4 sinking line and Scientific Angler's Hi-Speed Hi-Density lines are excellent choices for searching the bottom of lakes and quiet pools.

LEADERS

In choosing the appropriate leader, the prime consideration is, again, to keep the fly on the stream bottom. One of the most frequently repeated mistakes is selecting too long a leader. The conventional leader lengths of 7-½ to 12 feet have a tendency to be too buoyant to keep the fly on the bottom. A maximum leader length of six feet, and optimally three to four feet will suffice. Under extremely heavy water conditions, when fishing to spawning fish, I have shortened my leader to as little as two feet to eliminate the tendency of longer leaders to ride to the surface. Another means of keeping line on the bottom is to attach a one- to three-foot section of lead core trolling line to the butt section of the leader, then tie a two- to three-foot tippet onto the end of the trolling line. Lead core can be a misery to cast, but its rewards can be more than ample compensation.

The single most effective means of keeping the fly where the fish are is to use split shot, as a dropper, positioned one to two feet from the end of the leader. A good way to attach the split shot is to tie the tippet on to the rest of the leader with a blood knot. Then, rather than clipping one end of the blood knot, let that extra line extend down approximately one to two inches, forming an anchor line, and clamp the split shot to that extension. One of the shortcomings of using split shot as a dropper is that it often snags on the stream bottom, resulting in many lost flies. To minimize this, attach the split shot using a lighter pound test on the extended "anchor line," and then tie a knot both before and after the point at which the split shot is attached (see figure 1). Thereafter, if the split shot gets caught in the rocks, it has a tendency to break at the knots so that part of the extension, or "anchor line," is lost instead of the fly. Although this method may be aesthetically lacking to some, it will successfully keep the fly on the bottom when all else fails. During spring runoff conditions in New York's Finger Lakes region, I've found no better way to catch spawning rainbows with a nymph.

One further word of advice regarding split shot--I strongly suggest a horizontal cast to avoid snagging one's face or body. Author Charles Brooks has called casting with weighted flies "a form of Russian roulette with the eyes and ears as the stakes."

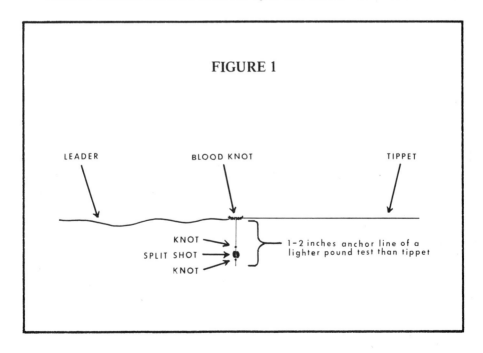

FIGURE 1

LEADER   BLOOD KNOT   TIPPET

KNOT
SPLIT SHOT
KNOT

1-2 inches anchor line of a lighter pound test than tippet

PATTERNS

When there are no visible rises, no hatch and often invisible fish, the angler must rely on other sources for determining what food is available to the fish. A wire mesh seine is a vital tool for collecting underwater insect life. By kicking up some stones and bottom turf, the angler, or his partner, can position a net downstream to intercept drifting specimens. If a seine is unavailable, a few moments devoted to upturning rocks and examining them should reveal the type of nymphal life in the stream. It is often useful to take some collected specimens back to the fly tying vise to assist in duplicating the exact nymph patterns in that water. A good collecting formula for temporarily preserving the specimens is a mixture of 80 percent rubbing alcohol and 20 percent water with a few drops of formalin added as a color preserver. There is no substitute for personally collecting and observing the nymphal life of a stream; however, when first-hand information is unavailable, Schwiebert's *Nymphs* is an excellent source book for investigating the types of nymph life that inhabit different types of rivers.

In the absence of other alternatives, exploring the water with an attractor nymph pattern can be successful. Attractors are generally tied in the sizes 2 to 12, with emphasis on the larger sizes. I usually tie them to simulate the ubiquitous stonefly. Most good trout rivers in the United States support at least a small population of various stoneflies, and fish seem to exhibit an affinity for these nymphs wherever they appear in their natural form. The stonefly genus, *Pteronarcys,* can be found on streams from the Adirondacks to the waters of Northern California and its commonality makes it a consistently effective attractor pattern throughout the states. Another stonefly of particular significance in the Finger Lakes region and Catskills is of the genus *Perla,* an excellent choice when in need of an attractor fly. Weighted *Perla* nymphs are particularly effective for tempting the large browns of New York's Mongaup River. When in need of a mayfly attractor nymph, I use a No.

12 impressionistic nymph tied to represent the common
Ephemerella genus. The following is a description of how to tie
these three attractor nymphs.

Pteronarcys **Nymph**	
Hook	Size 4-8, Mustad 9672, 3X long
Nylon	Olive 6/0
Tails	Grey quill fibers
Body	Grey dubbing mixed with hare's mask and ribbed with colorless, transparent swannundaze. Fine lead wire tied laterally along hook shank
Thorax	Grey dubbing mixed with hare's mask
Wing Cases	Brownish-grey quill fibers, should equal roughly half of insect
Legs	Grey partridge blended with thorax materials and "picked out" with a dubbing needle

This is a fly that I originated to represent the large *Pteronarcys*
flies of New York's Delaware River.

Perla **Nymph**	
Hook	Size 6-10, Mustad 9672, 3X long
Nylon	Amber 6/0
Tails	Woodchuck
Body	Amber, Australian possum blended with hare's mask and ribbed with fine gold wire. Fine lead wire tied laterally along hook shank
Thorax	Same as body, omit gold wire
Wing Cases	Amber mottled turkey quill, should equal roughly half of insect
Legs	Lemon wood-duck flank feathers mixed with hare's mask and "picked out" with a dubbing needle

Well known Adirondack fly tier and fisherman, Frances Bettors,
created this fly to initate the *Perla capita* stonefly of his native
Au Sable River. His skillful use of this nymph has produced an
enviable number of exceptional fish from these waters.

Ephemerella Nymph	
Hook	Size 10-12, Mustad 3906
Nylon	Amber 6/0
Tails	Partridge fibers
Body	Hare's mask. Fine lead wire tied laterally along hook shank
Thorax	Hare's mask
Wing Cases	Mottled brownish turkey quill
Legs	Light partridge hackle blended with thorax materials and "picked out" with a dubbing needle

I frequently tie attractor stoneflies as wiggle-nymphs which were first described in *Selective Trout* by Swisher and Richards. Personal experience has fashioned an adaptation which improves the effectiveness of these nymphs. When the abdomen is attached to the loop on the shank of the hook it is important that the loop be tied so that the opening is vertical. This is accomplished by lashing the loop onto the dorsal side of the hook shank which causes the abdomen when hinged onto this loop to flutter vertically, mimicking the natural vertical undulations of nymphs' movements. If the loop opening is horizontally tied such that the ends of the loop lie on the lateral sides of the hook shank, the abdomen will wag from side to side unnaturally. However, this horizontal loop *is* a superior device for designing jointed streamers, since this horizontal action strongly suggests the horizontal movement of a minnow's tail.

Technique

Big fish that are not actively feeding typically seek protective covering. These hiding places are provided either by the sheer depth of hollowed-out pools and stream channels, or by natural stream impediments such as logs, boulders, and undercut banks. Whatever form their cover takes, they tend to be on the bottom. Consequently, not only nymph equipment, but nymphing techniques must be designed to present the fly in a natural manner on the bottom of the river bed.

Charles Brooks, in his *Nymph Fishing for Larger Trout,* describes a number of useful nymphing techniques for a wide variety of stream conditions. When fishing to bottom holding fish my preference is Brooks' own method, which basically entails casting upstream to allow the fly to float dead drift along the bottom to a fish holding at a downstream angle to the fisherman. This method is well adapted to the deep waters of Fall Creek in Ithaca, New York, as well as to Western rivers like the Roaring Fork of Aspen, Colorado, where noted guide Chuck Fothergill uses a slight modification of this method and succinctly describes it as his "upstream, dead-drift, tight line, high rod, weighted nymph" technique. Regardless of the chosen method, success demands not only that the fly remain on the stream bottom but also that the fly move along at a rate not in excess of the speed of the current. Any nymph moving more swiftly than the current will be easily perceived as a fraud. Exception, of course, is taken to this rule when the angler deliberately imparts action to a fly.

Fishermen generally find one of the most taxing features of nymph fishing is learning when and how to strike a taking fish. The difficulty of detecting the strike relates to the fact that a fish will often take and reject the fly before a tell-tale pause in the line can be perceived. Thus, the object is to strike whenever there is an interruption in the natural drift of the line. In most cases, the fly will simply be snagged in the rock bottom, resulting in the loss of many flies. However, this is unavoidable. The angler who loses no flies is fishing the technique incorrectly. A good aid in learning this technique is to use a strike indicator. Often the hesitation in the line is so imperceptible that the angler doesn't realize a fish has taken the fly. The best remedy for deciphering this enigma is the development of that sixth sense so many nymph fishermen talk about, and that only comes from practice.

Basic information concerning proper casting and other fly fishing mechanics can be found in Chapter 7, "Fishing the Dry Fly for Fun and Challenge."

A secondary problem arises, especially for the Brooks method advocate, when the angler sets the hook on a downstream fish: the fly is literally pulled out of the fish's mouth. To counter this action, the angler must develop a slight hesitation in his strike to allow the fish time to take and turn on the fly. This is the same hesitation required of the Atlantic salmon fisherman and is also acquired through hours of trial and error. When a downstream fish is hooked in the front half of either the upper or lower jaw, the strike has probably been premature. If the fish is hooked in the corners of the jaw or in the rear portion of the mouth, then the hesitation hooking technique has probably been performed correctly. The reverse of this statement is true when striking a fish that is lying upstream from the fisherman.

There is a small variation of the Brooks method which I use when fishing specifically for spawning trout. Instead of

A slight hesitation in striking a downstream fish will result in proper corner of jaw hooking.

casting directly upstream, I prefer to throw an upstream curve in the line by means of a reach cast, as described by Swisher and Richards in their *Fly Fishing Strategy*. The upstream curve not only permits a deeper drift of the fly, but also allows for a more natural drag-free float of the nymph.

SPAWNING FISH

One of the greatest challenges when fishing to non-feeding fish is locating them. Frequently when large fish are migrating from the lakes into the streams, there is a concurrent influx of hordes of anglers. Consequently, on popular rivers where the spawning season is brief, crowds of fishermen invariably chase the fish off the redds and into the deep holding waters of the stream. The only practical defense against this situation is to either arrive at the stream very early in the morning before the fish have been spooked off the redds, or to be well familiarized with the holding water and resting places of spawning fish for that specific river. In working strange waters, a guide or friend who knows the nature of the stream is indispensable. I have found the "chuck and chance it" method relatively ineffective when fishing to spawning trout on unfamiliar water. Immediately after the height of the spawning season, the crowds begin to wane, enabling a resourceful angler to capitalize on a few weeks of relative solitude while fishing to some lunkers who have not yet returned to the lake.

Again the Charles Brooks method is the best approach when nymphing for spawners. The refusal of spawning trout to move great distances to take a nymph requires precise casting and bottom bumping drifts. If the spawning fish is sizeable enough to warrant the time, the typical number of casts presented to rising fish will not suffice with spawners. The angler's patience will be brought to bear by the necessity of passing the nymph in front of the fish for as long as endurance will permit. In fishing to surface feeders during a hatch, frequently the first cast is the best opportunity and every succeeding cast loses its impact. In fishing to spawners the first is still the best but it may require 200-plus casts to produce results. Changing angles to ensure a proper drift sometimes seems to be a deciding factor in a long awaited take.

Although arduously passing a fly over the same large fish can be frustrating in the extreme, netting a fish measured in pounds rather than inches is more than commensurate with the efforts required. The intrigue for the stream fisherman lies in the lure of lake bred fish of such great proportions. Once having captured a spawner, the intrigue quickly becomes an annual addiction, explaining the ever increasing popularity of this "young" Eastern sport.

9/Going Under with Hair and Feathers

by Gordon L. Eggleston

Without question, less has been written regarding fresh water streamer and bucktail angling than any other aspect of fly fishing. However, recently the fly rod has found favor with anglers in coastal salt waters and articles are beginning to appear on streamer techniques for ocean fishing. But there is still very little written on the use of these artificials for fresh water game fish.

I will attempt in this chapter to give the reader information on the various types of streamers and bucktails as well as the techniques which have proven successful for me over the years in quest of trout, landlocked salmon and bass.

Distinguishing Characteristics of Streamers and Bucktails

The major difference is the wing material used in the tying of each. Streamers are underwater bait fish and crayfish imitations tied with feather wing material such as rooster neck hackle, marabou and peacock herl. Bucktails are similar imitations which are tied with animal hair wing materials such as bucktail, bear hair or animal guard hair. Some imitations combine feather and hair wing material (*e.g.*, the Muddler) and are classified as bucktails since the primary wing material is hair.

Generally, streamers which are tied with a tail employ some short feather material. Some bucktails are tied with a tail while others are not. Bucktail tails are made of feather or hair material.

Various Types of Streamers and Bucktails

Primarily, there are six types: 1) Standard Trout Flies, 2) Salmon Flies, 3) Tube Flies, 4) Keel Flies, 5) Tandem Flies, and 6) Saltwater Flies (see Diagram I). Each, with the possible exception of tube flies and keel flies, has had numerous spinoffs. Streamers and bucktails, much like dry flies, may be tied either to imitate specific aquatic food sources or to attract attention in order to provoke a strike. Briefly, let us examine each type of streamer/bucktail in light of its design and purpose:

1) **Standard Trout Flies**. These flies are generally tied on long shank hooks in sizes 6, 8, 10 and 12. Two popular spinoffs are the Matuka (tied with 1 or 2 hackle feathers atop the body from head to extended tail to imitate a sculpin), and the Thunder Creek (tied on a ringed eyed hook with a bucktail and/or hair, with a bullet shaped head, which extends rearward as body and tail with painted or epoxy eyes). Some prime standard patterns today for trout and bass throughout the country are the Royal Coachman, Mickey Finn, Grizzly King, Gray Ghost, Muddler Minnow and the Black Nose Dace.

2) **Salmon Flies**. These flies are similar to standard trout flies except that they tend to be attention attractors rather than food source imitations. Salmon flies are generally tied on either single or double long shank hooks with eyes that turn up or down. The more popular sizes range from 2 through 8. The majority of these flies possess a tag of tinsel or bright colored floss wrapped around the hook shank at the top of the hook's bend just behind the tail material tie in. Some of the more popular patterns for landlocked salmon and steelhead fishing within this country today

DIAGRAM I

THE SIX PRIMARY TYPES OF BUCKTAILS AND STREAMERS

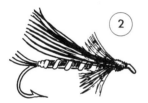

1. Trout Fly
2. Salmon Fly
3. Keel Fly

4. Tube Fly
5. Tandem Fly
6. Saltwater Fly

are the Goldeneye, Salmon Muddler, Rusty Rat, Jock Scott, Umpqua, Thunder & Lightning and the Silver Doctor.

3) Tube Flies. These flies are simple and flashy in design. Generally a long shank, No. 6, 8 or 10 double hook with ringed eye, is used with a section of woven mylar tinsel tubing about two inches long slipped over the hook shank. This, along with either white or dyed bucktail (or bear hair), is tied off at the head. The mylar tinsel is either left trimmed or is frayed at about ½ inch from the hook barbs, while the hair material extends in length to the hook barbs. Although not as widely known and fished as the other five types of streamers/bucktails, this fly is extremely versatile as an attractor for both fresh and salt water species of game fish.

4) Keel Flies. These flies are used in both trout and salmon waters where obstructions, particularly along the bottom, cause frequent snags when fished with standard streamer hooks. Keel fly hooks are constructed to float and work with the barb facing upward rather than facing down, therefore greatly decreasing the chance of snags. When tying keel flies, all the standard patterns can be achieved with only slight alteration. The names are: Keel Muddler, Keel Royal Coachman, Keel Mickey Finn, *etc.*

5) Tandem Flies. These flies are used extensively by fly fishermen in quest of such fresh water game fish as great northern pike, landlocked salmon, large and smallmouth bass, lake trout, coho and chinook salmon. Although designed for large fresh water fish, the saltwater fly angler can use them too, provided such flies have been tied with stainless steel hooks to prevent rusting. A medium to heavy gauge monofilament attached trailer hook is secured to the shank of the front hook. The trailer follows 1½ to 2 inches behind the forward hook and is dressed with body and tail materials only. The front hook is dressed in like body material, but contains the wing and cheek materials of the pattern as well. The wing material extends rearward so as to reach the tail of the trailer hook when the fly is straightened out. Like keel flies, all standard patterns are possible. The names are:

Tandem Gray Ghost, Tandem Grizzly King, Tandem Golden Darter, *etc.*

6) Saltwater Flies. These flies are generally of an attractor pattern and are tied in a wide range of sizes from small No. 2's through large No. 4/0's. These long shanked hooks possess ringed eyes and are of stainless steel to prevent saltwater corrosion. Most are tied with hackle, marabou, hair, pliable synthetics, or a combination of these wing materials which, contrary to fresh water streamers/bucktails, should extend well beyond the hook bend. Some of the more popular saltwater flies of today are the various Tarpon Fly patterns, the Sand Eel, the Menhaden, the Baracuda Streamer, the Lefty's Deceiver and the Pink Horror.

To weight or not to weight... that is the question.

It is generally agreed that an unweighted streamer/ bucktail will respond to stream currents in a more life-like manner than will a weighted fly. Also, weight (lead wire) often is improperly applied to the hook shank near its center and rearward. In so doing, the fly will float head up rather than level or head down. It may also turn on its side when worked. To prevent such improper balance, the angler using weighted flies should tie with fine wire near the head and cheeks when making flies. I prefer to tie weight beneath the hook shank rather than to wind the lead around the shank as most commercial fly tiers do.

Another problem facing the angler using a weighted fly is that it casts with more difficulty than does a similar unweighted pattern. The same problem faces the angler casting a line with a BB split shot attached to the leader ahead of the fly. One must remember that in any fly fishing the angler casts the weight of the fly line as balanced to the rod (not the fly), and that the wind-resistant bulkiness, size and weight of either streamers or bucktails all contribute to the difficulty in casting as opposed to the lightness and smallness of a dry fly.

Of course the purpose of fishing either a weighted fly, leader and/or line is to place the fly well beneath the surface or near stream bottom where bait fish are generally located. Actually there are seven main factors which affect the rate at which a streamer or bucktail will sink in fresh water:

1) **The Speed of Current Flow.** The faster the flow affecting the drift or retrieve, the slower and shallower the fly will descend.

2) **The Fishing of a Weighted Fly.** Heavy wire, larger hook sizes and lead wire all tend to increase the rapidity of sinking.

3) **The Fishing of a Split-Shot Weighted Leader.** BB split-shot attached to the leader from 10 to 12 inches ahead of either a weighted or unweighted fly increases its sinking.

4) **The Type of Materials Used in Fly Construction.** Hair wing and body material, which constitutes the main portion of a bucktail, tends to cause far greater buoyancy than do the feather, tinsel and floss materials which comprise the main dressing of a streamer. Therefore, streamers tend to sink more rapidly than bucktails.

5) **The Amount of Dressing Used in Construction of the Fly.** Sparsely tied flies sink more rapidly than do heavily dressed flies.

6) **The Use of High Density Sinking Lines.** Obviously, a sinking line will draw a fly deeper and faster than will a floating line where only the weight of streamer and/or weighted leader cause the fly to sink.

7) **The Amount of Water Absorption by a Fly Before It Is Fished.** A fly which has been submerged in water and worked with the fingers, so as to absorb water before being fished, increases its sinking ability. Also, along the same line, avoiding excessive false casts (which tends to whip water from the fly and dry it) helps maintain sinking ability.

Many anglers are of the opinion that a streamer must be fished deep for results. This is the usual rule. However, there are exceptions. Many times bait fish will rise to a level within less than 12 inches from the surface; particularly when either caught in heavy current or chased by a predator. In fact, I think perhaps 25% of the trout and bass I have taken on streamers and bucktails were the result of fishing the fly either in or just beneath the surface. Then too, there are certain bucktail patterns (*e.g.,* the conventional Muddler) which are purposely tied unweighted and, due to the buoyancy of materials used in their construction, lend themselves to surface, or very shallow, floats.

Certainly, fishing a streamer/bucktail with a floating fly line, as in shallower stream areas, offers easier line mending for adjusting line position during a float as compared to using a full sinking line or a sinking tip line. Such a line offers these advantages: a broadside float of the fly can be easily maintained; a slower drift of the fly can be achieved; and a visible line tip indicates where the fly is and what is happening to it. However, one must always remember that even with these advantages the angler must place the fly to within easy view and striking range of the fish in order to be effective. As such fish are generally located near the bottom and within either the main current itself or its edge, weight of one type or another is required in most situations when using the floating line outfit.

The fishing of streamers and bucktails with a floating dry fly line cannot do justice to all conditions. Therefore, I prefer to carry an extra reel spool loaded with a sinking tip line for use in fishing nymphs and streamers/bucktails in waters 5 feet deep or deeper whenever there is a lack of dry fly action. In so doing, I am able to fish a shorter leader with heavier tippet (3½ to 4½ pounds stress) than the longer, lighter tippet leader employed on my dry fly line. However, if I desire to fish a nymph or bucktail in waters of less than 5 feet, such as riffs and runs, I prefer to use my floating dry fly line with its long, light tippet leader. When going with the sinking tip (the same would apply for either a shooting head or a sinking line), I prefer to use a leader which does not exceed 7½ feet in length. Not only will a shorter leader cast easier when streamer/bucktail fishing, but it will also prevent excess planing during the float and retrieve. Ideally, the line should be at, or above, the working level of the fly whenever possible, thus preventing the line from either spooking the fish or becoming snagged on obstructions along the bottom.

I carry and fish both weighted and unweighted streamers and bucktails. Once these are tied, it is next to impossible to tell which is which. Therefore, I tie all my own weighted patterns with a fluorescent head and finish off the unweighted flies with a natural color thread. Sometimes I could swear that the tiny fluorescent orange at the head of my weighted flies aids in prompting an attack.

Yes, there are pros and cons to weighted flies versus unweighted flies, leaders and lines. However, in the final analysis, it is strictly up to the individual. Fish can be taken in many ways. One must settle for that particular system which affords the greatest confidence and enjoyment.

Prime Time to Fish a Streamer Fly

There are certain times of the year, just as there are certain times of the day, when streamers and bucktails are more productive than at others.

Early Spring. Although I am primarily a dry fly fisherman at heart, I believe in taking fish whenever and however I can. During early spring the water conditions are usually cold, high and often roily from winter runoffs and frequent showers. Major fly hatches are generally not yet established and a trout's ability to see any surface floating insects which may have emerged, is often nil. At such times I have found that working a streamer/bucktail deep and slow is often the most productive way of taking trout. Fishing such flies can bring results at any time of day.

Mid-Season Periods. I tend to rely on dry flies for taking trout once the major hatches begin. I must admit that my streamers take a back seat to my dry fly selections at this time of year. Nevertheless, there are times during the heart of the season when I fish nothing but a streamer or bucktail, for example during and immediately following a sudden downpour when a clear stream rises and begins to color to the point that dry flies float unseen to all below the surface. This is one of the few times during daylight hours when the angler may be glad to have fished a heavy 1X, 2X or 3X tippet, as it is a prime time for really big fish to leave their cover in search of a meal, a meal which often centers on bait fish which the streamer imitates.

Late Fall to Early Winter. For me, fall means back to work college teaching and coaching duties. Summer on the stream turns, like the changing leaves of autumn, into a time of changing patterns. There is less time for the pleasures of casting the fly. However, there are times when I manage to hit our Cayuga Lake Tributaries in quest of landlocked salmon and brown trout in their spawning migration, a time when these streams also find rainbow feeders in a responsive mood to the angler's presentation. The dry flies are carefully stored away for hibernation over the long winter months, but the streamer and bucktail continue to produce for the remainder of the New York State special stream season through December 31st. Once the chill of late fall rains and snow bring the water level and its accompanying color up, both salmon and trout respond to the call. Most of these lake fish are truly a trophy catch when taken in these streams *via* streamer or bucktail. At such times I prefer to fish either a Muddler or a Goldeneye slowly along the bottom using a strong 2X or 1X tippet as these fish are heavy and full of fight. I am certain that similar success with streamers can be found throughout the northern waters of this country during this time of year for the fly fisherman seeking both steelhead and salmon.

Braving inclement weather and water conditions requires both dressing properly and accepting the fact that many times de-icing rod guides is the order of the day. Nevertheless, the results are often compensation for the inconveniences encountered. One thing is in your favor. You don't have to worry about getting up early in order to beat a crowd to your favorite stretch of water.

Usually the stream will be all yours ... unless you start to show and tell.

Any Given Day. I have found that a consistently prime time for fishing streamers and bucktails for trout is from dawn to just before the sun hits the water. On overcast days this productive time span can generally be extended with success well into the morning hours. Should it begin raining, which tends to mask the water so as to inhibit visibility for fish and angler alike, be prepared to continue swimming the streamer/bucktail as long as it produces before switching to nymphs or dries. Usually I will read the water as well as the weather and start the day off in accordance. If it is a clear, cool morning and no surface rises are in evidence I will begin with a streamer or bucktail. If I fish one or two "fishy" looking areas without success for 15 to 20 minutes, I will switch to a nymph pattern before changing to my dry fly outfit. At midday I prefer to work dries as long as they produce. However, should a lull in midday dry fly action occur, I will usually go under with either nymph or streamer. The evening hours can generally be counted on to produce the day's prime feeding time for trout. The problem is which way to go, dry or streamer, as each is likely to produce. I enjoy dry fly fishing, therefore I seldom forsake such flies during the fleeting hour of daylight unless absolutely necessary.

What is the best way to work a streamer or bucktail?

We were fishing the East Branch of the Owego Creek, one of my favorite local trout streams, and I had just handed my son one of my favorite early season bucktail patterns (a size 8 Eggleston Brook). We had each done well on our Adams dries, but the surface action had slowed to a standstill. Actually, this

---

Basic information concerning proper casting and other fly fishing mechanics can be found in Chapter 7, "Fishing the Dry Fly for Fun and Challenge."

was my son's first year on the stream with flies and he had never fished anything but a dry. As we clipped and changed to the weighted bucktails my son asked, "What is the best way to work a bucktail?" My immediate answer was, "The best way is the way which will take fish." I had not meant to be facetious but in afterthought I realized the depth of the statement. There are many ways to take a fish. What works under one situation may fail under another. Certainly the right pattern for the water being fished will generally fail if presented and worked improperly.

A gut feeling, which develops slowly over a long period of fishing experience, often will dictate fly selection and its mode of presentation. Yet, for the novice such a statement is meaningless. The best advice for such an angler is to become proficient at the standard bread-and-butter presentations involved in streamer fishing as rapidly as possible: the Broadside Float (see Diagram II), the Down-and-Across Cast, and the Downstream Drift. Once these are mastered, the foundation will have been laid for your own intuition. Following is a brief description of these basic presentations, as well as certain innovative techniques which have proven their worth in working various streamers/bucktails.

The Broadside Float. I feel that the most important of all presentations to learn and use is the Broadside Float as it presents the fly in a natural position—natural speed swim. Receiving its name from the fact that, when properly employed, the fly is dead drifted with its body traveling downstream in a side-to-current (broadside) position. This is a far more life-like position for a bait fish than is a facing downstream drift or sweep and, after all, this is what the angler seeks to duplicate: the normal motion of whatever's being imitated.

The Broadside Float is best suited to waters possessing moderate to turbulent current flow. I prefer to cover such areas completely by first presenting the fly on a short line (short cast) so as to cover the near side water, beginning at the head of a run. Remaining in the same casting position, each successive cast and float is lengthened until the entire width of the stream has been covered. Each cast travels the same up-and-across stream line and

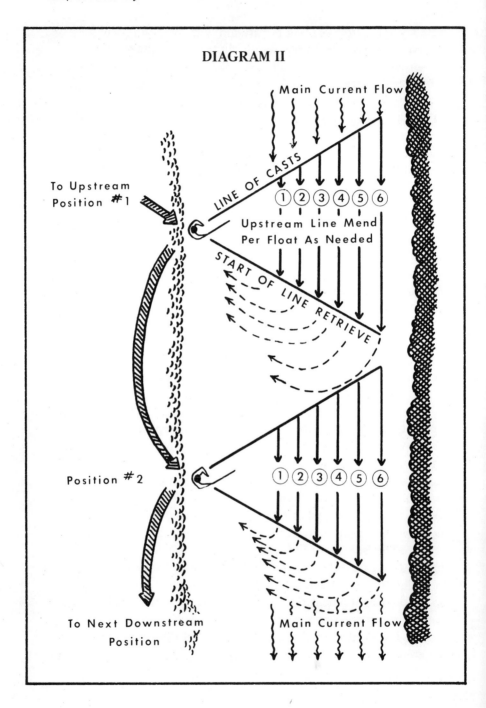

DIAGRAM II

each float is maintained in a broadside presentation of the fly
through continual mending of the line as needed to prevent line
(or fly) drag. The line mend may be either upstream (*i.e.,* when
the fly is floating slower than the line) or downstream (*i.e.,* when
the line is floating slower than the fly). Occasionally the angler
may wish a longer dead float than line mending will provide at
the down-and-across position. At such times a Roll Cast of
stripped (from reel) running line outward into the current will
provide a few extra feet of drift than would otherwise be
possible. Each retrieve, at the end of the float, should begin at
the same down-and-across stream line and may be whatever
method the angler feels appropriate for the fly pattern in use;
e.g., short and quick stripping, slow and steady stripping,
alternate strip and stop, alternate rod tip lifts and lowering to
strip, *etc.* Once the head of the run has been covered, the angler
should carefully move downstream to a position where the line of
casts will cover the lower edge of the retrieve waters fished at the
first position. The series of broadside floats is then repeated,
each float being spaced from 3 to 4 feet apart as in the first series.
Thus, the angler continues the downstream positions to fish the
entire stretch of water.

    The Down-and-Across Cast. Probably one of the most
commonly used techniques for working streamers/bucktails is the
Down-and-Across Cast. The length of float is not nearly as long
as that of the Broadside Float where the drift begins from an up-
and-across cast. However, in many cases obstructions prevent all
but either a Cross-Stream or a Down-and-Across Cast. Current
force from slow to moderate is especially conducive to the use of
the Down-and-Across Cast presentation. Line mending and/or
roll cast of slack line is required during the dead drift phase to
allow the fly to continue sinking and coasting with a natural at-
current pace. Should the angler wish to raise or increase the speed
of the fly, the line may be mended downstream. As with any
method of swimming a streamer/bucktail, nymph, wet fly or dry
fly, the angler should be especially observant of a strike indication
(*i.e.,* feel through rod and line, line hesitation and straightening,
or a visible flash of a fish at the estimated location of the fly). The

prime time for such an indication of a strike to occur is as the fly is swept upward and into the current's main flow. The retrieve at the float's end may be executed in any one or combination of the various traditional methods.

The Downstream Drift. Situations sometimes arise where the only way to fish a run is by means of a Downstream Drift; *e.g.,* when obstacles along each streamside prevent a conventional cast. In such drifts, the fly should be allowed to hang and wash about a few seconds between either swimming it forward or allowing it to drift downstream a few feet to hang and wash once again. By moving the rod tip down and to one side or the other, the fly can be directed to dart sideward due to the current's action against the redirected line. At such times the strike will occur not as the fly darts across the current but, rather, as it stops, sinks or rises to dart back into the current. Generally, those fish enticed into a take provide the angler with a spectacular, hard-hitting, splashy display due to the fact that the fly is current-forced (even if weighted) to or barely beneath the surface. Therefore, a trout on the take will rise in a rush, anxious to retreat immediately to the less forceful stream bottom flow where little energy is required to station within the current.

Most presentations consist of three parts: the cast, the drift or float, and the retrieve. As the first two aspects have been discussed, let us now examine the retrieve. It should mimic the actions of bait fish. Such fish can be observed to hold or lie nearly motionless either at or near the bottom, to slowly swim upstream or about in a current's eddy, to swim or dart upward only to settle back with the current, to dart to the side in a change of station, to quickly half-roll with a flash of the side when sunning themselves and to dart in erratic directions and speed when frightened. Regardless of the retrieve employed, the angler should always maintain a proper rod tip angle throughout. This requires a continual conscious effort in preparation for a possible take. The angle should be at about 45 degrees and very slightly leading the fly downstream. Without such angle to absorb a sudden, forceful strike, the chance of an immediate breakoff of both fly and fish is greatly increased.

Due to the nature of tackle and techniques utilized in fly fishing, all retrieves are hand drawn in what is referred to as strip retrieves. Such retrieves may in some instances also employ the use of rod tip and/or stream current action for imparting a lifelike swim to the fly. The following retrieves are those which have found favor among streamer/bucktail fly fishermen over the years. Some are traditional tactics, while others are newer innovations.

Slow and Steady Strip. This retrieve is carried out through either a Figure 8 (see Dry Fly chapter retrieves diagram) or a steady strip from either in front of or behind the rod hand supported line. It is especially good in working eddies and cross current.

Short and Quick Strip. This retrieve is carried out from behind the rod hand supported line using short (usually from 3 to 6 inches) and rapid line hand strips. It is especially effective in retrieving a properly weighted fly which, due to the forward weight, attains a nose down attitude between strips. Thus, the fly responds in a bobbing action very similar to that of a jig as it travels through the water.

Long and Rapid Strip. This retrieve, like the Short and Quick, is carried out from behind the rod hand. However, instead of short wrist stripping, the line hand strips downward as initiated from the elbow. In so doing, each strip of the line moves the fly forward from 15 to 20 inches. It is an especially good retrieve to use in casting cross stream to opposite bankside areas containing cover such as overhanging grass or bushes, log jams, rock ledges, *etc.*, where predator fish (*e.g.*, trout or bass) may be located. In fishing such a cast, the retrieve should be immediate upon entry so as to imitate a startled bait fish attempting to escape an unpleasant situation. Often this tactic will prompt an attacking response within the fish before it actually realizes what is happening.

Two Handed Haul. This is an innovative fast strip retrieve technique popularized in recent years by Doug Swisher. In executing the retrieve, the rod grip and attached reel are placed under the line hand armpit while line is stripped from behind the rod's first guide (stripping guide) in a rapid hand-over-hand method. However, due to the rapid force of the retrieve, compounded by the rapid force of a striking fish, the angler should be especially conscious of keeping a high rod tip during the tactic. Also, one should never attempt this retrieve if fishing a light tippet. Like the Long and Rapid Strip, this retrieve imitates a frightened bait fish and should be reserved for fishing situations which call for an especially rapid retrieve unattainable via other more traditional means.

Alternate Strip and Stop. This retrieve is especially good in any of its spinoff versions and is very adaptable to fishing all types of water encountered in streamer/bucktail fishing. In executing the retrieve, an angler may strip line either slowly or rapidly, short or long in length. He may stop or hesitate after each strip, thus allowing the fly to either hold or settle. Then again, he may stop or hesitate after a series of either fast or slow strips of the line to allow the fly to hold or settle. Regardless of which version is used, the angler should be ready for a strike either as the fly stops to hold in the current or as it settles.

Alternate Lift and Strip. This retrieve is executed by slowly lifting the rod tip on a taut line and then quickly lowering it to strip the resulting slack line. The rod and line hands coordination continues to move the fly forward in a series of raise and settle maneuvers during the retrieve, a retrieve which is often utilized in either a downstream drift or a down-and-across cast.

Alternate Rod Twitches and Strip. This retrieve, which I call the "Palsy Shake," is executed by rapidly twitching or jiggling the rod hand with a stiff wrist while slowly moving the rod upward and upstream on a taut line. Then, as the rod is returned to its starting position, the line hand either slowly or rapidly (according to the angler's option) strips in slack line. The rapid rod tip twitches, in accompaniment with the upstream movement of the rod, generates a typical swimming action within the fly. As it drifts and settles backward, during the stripping phase of the retrieve, the angler should be prepared for a strike by keeping a high rod tip to prevent a breakoff. This technique

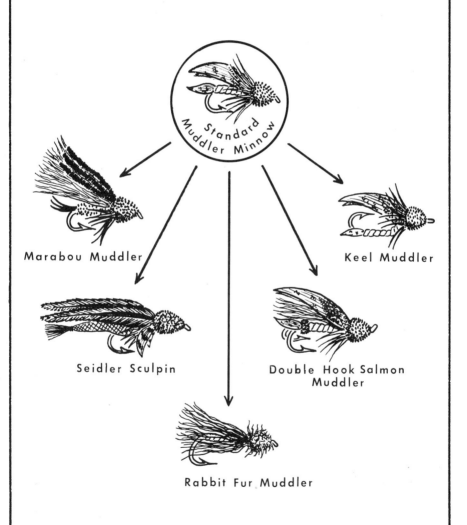

DIAGRAM III

THE STANDARD MUDDLER MINNOW
AND ITS VARIOUS SPIN-OFFS

Standard Muddler Minnow

Marabou Muddler

Keel Muddler

Seidler Sculpin

Double Hook Salmon Muddler

Rabbit Fur Muddler

performs best when working either streams of from slow to
moderate current or in working placid waters.

What is so Great about
a Muddler?

Without question, the most famous bucktail of all is the
Muddler Minnow. This is attested to by the fact that very few fly
fishermen can be found on the stream without at least one of
these patterns among their fly selection. While it can double as a
grasshopper when fished dry, its underwater disguise is of a
somewhat prehistoric looking sculpin, a small bottom-hugging
fish that frequents stone and rocky bottomed streams in this
country as well as abroad.

The standard Muddler pattern is tied with turkey feather
wings and tail, tinsel body, untrimmed spun deerhair cheeks and
a closely trimmed spun deerhair head. Two spinoffs are the same
except one is dressed with marabou wings, while the other is
dressed with spun rabbit fur head and marabou wings.

A standard Muddler as well as certain specific patterns,
the Letort Hopper and Letort Cricket, may be fished in three
methods: as a dry fly, a wet fly, or a bucktail. In fact, it is
possible to do so all in one float providing the fly is tied
unweighted and is presented in a Broadside Float. The fly begins
atop the water as a grasshopper drifting downstream in a dead
float. Line is mended to maintain the float as long as possible
(usually until about opposite the angler) and, once it submerges,
is allowed to dead drift to a quartered downstream position in
imitation of a wet fly (drowned terrestrial). During this second
phase in the presentation the line mending continues so as to allow
for a natural dead float. The third and final phase begins as the
angler discontinues line mending, whereby the current acts to
cause line drag. Consequently, the fly is swept cross-current to a
straight downstream-to-angler position as it takes on a new

disguise, that of a sculpin. As the sculpin is generally a slow mover, its imitation calls for a very slow retrieve with frequent hesitations and drifts backward. In order for sculpin patterns such as the Muddler to be effective, they must be fished deep. To attain such depth, I prefer this buoyant fly to be well trimmed to a small, bullet shaped head and to be sparsely dressed. As weight cannot be utilized when working the fly in all three phases, it is essential at such times to fish shallower waters of slow current flow for best results.

Some Parting Words of Advice

Streamer and bucktail fishing is simple, yet complex. It is enjoyable, yet frustrating. Nevertheless, it can become one of the most rewarding of all fly fishing alternatives providing the angler remembers four important points.

1) To match the fly pattern to the known bait fish or food source of the waters being fished and work it in an appropriate, realistic manner.

2) To keep the rod tip at a 45 degree angle to the surface rather than pointed directly at the fly in order to hook a taking fish and prevent a possible breakoff.

3) To stay with one style of retrieve as long as it produces results.

4) To check the fly often while fishing to insure its functional security. A fish cannot be hooked if the barb has become either dulled or broken by striking a rock while casting or while working the bottom. Also, a lifelike action will not be maintained should the leader tippet become caught behind the hair wings, or if streamer hackles become twisted around the hook shank.

10/Nymph Fishing to Surface Feeding Trout

by J. Michael Kimball

Although trout fishing literature has existed for five hundred years, it is remarkable that until the turn of this century only cursory mention was made of nymphs or nymph fishing. Moreover, no comprehensive source book on the subject could be found prior to this decade. As early as 1600, John Taverner made mention of immature underwater insects in his scientific publication on *Certaine Experiments concerning Fish and Fruite.* During the 1700's and 1800's, contributions were added to the foundation of nymph fishing by such writers as Richard and Charles Borulker, who dominated eighteenth century flyfishing with *The Art of Angling,* Alfred Ronald, who wrote the 1836 classic *Fly Fishers Entomology,* John Younger with the 1840 *River Angling,* W. C. Stewart, who promoted upstream wet fly technique in his 1857 *The Practical Angler,* and T. E. Pritt, who in 1885 wrote of soft hackle wet flies in his *Yorkshire Trout Flies.* But it wasn't until the early 1900's when the Englishman George M. Skues broke with tradition and jolted the fishing world with his famous "Halford debates" that nymph fishing as we know it today was permitted its first recognition. Skues supported his experimental use of nymphs as a viable alternative to F. M. Halford's purist dry fly methods. His studies of nymph fishing, *Minor Tactics of the Chalk Stream* in 1910, *The Way of a*

Trout with a Fly in 1921, and *Nymph Fishing for Chalk Stream Trout* in 1939 remain as required reading for the serious nymph fisherman.

For all the controversy he aroused, it's apparent from his writings that Skues and his followers had acquired only a superficial understanding of the nymph. Its habitat and individual characteristics as related to fishing technique eluded him. However, once the idea of nymph fishing had been introduced, several writers carried the flag throughout the twentieth century, each building on the scant information at hand. Edward R. Hewitt is considered to be the first from the United States to write of nymph fishing. Although his works of the 1920's, 1930's and 1940's are at times contradictory, vestiges of his methods still are practiced today. Other authors like James Leisenring (*Art of Tying the Wet Fly,* 1941), Alvin Grove (*The Lure and Lore of Trout Fishing,* 1951), Sid Gordon (*How to Fish from Top to Bottom,* 1955), and Poly Rosborough (*Fishing and Tying the Fuzzy Nymphs,* 1969) all anticipated the explosion of present day enthusiasm for nymph fishing.

The 1970's ushered in the first fisherman-author who attempted to write exclusively about nymphs in the same manner that had for centuries been reserved for dry flies. Ernest Schwiebert's monumental book, *Nymphs,* published in 1973, was the first work of its kind. Prior to its release, fishing literature had not yet comprehensively explored the ecology of the "underwater insect." In *Nymphs* Schwiebert bridged the literary gap from the general to the specific. During the first part of this century many fishermen and some anecdotal writers expressed the commonly held theory, "When all else fails, try a nymph." The corollary spoken by an experienced dry fly fisherman would be unthinkable, "Try a mayfly."

The concept of the *right* nymph was a long time in evolving. Schwiebert's book attempted to answer the question, what kind of nymph, even perhaps, before it occurred to many fishermen to ask. Fishes' selectivity to specific nymphs had not often been considered a major factor, and transitions in habits are hard fought.

Although Schwiebert touched on how to fish the nymph, it was Charles Brooks in *Nymph Fishing for Larger Trout* who compiled under one cover the earlier works on nymphs and nymph fishing techniques. Brooks' book summarizes fishing the nymph, while Schwiebert's book focuses more on identifying the specific attributes of important nymph species and how they can be represented at the vise.

The book *Mayflies, The Angler and The Trout* By Fred Arbona, Jr. is a work expected for release sometime in late 1979 or early 1980. I have read the galleys of this much anticipated study of insect life as it pertains to the fisherman and it will be an invaluable source book for both the dry fly and nymph fisherman of the 1980's.

These literary achievements, as well as Doug Swisher and Carl Richards' informative books *Selective Trout* (1971) and *Fly Fishing Strategy* (1975), which are not exclusively related to nymphs, seem to be meager accomplishments when compared with the vast library of volumes on dry fly fishing. However, nymph fishing, still in its infancy, has only recently been granted the status it deserves. I strongly suspect that the current research and written work on the subject will continue to gather momentum as the fastest growing form of fly fishing.

Generally speaking, there are two kinds of nymph fishing, each offering its own challenges and each requiring its own specialized equipment. The two categories are directly related to the diverse feeding behavior of surface feeding fish and non-surface feeding fish.

Nymphing for Surface Feeding Fish

Although Skues and others have written very literate studies on nymph fishing England's chalk streams, their works never attained the sophistication demanded of the nymph fisherman today. Nymphing for rising fish, feeding visibly on the surface, requires the angler to identify the types of nymphal life found in the stream. Once the dun of a given species is recognized on the water the fisherman must associate not only the physical appearance of the nymph but also the correct behavior and motions for that particular species. Armed with this information, the angler will be more likely to choose the appropriate fly and to discern what technique should be applied to its presentation.

The Latin names of each insect species are by no means a prerequisite to skillful fishing, but it is essential to have a clear concept of size, shape, general coloration, and emergence habits of the various orders of nymphs. For instance, certain mayfly nymphs such as *Isonychia sadleri* will emerge by crowding onto rocks protruding above the water's surface, whereas *Ephemerella dorothea* will emerge midstream. Consequently, the informed angler would surmise that during an *Isonychia* hatch, fish would tend to congregate in the shallows in order to intercept nymphs migrating to the rocks to hatch. If fishing to a *dorothea* hatch, the concentration might be best directed to areas where the stream creates food channels for feeding fish.

There are four main orders of nymphs that are of significance to the fisherman: 1. *Ephemeroptera* (mayflies), 2. *Trichoptera* (caddis), 3. *Plecoptera* (stoneflies), and 4. *Diptera* (midges). There are also other categories such as *Odonata* and *Neuroptera* and of the class *Crustacea* that contain flies which may be of local interest to regional fishermen. Of the big three, *Ephemeropterans* tend to be recognized as the most numerous and consequently the most important to the nymph fisherman. Though less renowned, I have found *Dipteran* pupae of the family *Chironomidae* to be a highly underrated food source deserving of greater angler attention. The following is a very brief summarization of some relevant details of important *Ephemeropteran* nymphs and their behavioral characteristics in the United States. For the more serious student, a more detailed format can be found in many of the recent volumes on nymph fishing.

Summary of Some Important *Ephemeroptera* North American Nymphs and Their Characteristics[a]

Nymph	Common Name	Size (mm)[b]	Location[b]	Water Type[b]	Hatching Time[b]	General Coloration
Gen. *Ephemerella*						
Sp. *subvaria*	Hendrickson	9-13	E, M	F-Md	A	mottled brown
Sp. *rotunda*	Sulfur	7-9	E, M	Md-F	A, E	mottled brown
Sp. *dorothea*	Sulfur	6-9	E, M	S-F	A, E	mottled brown
Sp. *infrequens*	Pale Morning Dun	7-9	W	F-Md	A	brown
Sp. *inermis*	Pale Morning Dun	5-9	W	S-F	A	olive brown
Sp. *grandis*	Western Green Drake	14-17	W	S-Md		brown
Sp. *falvilinea*	Slate-Wing Olive	8-10	W	Md-F	A-E	brown
Gen. *Ephemera*						
Sp. *guttulata*	Eastern Green Drake	18-22	E	S-F	A-E	pale olive
Sp. *simulans*	Brown Drake	10-15	E, M, W	S-F	E	mottled brown
Gen. *Pseudocloeon*						
Sp. *anoka*	Blue-Wing Olive	4-5	M	S-Md	A-E	olive
Sp. *edmundsi*	Blue-Wing Olive	4-5	W	S-Md	A-E	olive
Gen. *Epeorus*						
Sp. *pleuralis*	Quill Gordon	9-11	E	F	A	grayish-brown
Gen. *Tricorythodes*						
Sp. *stygiatus*	Trico	3-4	E, M	S	Mo	brown
Sp. *minutus*	Trico	3-5	W	S	Mo	medium brown

	Common Name	Size	Location	Speed	Time	Color
Gen. *Paraleptophlebia*						
Sp. *adoptive*	Red Quill	6-8	E, M	Md-F	A	brown
Sp. *heteronea*	Slate-Wing Monogany Dun	7-9	W	S-F	Mo	brown
Sp. *debilis*	Dark Blue Quill	7-9	E, M, W	Md-F	A	brown
Gen. *Baetis*						
Sp. *vagas*	Blue-Wing Olive	6-8	E, M	S-Md	A	olive brown
Sp. *tricaudatus*	Blue-Wing Olive	6-7	W	S-F	A	olive brown
Gen. *Stenonema*						
Sp. *fuscum*	Grey Fox	9-12	E, M	Md-F	A-E	amber brown
Sp. *vicarium*	March Brown	10-16	E, M	S-F	E	amber brown
Sp. *ithaca*	Light Cahill	10-12	E, M	Md-F	A-E	amber brown
Sp. *canadense*	Light Cahill	10-12	E, M	Md-F	A-E	amber brown
Gen *Isonychia*						
Sp. *sadleri*	Leadwing Coachman	12-15	E, M	F	A-E	dark brown
Gen. *Callibaetis*						
Sp. *coloradensis*	Speckled-Wing Dun	9-12	W	S	Mo	greyish-brown
Gen. *Potamanthus*						
Sp. *distinctus*	Paulinskill	13-16	E, M	S	E	brown
Gen. *Hexagenia*						
Sp. *limbata*	Giant Michigan Caddis	16-35	M, W	S	E	amber brown

a A more complete list of nymphs and their characteristics can be found in Al Caucci, Bob Nastasi, *Hatches* (Comparahatch, Ltd., 1975) and Doug Swisher, Carl Richards, *Selective Trout* (Crown Publishers, Inc., 1971).

b E = East   W = West   Md = Medium   F = Fast   Mo = Morning   A = Afternoon   E = Evening
   M = Midwest   S = South

Tackle for Surface Feeders

RODS

The tools in a fisherman's arsenal can fluctuate greatly depending on his game. When nymph fishing to surface feeders, special equipment is needed for the task. My personal choice is a medium to fast action rod of 8½ feet for a 5 or 6 weight line, but most rods of dry fly action are a good choice. This personal endorsement for dry fly tools is not the typical selection for nymph fishing equipment and may require some further background discussion.

The consensus of current opinion agrees with the axiom that fish feed on nymphs before a hatch, then as the hatch progresses, they switch their affinity to the duns. Thus we have

A stomach pump proves conclusively what trout are feeding on. The next step is to imitate those insects.

This 23 inch rainbow was taken on Henry's Fork of Idaho's Snake River and fell victim to a nymph fished in the surface film.

been told that preceding a hatch we must scrape the stream bottom with the appropriate nymph pattern, and after the hatch moves into full swing, we must switch to a dry fly pattern representing the dun of that species.

In my experience I have encountered the opposite of that axiom more frequently than its rule. Trout, and most particularly good trout, will feed on nymphs right up to the last insect inhaled, therein violating the "before the hatch only" limitation on the nymph. It wasn't until the recent popularization of the stomach pump (used to extract the contents of fish stomachs) that many fishermen have begun to realize trout feed on nymphs not only before the hatch but will also nymph right through the hatch, *and,*many trophy fish will select nymphs exclusively through even the heaviest hatch of duns.

I have witnessed this event many times in my fishing life. I recall a mild afternoon in early August while fishing the Henry's

Fork of Idaho's Snake River, when *Ephemerella inermis* had first started to appear. This hatch is one of the better ones on this prolific river and large fish began rising all over the flats. One especially large trout was rising not six inches from the bank, making the unmistakable dense boil of an outsized fish. A hatch of pale sulfur duns now blanketed the water around me but repeated casts with a number 18 *inermis* dun were consistently refused. To my right was an island fringed with some exposed grass which formed a natural collecting spot for floating debris. A close inspection revealed a relatively large quantity of empty *inermis* nymphal shucks.

My fish's rise form was not the bulgy type normally associated with nymph feeding but was instead the classic head and tail rise of a surface feeder. Nevertheless, with so many nymphs on that nest of grass beside me, I switched to an *inermis* nymph. Fifteen minutes later, the pumped stomach of a 23-inch rainbow revealed a capacity crowd of nymphs. This nymphing phenomenon has repeated itself innumerable times on innumerable rivers. As a result, during most hatches, my first choice is a nymph fished in the surface film for the duration of the hatch.

The discovery that good fish often feed exclusively to nymphs through the duration of a hatch should put to rest some of the equipment dictates for nymph fishing. For years we have been told to use slow action rods to keep our nymphs soaking wet during casting and to allow us to feel a taking fish's gulp right down to the butt of the rod. However, the slow action rod lacks the accuracy and power of a classic dry fly rod. On western water where wind is an everyday foe, the medium-to-fast action rod better enables the angler to deliver the fly to the narrow feeding lanes so often frequented by rising fish.

LINES

Similarly, nymph fishing of this type should be done with a floating line. When fishing crystal clear, smooth current spring creeks where conditions require exact and subtle presentations, it is generally difficult to use larger than number 6 weight line and lines of 4 and 5 weight are preferable. Larger lines have a tendency to create friction during the pick-up and set-down of a cast. These wakes on the water's surface can put sophisticated fish on streams like Pennsylvania's Letort down for the day.

Cortland Line Company has recently come out with a new line called a Nymph Tip with a strike indicator built into the tip of the line. For the beginning nymph fisherman, the fluorescent indicator is a great asset in detecting a fish's take. However, I prefer to stay with conventional lines which force the angler to use greater concentration. When the fisherman's eye is on an indicator, his attention is diverted from the true target. As a result, important stream data is lost, such as subtle leader drag, type and frequency of the rise form, and the general behavior of the fish. For this reason, I don't recommend it for nymph fishing to rising fish, but it can be an indispensable aid when fishing nymphs to fish that are not visibly feeding.

LEADERS AND TIPPETS

Much research has been dedicated to the design of leaders and leader tapers. There is a never-ending quest to design a small diameter leader with large diameter strength. Two of the more recent breakthroughs are Cortland Line Company's Nylorfi and Japanese-manufactured Aeon. Both are superior materials for offering maximum strength with minimum diameter. They do, however, tend to be limp, which is suitable for the terminal end of the leader; but I prefer a more rigid material such as Maxima for the butt section of the leader. One further problem with Aeon is that knots tend to slip. The angler can compensate by snugging up his knots more tightly and lubricating them with saliva as they are being tied.

Most manufactured leaders do not come with a tippet point longer than two feet. For fooling difficult fish I prefer a tippet length of approximately four feet. By using a four-foot tippet, what is sacrificed in accuracy is regained in a more natural presentation. The longer tippet allows the nymph to drop lightly on the water, trailing corkscrew coils of extra tippet which uncurl as the fly floats downstream to the holding position of the fish. This technique allows for a longer inspection by the trout before drag sets in. The slow current of most spring creeks makes this feature more critical than on the fast choppy waters of freestone streams.

FLY PATTERNS

When tying nymphs to be used for rising trout a premium should be placed on the following essentials: (a) lifelike materials which match natural colors, (b) appropriate size of the imitation, and (c) appropriate shape of the fly. The primary attribute of an effective nymph is one that will act naturally in the water. An impressionistic representation which doesn't adhere strictly to each insect feature but moves pliantly when immersed will likely produce more consistently than a rigid counterpart. Ostrich and peacock herl, marabou, rabbit and other "soft" materials lend themselves to a less static appearance and should be employed whenever possible. These, blended with Seal-Ex for sparkle and translucency, literally breathe when placed in water and offer the angler very lifelike imitations.

It is common practice to use partridge flank feathers as the legs on nymphs since the mottled partridge represents the coloration of so many numphs but this material, when used to construct legs for *small* flies, appears brittle and static. The tapered ends of partridge do not retain the flexibility of the longer length hackle and cause the short leg projections of smaller nymphs to look like tiny metal needles when wet. The soft, webby fibers of dyed ostrich herl are far superior for constructing nymphs of sizes 18 and smaller. Partridge can be most successfully used to construct large insects' legs since the longer fibers retain their pliability and offer less resistance to water currents.

One can't mention fly tying without Poul Jorgensen's name coming to mind. He has popularized an extremely lifelike pattern for larger nymphs which combines a fur underbody with an outer shell of dyed latex. By picking out the fur along the abdominal and thoracic segments it gives the fly a very "buggy," realistic appearance. Latex is well adapted to the construction of the larger caddis and stonefly nymphs and are time tested big fish takers. Poul's imitation of a *Pteronarcys* stonefly recently lured a handsome six-pound brown from the headwaters of Montana's Madison River. Their specific construction is well defined in his *Modern Flydressings for the Practical Angler.*

When choosing fly tying material, I prefer to give first priority to their lifelike properties and second place to exact coloration. Often both can be combined with successful dying. Although precision color coding is not vital to me in constructing flies, it is notable that water will darken most tying materials and a cognizant tier can compensate accordingly. I generally carry a selection of colored waterproof pens as a streamside aid for on--the-spot color coding when flies need to more closely match the hatch.

SIZE

When trout are selectively feeding, size becomes an exacting contender in matching the hatch. As Swisher and Richards point out in *Selective Trout,* size is most critical when fishing to midges. The percentage difference of fly size when comparing a size 22 to size 24 is far greater than the percentage change going from size 8 to size 10. The first example represents roughly 22% difference in overall size, whereas in the other case the difference is approximately 13%. Consequently, a miscalculation in the midge classification will likely lose far more fish than a comparable error in the large stonefly category.

SHAPE

An often overlooked feature in tying imitations is the form or shape of the fly. A final trim job at the vise can significantly alter a well tied pattern for better or for the worse. Nymphs, depending on their species, can vary from flat, linear shapes to rounded, cylindrical ones. The angler must have a working knowledge of the stream habitat and the shape of the nymphs it engenders. The inverse of the rule regarding size applies to the importance of shape; that is, as the fly becomes larger, the appropriate shape is more crucial. A case in point is the stonefly, *Pteronarcys dorsata,* which has a flat linear body. The angular configuration is well suited to the rock bottom, fast water stream in which this insect typically thrives. Fishing a fly of the same size and pattern but with a rounded shape will not likely be as effective for fooling the sophisticated fish of today's hard fished waters.

On the other hand, the Brown Drake, *Ephemera simulans,* has a convex, cylindrical body designed for burrowing into the sand and gravel of slower moving streams. Its rounded anatomy is well adapted to its stream behavior. Selective fish seem to have no difficulty perceiving a misshaped substitute. Fortunately, flies of the midge category, such as tiny *Pseudocloeon* nymphs (4 to 5 mm) offer the fly tier some artistic leeway in refining their shape since the importance of exact configuration diminishes somewhat with pattern size. However, the discerning fisherman would be wise to attempt to duplicate exacting shapes even in the smaller sizes.

WIGGLE-NYMPHS

In 1971, Swisher and Richard's *Selective Trout* popularized a new design of nymphs called the "wiggle-nymph." The wiggle-nymph is a jointed body nymph which allows the abdominal section to swing freely in the water imparting a very lifelike action to the fly. I have fished the wiggle-nymph extensively and have found this fly to be best for fishing large imitations in slow currents. In fast water such as Ithaca, New York's Fall Creek (below the falls), the force of the water tends to negate the jointed effect since the heavy current straightens the fly out. This pattern is especially effective when fished in deep quiet pools or lakes, since the still water allows the wiggle-nymph's abdominal section to flex and float freely in the water. A jiggling action imparted in the angler's retrieve will cause the jointed section to undulate in an enticing motion. When fishing

The wiggle-nymph can be deadly, especially in deep pools.

the wiggle-nymph dead drift, the slower currents will induce a similar motion. This pattern is an excellent choice when used for the larger burrowing flies, like *Ephemera simulans* and *Ephemera gluttalata,* or when fishing the outsized *Hexagenia limbata* hatches, for which Michigan's Au Sable River is so famous. I have fished the smaller jointed flies representing nymphs of *Tricorythodes, Beatis* and *Pseudocloeon* tied as small as No. 24, but I have not found them to be more effective than conventionally tied nymphs. However, when fished to the Brown and Green Drakes or the larger *Hexagenia* hatches, the wiggle-nymph has my strongest personal endorsement.

EMERGERS

One popular group of flies today is the emerger. This is the transitory state between the nymph and the dun, and for many has practically rendered traditional wet flies obsolete. Many emerger patterns are tied as floating extensions of wet flies.

But for most hatches, I feel the emerger should be tied to look
more like a nymph than a wet fly. Specifically, the concept of
the nymph-like emerger pattern is to imitate that phase of
development in which the wing case splits and the adult wing
begins to emerge along the dorsal side of the nymphal shuck.
Since the wings have not *fully* emerged, they should be much
shorter than the wings on conventional wet fly patterns.

    Many emergers are tied with quill wings. However, these
appear rigid and quite unlike the fluid, membranous wings of a
natural fly. Many flexible materials such as marabou, dyed silk
stockings, rabbit (applied by the spinning loop method), longer
strands of partridge hackle, and the soft "downy" fibers at the
base of many hackle stems can be used for designing the partially
emerged wings of this important hatching stage. Furthermore,
since emergers represent a surface developmental stage, this
pattern should be tied with buoyant materials and fished in the
surface film.

    In many cases the emerger pattern is superior to the real
nymph, particularly in species that are characterized by a
prolonged emergence period. This is a great advantage to the
fisherman since the longer the time interval needed for the adult
insect to break through the nymphal shuck, the greater success an
angler can anticipate from that pattern. Many insects of the
genuses *Ephemerella* and *Stenonema* have this character, and
emergers tied to imitate these flies can be superior fish takers.

    Last fall Mike Lawson, talented fly tier and proprietor of
Idaho's Henry's Fork, Inc., and Fred Arbona, author of *Mayflies,
The Angler and The Trout,* showed me an emerger they developed
for two of Henry's Fork's more well known *Ephemerella* hatches,
Ephemerella grandis (Green Drake) and *Ephemerella inermis*
(Pale Morning Dun). I was told that the fly, tied with a few turns
of grizzly hackle (swept back and kept short) and a body of pale
olive-yellow Fly-Rite, was a "winner" when fished nymph-like in
the surface film to the Ph.D.'s of the river. This spring I tied a
similar pattern, with a slightly darker body for the *Ephemerella
subvaria* (Hendrickson), of New York's West Branch of the
Delaware River. Five browns in eight casts, between one and

two-and-a-half pounds, has me more than a little interested in the
future of the "Lawson-Arbona emerger." The fly reminds me of
the popular soft hackle, emerger-like flies found in Sylvester
Nemes' *The Soft Hackled Fly.*

Poul Jorgensen has also created some excellent emerger
patterns to represent the sulfurs, *Ephemerella dorothea* and
Ephemerella rotunda, so prevalent on the limestoners of
Pennsylvania's Cumberland Valley. He uses the spinning loop
method to apply a soft, natural fur wing to represent this
developmental stage. This is a highly successful pattern for
fishing the sulfur hatches of Pennsylvania's Big Spring, Letort
and Falling Spring Run.

Brilliant writer Art Lee, northeastern editor of *Fly
Fisherman* magazine, has also developed a series of midge emergers.
These are tied in sizes 22 to 24 with short strands of mallard
shoulder fibers. They are his "ace in the hole" for the August days
on the Willowemoc which borders the backyard of his cottage in
Roscoe, New York.

STILLBORNS

Another fly increasing in popularity today is an imitation
of a stillborn insect. Stillborns are flies that die or become
crippled in the process of attempting to crack the nymphal shell.
They can be seen floating awash in the surface film often still
trailing their nymphal shuck. The innovative researchers, Doug
Swisher and Carl Richards, introduced this fly in their 1975
edition of *Fly Fishing Strategy,* but most of their patterns were
geared to dry fly imitations. Their style is to tie the insects as dry
flies with a spray of hen hackle at the tail to simulate the trailing
shell. Whenever stillborns appear in reasonable numbers, trout
seem to be more selective to this stage of the nymph. This
preference may be explained in part through fishes' need to
conserve energy. In order to stay alive, the energy received from
the food must exceed the energy expended in its capture. The
stillborn's struggle to be free of its shuck must broadcast its

vulnerable condition and the energy used in its capture is rarely wasted, for the chase generally results in a guaranteed meal.

I prefer a slight variation of Swisher and Richards' stillborn dry fly representation. I have found it most effective to tie these flies as floating nymphs with an adult insect emerging from the partially empty shuck. Using a Mustad 95831, 2X long hook, I tie an imitation of the actual nymphal shell onto the rear of the hook shank. In most cases the abdominal section of the shell should be tied with transparent-like materials such as dyed micro-web to represent a shuck that no longer fully contains a nymph. I have also tied this shell as a wiggle-nymph to simulate the soft, flexible nature of the paper-thin, half-empty nymphal container. Then to the front section of the hook, a no-hackle dry fly is tied in the usual way except that one or both of the wing tips are trapped by the nymphal wing case. This differs from the typical Swisher and Richards pattern which has a nymphal case only suggested by clumping trailing hackle and slightly protruding adult wings. In my "trailing nymph" variation, the adult is exposed to emulate a phase of development in which the front half of the dun has emerged but is still trailing its nymphal shell. This fly is tied with buoyant materials and fished in the surface film in much the same way an emerger is fished.

I've found this stillborn "variant" to be more effective in the orders of *Diptera* and *Trichoptera* than in the *Ephemeropterans*. During a midge hatch there is no better fly than this pattern to represent the *dipteran* stillborns of Montana's spring creeks. I have used this pattern with consistent success from the East to the West Coast, particularly during heavy hatches, and would expect that further research on stillborns will prove them to be more universally effective than is now claimed.

Technique

HATCHES

When an angler is confronted with the complexities of a hatch, the first task is to identify the insect on the water. For the nymph fisherman the next procedure is to differentiate the developmental stage the fish are selecting whether nymphs, stillborns or emergers. After observing the dun, a knowledge of entomology can be used to deduce the nymph of the same species. Nymphs, or their shells, that may be floating on the water often provide useful clues for solving the puzzle of the right nymph.

The angler's challenge is heightened during a multiple hatch in which two or more species of insects are hatching concurrently. The problem becomes further compounded when various developmental stages of these insects occur simultaneously. When the information at hand is conflicting, observing the rise form can help in decoding the appropriate fly. Angling literature is replete with attempts to categorize the relationships between the rise form and the type of fly being taken. For instance, a trout's back bulging through the water generally indicates he is taking a nymph. A sipping rise suggests an immobile fly--often a spinner off the surface film. Typically, a slash rise is associated with an active insect like a caddis. A head and tail rise is usually to a dry fly. Unfortunately, I have witnessed repeated violations of this categorical analysis, but most commonly I find exceptions to the last view. Often I have encountered textbook perfect head and tail risers whose stomach contents were not full of duns but rather were packed almost exclusively with nymphs. The understanding that fish surface feeding during a hatch are more apt to be nymphing than sipping drys is a long overdue concept. Halfordian doctrine has undoubtedly stymied this discovery but knowledgeable anglers are beginning to capitalize on this behavior of nymphing fish.

A variation of the multiple hatch that can be very deceiving is a masking hatch. This is a situation in which there

are two different insect species simultaneously on the water, a
small fly coupled with the presence of a usually more numerous
larger fly. The angler's eye first perceives the larger fly so that
the fish's preference, as a rule, for the smaller fly is concealed.
Masking hatches are often the cause of fishless days. I recall a
classic example of a masking hatch which occurred a few years
ago on a small Wyoming spring creek. Two flies, *Ephemerella
inermis* and *Centroptilum elsa* were concurrently hatching on a
frosty, late September day. The large *E. inermis* had been
hatching since August in this area and No. 18 *Ephemerella*
nymph had been a sure bet to fish to the *inermis* hatch. Even
though I had recognized *C. elsa* on the water for at least a week,
habit and previous success with the *inermis* nymph had obscured
their presence. This day, however, brought a change of pace–it
wasn't until the hatch was almost over that one of the less
educated fish finally accepted the *inermis* nymph. The stomach
pump revealed his preference for the tiny *Centroptilum* nymphs.
I've witnessed numerous comparable masking hatches around my
home waters of Ithaca, New York, which have disguised fishes'
preference for *Paraleptoplebia adoptiva* in the presence of the
larger *Ephemerella subvaria* (Hendricksons).

One of the least understood aspects of multiple hatches
is the individuality of fish. It is commonly believed that once a
fly raises a few fish, this fly will be successful for the remainder
of the hatch. But there is no guarantee that all fish in the river
are feeding on the same fly. When two or more distinct species
of insects are hatching, it is sometimes possible to observe some
fish along the same stretch of water, and sometimes even in the
same pool, feeding on not only different insect species but also
on different stages of the same insect. This phenomenon further
elevates the indispensable nature of the stomach pump in solving
the food enigma. In addition, a monocular can assist in
disclosing surface activity; and the rise form, though not a
foolproof clue, can provide some missing links. The
individuality of fish is a study that will probably be examined
more closely in future research and hopefully in the depth that
it warrants.

CASTING APPROACH

The manner in which a nymph is presented is dependent in part on the character of the stream. Charles Brooks in *Nymph Fishing for Larger Trout* has extensively covered the delivery of the fly as related to a broad spectrum of stream conditions. This long overdue synthesis of methodology is an excellent reference for the nymph fisherman. No one method is ever adequate all of the time. A thorough understanding of each approach as described by Brooks is fundamental to fishing a large number of streams and can provide practical alternatives even on one familiar stream.

Fly fishing doctrine has dictated that something approximating a three-quarters upstream cast is the most effective means of achieving a drag-free float. However, unless a three-quarters upstream cast is accompanied with either a very wide upstream curve, or lots of slack line, the nymph fisherman is faced with only short intervals of dragless drifts. Also, nymph fishermen that use roll casts as part of their delivery frequently find it difficult to consistently throw good upstream curves, especially when faced with windy conditions. This is another case where tradition has hindered the development of fly-fishing technique. It has been my experience that best results can be achieved by varying the appropriate casting position from any point directly above to directly across from a feeding fish. It is much easier to throw wide reach curves (both positive and negative) when quartering downstream than when adhering to upstream tradition. Roll casting, when accompanied with a reach curve and a mend as soon as the fly meets the water, achieves a much more natural float than its upstream counterpart.

The downstream dead drift method is a technique born of necessity on the Western spring creeks and the limestoners of the East. These waters contain fish that do not recognize hatchery pellets and whose banks read "No-Kill." The fish are

---

Basic information concerning proper casting and other fly fishing mechanics can be found in Chapter 7, "Fishing the Dry Fly for Fun and Challenge."

generally large and sophisticated and angling success often requires breaking the rules. For some, downstream dead drift fishing does break with tradition but I suspect its success will someday make it the rule rather than the exception. Very simply, under most conditions, when properly executed, the three-quarters downstream cast can achieve longer, more natural drag-free floats than conventional upstream casts!

There are advantages of downstream casting other than long, dragless drifts. With the help of a downstream mend, the fly can easily be made to arrive at the holding position of a feeding fish before the arrival of the leader. Also, once the nymph has passed over the fishes' station, the angler, being above the fish, can often induce a take by very gently twitching the nymph in the vicinity of the fish.

Downstream dead drift nymphing is not without its disadvantages and an understanding of these shortcomings can help to more completely perfect the technique. In order to achieve a natural drift over a downstream fish, the fly should be cast approximately two feet ahead of the fish with enough slack and curves in the line and leader to allow the nymph not only to reach the fish but to pass at least three feet beyond its feeding position. A fly cast with too little slack in the line and leader will drag too close to the fish and may put him down for the day. But casting slack lines has its problems. Setting the hook while attempting to take the slack out of the line can be difficult. A long rod, held high overhead, can help remedy the problem of cumbersome slack in the leader. Occasionally, however, the fish's take occurs immediately upon the fly reaching the water and a rod held high overhead becomes of little use for striking in the conventional manner. In this case the best hook setting method is not to attempt to raise the rod even higher, but rather to thrust the rod tip forward in much the same way a roll cast is accomplished. In extreme cases when a roll cast is not enough to remove all the loose coils from the leader, then a simultaneous downward pull on the line with the left hand (for a right-handed caster) will help to correct this situation. Assuming the fly is not instantly taken, a gradual lowering of the rod tip combined with continuous line mending should keep the nymph floating drag-free over the feeding station of the fish.

It is important to have placed enough slack in the line to allow the fly to pass well beyond the fish's suspected location, for as renowned author and limestone fisherman, Vincent C. Marinaro, points out in his 1976 *Ring of the Rise,* fish inspecting a fly will often drift back many feet before an actual rise occurs. Vince calls this feeding habit a complex rise and it is thoroughly discussed in this innovative work. I have found this rise type to be a frequent occurrence on Eastern and Western spring creeks and particularly important on his home waters of Pennsylvania's Letort.

Another reason for insuring a drift well beyond the fish is to minimize the effect of any surface disturbance during the pick-up of the fly. As the fly continues past its original target, the rod tip should be moved laterally away from the fish. A sharp downward movement of the rod tip will initiate waves in the line that will cause the fly to literally jump from the water. A conventional pickup executed from a location above the rise form will frequently cause fish-frightening wakes on the water's surface and should be avoided whenever a "snap" pick-up can be used. If the snap pick-up cannot be applied, then a slow retrieve *under* the water's surface is far safer than risking a potential drag-causing pick-up.

Occasionally an angler will be faced with a cast that is short of its target. This frequently happens when a fish changes his feeding position to a location below the original rising position or when the distance from the rise form is underestimated. The danger here arises in the potential for drag occurring directly in front of the fish. When this situation is recognized, a quick lowering of the rod tip and a mending motion while simultaneously feeding line through the rod guides will generally get the fly past the fish without drag. This technique of mending and feeding line to downstream fish is a not so well guarded secret of those who chase the wild rainbows of Northern California's Fall River.

If the short line situation is recognized too late, then a very slight raising and lowering of the rod tip, causing a deliberate but

controlled drag (*a la* Leonard M. Wright, Jr.) will often effect a
quick strike. In fact this action, when properly executed, can be
a deadly technique for fooling difficult fish. Leonard M. Wright,
Jr.'s 1972 *Fishing the Dry Fly as a Luring Insect* explains this
method in detail and I have found it equally applicable to fishing
nymphs for rising fish.

A major disadvantage of downstream dead drift fishing is
the lack of concealment of upstream objects. Practitioners of
this technique should recognize the increased exposure of person
and equipment and take appropriate corrective measures. Keeping
a low silhouette, with clothes matching the backdrop of the
particular river, will increase the angler's chance of success. On
many of the West's famous trout streams, and notably on the
Railroad Ranch of Henry's Fork, large areas are without
prominent backdrops. When confronted with these conditions,
hats and other clothing resembling the horizon or the sky color
can facilitate the merging of angler and environment. The need
for low profiles and camouflage clothing is particularly important
on this country's spring creeks and absolutely critical for stalking
such placid waters as the Letort.

Another factor to consider when determining a casting
approach is the direction and the intensity of the wind. If there
is a strong wind, then the angler must decide whether to cast into
the wind, or with the wind at his back. Many fishermen prefer the
latter. However, experts like Phil Wright of Montana's Wise River
contend that a good fisherman will cast better facing into the
wind than *vice versa*. Wind is an almost everyday hindrance in the
West and is often prevalent in the East during the blustery spring
months of March, April and May. Personally, I opt to first
determine whether my imitation should float naturally on the
water or whether it should be fished with a twitching retrieve. If
I interpret that a natural float is required, I cast against the wind
as its force will often cause the leader tippet to stack up on the
water and the gradual uncoiling will produce more drag-free float.
Although this type of casting demands practice for an angler to
hit his target, it is far preferable to casting with the wind at his
back. Casting with the force of the wind insures a more effortless

delivery, but will also straighten out the leader rendering an almost simultaneous occurrence of the touchdown and drag of the fly. If, however, the intent is to twitch the fly, casting with the wind helps to set up that circumstance most easily.

RHYTHM FEEDING

Many anglers naturally assume that when a rising trout repeatedly ignores a well placed fly, the refusal requires a change of pattern. I contend that a little observation and timing might provoke more favorable results than frequent pattern changing. It is important to recognize that a trout feeding during a heavy hatch won't consume every live insect which passes over him, but will often rise in well defined *rhythmic* patterns attuned, in part, to its assimilation rate of food. What I am suggesting is that the angler may often have chosen the right fly but is presenting it at the wrong time. To understand rhythm feeding, an important distinction must be drawn between a heavy and a light hatch. During the latter, rhythm feeding becomes secondary to survival. The flies drifting over the trout's feeding station are already intermittent enough to allow time for digestion, and fish will be inclined to capture a larger percentage of the insects that pass during times of sparse food supply. In a light hatch situation, once a fish determines a preference for an insect, he is apt to take a major portion of the flies drifting over him. Under these circumstances, rhythm feeding ceases to be a factor and changing patterns to match the "naturals" takes precedence as the more productive angling technique.

Most work on rhythm feeding has been of a very superficial nature. Only cursory allusions are made to its significance in today's fishing literature. Discussions typically take the posture, "It is important to cast the fly to coincide with the feeding rhythm of the fish." Little reference is made to the nature and complexity of the rhythm. A fish may alter its feeding pattern many times during a given feeding period. The rhythms can speed up and slow down periodically during any one feeding siege, but nevertheless often seem to maintain well defined patterns. Rhythm changes during a hatch may depend upon the quality and quantity of food, the state of hunger, the competition with other fish and many physiological and genetic factors which fishermen may never completely understand.

During periods of heavy feeding activity, as is customary in *Tricorythodes* hatches, the fisherman must determine the feeding rhythm of the fish at that particular point in time and deliver the fly at the appropriate moment. A very familiar feeding rhythm often noticed at "Trico" time is a rise, a few seconds' pause, and then two or three quick takes. But established rhythms change, frequently for no obvious reasons; however, the change is often to merely another set of feeding rhythms. The only method to combat this complexity is to time the intervals through observation.

One unique exception to varying rhythms occurred a few years ago on the Letort when I witnessed a small brown sipping *Diptera* according to a repeated time progression of 30 seconds, 12 seconds, 12 seconds, 50 seconds; 30-12-12-50; and so on. The fish fed as if cued by a bell; his progression was interrupted only three times in the course of twenty-five minutes! This little brown was the most consistent rhythm feeder I have ever witnessed. However, this is not surprising, since the Letort holds many "mosts" in my mind.

If your patience allows, and if the feeding intervals fall into a numerical sequence, a good understanding of rhythm feeding can provide a disarming technique. However, landing a cast on target at the split second of a fish's countdown is almost reward enough in itself, as anyone will discover once he tries to cast "on command." Although not a panacea for fishless days, an understanding of rhythm feeding has at times been an invaluable tool when sophisticated fish are exposed to heavy hatches.

11/Fishing for Spawning Rainbows

by Ron Howard, Jr.

From everything I had read and heard, fishing for spawning rainbows in the Finger Lakes tributaries was a crowded affair. When I first started fishing for rainbows, I decided to avoid the spawning streams for the first few days, hitting them after the pressure faded. A Sunday afternoon drive to look at the stream wrecked my resolve. The water was high, but clear; and fish were visible on the shallow gravel bars. My wife, Susie, and I were impressed, seeing perhaps 100 big trout in about an hour. Susie pointed out a particularly good fish, about 5 pounds, lying beside a sunken log; and as we watched, the "log" rolled on its side and began to dig a redd (a nest). That did it! We would join the crowds the next morning.

A heavy shower overnight had raised the water about 2 feet and colored it a creamed-coffee brown. I helped Susie rig an orange yarn sack and slipped a small night crawler on a weighted hook for myself. Her first cast overshot the pool and fouled a small cedar on the opposite bank. She muttered something about "feeling funny enough about being the only woman on the stream without hooking trees" and broke the lure off. A week later that little tree looked like it had been decorated for Christmas, brightly hung with red, pink, yellow, and orange sponges.

Two hours later we were still waiting for our first strike. A young fellow walked up to the head of the pool we were

The spring spawning run of rainbow trout into The Finger Lakes tributaries brings anglers from all over.

fishing, flipped a rig into the current, and started a drift. Within seconds he set the hook and was fast to a bright silver male of about 4 pounds. A few minutes later he repeated the performance, completing a three fish limit, weighing about 12 pounds.

"He must know something we don't know," I thought. Just then an old gentleman walked up to us.

"You gotta use sponge," he said. "And, you gotta fish right on the bottom. Here, give these a try." He offered us a few pale orange balls cut from a kitchen sponge.

"Thanks," I said, "we will." We drifted those sponges for another hour or so without success. The fish were not buying any, so we decided to drop by a store for an assortment of kitchen sponges, then have lunch and regroup.

When we got back, the water had dropped significantly and begun to clear. We rigged samples from our newly cut selection of trout tempters and began casting. Remembering the salmon eggs I had used as a kid in Pennsylvania, I selected a pink one. My first cast was designed to drift an eddy where a break in the stream indicated a large midstream rock. I felt the split shot bounce along the gravel, then pause. As I flicked the rod tip to free the lure, the line came to life, and a small male rainbow came thrashing to the surface. That 13-inch jack worked wonders for my confidence in sponges as trout lures. When we finished that opening day we had caught a total of 8 trout, the largest an average fish of about 18 inches--not bad for a couple of beginners!

Since that April Fool's Day in 1968 we have taken many of these spawning rainbows using a wide variety of tackle and techniques. This chapter is designed to help you in catching some yourself.

Understanding Your Quarry

The rainbow trout, *Salmo giardnerii,* is not native to the eastern United States. A highly regarded sport fish, the rainbow was widely planted, expanding its range far beyond the streams flowing into the Pacific Ocean, which was its original habitat. Rainbows are frequently migratory, dropping down into lakes or salt water to feed and grow, then running up their natal streams to spawn. Both the Great Lakes and the Finger Lakes are famous for their spawning runs, but many lakes have similar runs of large fish.

Our success on that first opening day was at least partially due to our understanding of where the fish were likely to be lying. Knowledge of their habits and requirements can be very useful to anglers. A brief summary of rainbow trout natural history is included to provide background information.

After hatching and emerging from their gravel redd, the young rainbows spend a few weeks to several years in the nursery stream before dropping down to the lake. In general, the better the nursery stream, the longer their tenure there. Since rapid growth is associated with the rich food resources in the lakes, poorer nursery streams often yield larger fish.

After one to three years in the lake, the fish return to their hatching streams to spawn. Although spawning takes place in the spring as waters warm toward 40 degrees F, trout will enter the streams during high water periods in the fall as well as during the spring run-off.

Most salmonids, including rainbow trout, spawn in nests, called redds, excavated from gravel bars. Each redd contains a series of egg pits oriented with the flow of the stream. Male fish will actively defend a female, often fighting each other for dominance and the right to spawn. When the combination of reproductive behavior, time of year, and water temperature has brought the female into reproductive condition she will move out of cover onto a gravel bar, frequently in a riffle or at the tail of a pool where there is good water flow. Turning on her side, she will dig a pit in the gravel using the thrust of her tail to displace the stones. She will continue to dig until the shape and size of the pit suits her instincts. After a bout of spawning where she deposits eggs as one or more males deposit milt, she will dig another pit upstream of the first, covering the fertilized eggs with the gravel displaced from the new pit. The sequence is repeated until the female is spawned out.

After spawning the fish drop back toward the lake, feeding actively as they do. The drop-back period may involve hours to weeks, and some stream fishing for lake-run fish may be available into early summer. Rainbows have the potential to spawn again, usually on a 2 or 3 year cycle. Relatively few survive to spawn more than once, so most of the spawning population is made up of first-time spawners.

The selection of holding lies depends upon a combination of three major factors: 1) cover, either in deep water or some type of physical cover; 2) shelter from heavy currents; and 3) proximity to suitable spawning sites. When these factors are found in combination, trout should be present. Even in the best pools or riffles, the bottom will not be paved with trout. They will be lying singly or in small groups in selected locations where their needs are met. Skill in identifying those locations will greatly increase your efficiency in finding and catching these trout.

Gravel has been discussed a bit earlier. These fish seem to prefer rather coarse gravel, from large pea-size up to about 2 inches in diameter. Similar-sized stones may be used on some streams, but gravel is preferred. Suitable gravel must be in areas having upwellings or considerable current so that the eggs will be well oxygenated while they are developing in the redd. Since anglers may not be as adept as trout in identifying upwellings or "sufficient" flow, gravel bars should be carefully fished. Particular care should be paid to fishing them in early morning or late afternoon when spawning fish tend to be most active.

Cover comes in many forms. Cut banks, submerged or surface logs or brush, large rocks, and ledges are all good forms of cover. Where stream improvement structures have been placed, the cribbing is frequently used as sheltering cover by spawning fish. Thus, these trout often are found in exactly the same kinds of holding lies favored by stream-dwelling brookies or browns. Deep water, particularly where the surface is broken by turbulence, is also effective cover. Even relatively smooth shale bottoms will hold fish if the water is sufficiently deep. "Sufficient" in this context may be on the order of 2 to 3 feet.

Since these trout are conditioned to an existence in the relatively calm waters of large lakes, shelter from heavy currents commonly encountered during the spring spawning season is important. Frequently, areas that provide such shelter may be obvious, like eddies, or more subtle, like the counter currents created by falls. Depth and bottom structure also influence current flows. Water, like wind, shows some elements of laminar flow, that is the currents tend to be slower near the bottom than at the surface of the stream. Surface disruptions, broken bottom structure, and energy dissipators like waterfalls all produce areas where the flow is either reduced or even reversed. Holding in those areas eases the energy demand on the fish, and they actively seek such locations. A prudent angler would do well to seek out these locations as well.

An example may be useful in illustrating this point. On April 1, 1969, I was fishing a tributary of Cayuga Lake in New York's Finger Lakes region. The afternoon was beautiful, with mild temperatures, a light breeze, and partly cloudy skies. The upper reaches of the stream were mobbed with hopeful fishermen, but as I worked my way down toward the lake the crowds thinned to a scattering of anglers. In a couple of hours of fishing I had taken 9 trout in the 1-½ to 3 pound class, mostly from a section of deep runs and riffles with a coarse freestone bottom. The first big pool below that section was well stocked with anglers, so I by-passed it. Just downstream was a long, deep pool, a lone angler fishing the white water at its head. Sizing up the pool as I watched him cast, I noticed that it was deep for about ¾ of its length, brawly at the head, smooth and deep in a central eddy, and shelving up to a good gravel bar at the tail of the pool. The other angler sat down and continued to cast his sponge lure mechanically, fishing the white water chute. A break

---

This fine 6 1/2 pound rainbow succumbed to a pink sponge fished on 4 pound test monofilament in Salmon Creek in Ludlowville, New York.

at the upstream edge of the central eddy suggested a large rock or
a sharp drop off, and my first cast went just above the break on
the current edge. That cast yielded a nice 2 pound male. Three
casts later a 5 pound male rolled out of the current at my strike.
A few minutes later I slid the exhausted fish onto the sandy bank.

"You sure are lucky!" yelled the fisherman above me.
"I've been here all afternoon without even getting a hit, and you
catch 2 nice ones just like that--out of the same pool, too."

Same pool, yes; but from a spot with particular
attraction for the fish. That spot, less than 5 x 15 feet, yielded
5 trout and several white suckers in a span of about one hour.
The other fellow was using the right tackle in the right way, but
fishing the wrong places. Without shelter from the current, that
white water chute was barren of fish. As in many other forms of
field sports, *where* is frequently as important as *when* and *how.*
Concentrating on likely holding water greatly increases any
angler's probability of success.

Before leaving the topic of where to locate fish, we
should mention that good holding water may exist in very small
pockets. These small pockets, often in seemingly shallow riffles
or in a stretch of white water, are frequently passed over by the
majority of anglers, leaving their fish to the careful and thorough
fisherman who learns to read holding water. This is a good place,
also, to note that holding waters should be *fished* rather than
waded. Too many anglers end up standing where the fish want
to be and fishing barren areas.

Fundamental Techniques

Successful techniques for taking spawning rainbows are
as variable as the anglers that use them. A few generalities
emerge when all methods are examined, however. The best
fishermen work at it, they spend time on the stream, and they
believe they are going to take fish. They use tackle they feel
comfortable with, and they use the most sensitive equipment
they have. They concentrate their efforts on likely holding

water, and they keep their baits or lures down and under control. They maintain their concentration, and they remain adaptable, willing to try a new wrinkle to tempt a trout.

Many writers have stated that spawning fish do not feed while on their pre-spawning runs. Very seldom, however, have I autopsied a spawner with a completely empty stomach. Most often they have an assortment of real and artificial trout eggs, sucker eggs (they are spawning at the same time), small aquatic insect larvae, and small worms. The fish do not cruise around seeking out meals, however. Instead, they seem to feed on things that drift into their holding lie. My observations indicate that the fish will only rarely move as much as 2 feet to take a bait or lure. You must take the bait to them; in fact, you should try to hit the fish right on the nose with your drifting lure. In addition, since the trout are rarely on the surface or at middle depths, your efforts should be concentrated on the bottom.

Although post-spawning fish may aggressively smash a bait or lure, most strikes will be soft, brief, and tentative. Sensitive tackle is essential to consistent success. For years, the standard in the Finger Lakes was a glass fly rod of 8 to 9 feet, and a reel spooled with 10 to 15 pound-test monofilament. That combination provided adequate range for most fishing situations and had excellent sensitivity. Light spinning tackle, using 4 to 8 pound-test lines and soft or fast tip rods, is increasing in popularity. Although bait casting and spin cast equipment is adequate in the right hands, it is *not* the optimum tackle. My personal choice for bait and sponge fishing is a soft ultra-light spinning rod with a high speed reel and a clear fluorescent line of 2 to 4 pound test. For flies I use an assortment of rods, preferring an 8-½ foot, 7-weight stick and either weighted leader or a leadcore "downrigger" shooting head.

Light lines are a significant aid. Their smaller diameter results in less drag, a shorter belly, and better "feel." The long belly resulting from 15 pound-test monofilament in heavy currents may require 2 or 3 seconds to reveal a strike, resulting in a failure to detect the stike or a missed fish. Good advice would be to use the lightest line you can handle consistent with the size of the trout, the strength of the current, and the abundance of obstructions.

Light lines also require less weight to maintain contact with the bottom. That weight can be attached in several ways, each having its proponents. My method is to place the smallest number of shot necessary to get good bottom feel directly on the snell loop. Snells should be twice the strength of the main line and used with light wire, short shank hooks (size 8 to 4).

Others use a series of several small shot placed a few inches apart on the line or leader. Users claim this technique reduces hang-ups. Still others put their weights either on a light, fixed dropper or on a sliding dropper attached to a split ring. The use of pencil lead in a rubber snugger, very popular among western steelheaders, has not caught on in the East.

Sponges, yarn sacks, or spawn sacks should be sized with an eye to realism rather than using the "big bait, big fish" philosophy. Under normal conditions these lures should be dime-sized or smaller. Under low, clear conditions baits as small as single eggs or 2 or 3 egg clusters are to be preferred. Spawn sack material and sponges in pale yellow, orange, pink, and red are useful. Often the yellow-orange colors are most effective under the clear water conditions found later in the season, but having something different on the line may help when lots of anglers are on the water.

Much has been said about odor in fishing for spawning trout. If using spawn or some cleverly concocted and foul smelling bait gives you confidence, by all means use it. Under murky water conditions, such tactics may help; but the fish are probably motivated to feed more by visual cues than by olfactory ones. The ability of these fish to detect minute quantities of some odors, including some commonly found on human hands, has been very well documented by scientists; so the "secret odor bait" school cannot be completely discounted. Most of those baits had a combination of cod liver oil, oleum percomorphum, and a vaseline base.

The bait fisherman covers all likely holding water carefully and persistently, quartering casts upstream and following the downward drift with a high rod to reduce drag. Watching the line for any signs of a light hit, the angler will feel the sinkers along the bottom, striking at any differences in feel. Very frequently the strike on a sponge is like a momentary hang-up, a soft rock. If you are taking suckers, but no trout; have faith. You are doing the right thing.

Spinners can be effective in teasing strikes from fish on redds. Since they may aggravate the fish and move them off the redd, an angler would do well to start with dull finished blades and progress toward bright blades if the fish fail to respond. Upstream or quartering casts and a slow retrieve resulting in a fluttering spinner are usually the best bet, but a cast designed to place a wildly spinning lure a few inches above and to the side of a redd-guarding male is almost certain to produce a vicious strike. Breathing streamers, like marabous, will produce results very similar to those produced by spinners; and, like spinners, they are most effective in teasing fish that are on redds or otherwise visible.

Flies can be used effectively in fishing holding water, too; but they require more careful attention and a quicker strike than either spawn or sponges. Flies in white, yellow, orange, pink, red, chartreuse, black, and silver have been effective in Finger Lakes tributaries. Here, again, the flies must be on the bottom. In small streams a weighted leader, although miserable to cast, can be used with excellent results. Attaching the extra weight to a dropper tied of lighter leader material can save a few flies. The trout are not extremely leader shy, and leaders should be on the heavy side (and checked frequently) because of abrasion on the bottom structure.

When fishing bigger streams or heavier currents, an angler can profit by using a specialized high density shooting head made of plastic-coated leadcore line. I have even constructed a "downrigger" by braiding an appropriate weight of the leadcore and splicing it to a light floating running line. Very short leaders should be used with these specialized lines in order to keep the flies deep. Fly rod tactics differ slightly from those used by bait fishermen. I find that leading the fly through the drift with a low rod and sweeping the rod to the side to strike results in better catches. Later in the season, as drop-back fish predominate, wet fly and nymph fishing tactics can be deadly.

Optimum Conditions for Taking Fish

Anglers often ask when they should concentrate their fishing efforts. These fish seem to hit better either early or late in the day, and new fish tend to arrive with high water periods. Water with visibility of less than 8 to 10 inches is too murky for best results, but clear water tends to make the fish very sensitive to movement and angler pressure. A very good time to fish is just as the water begins to drop and clear after a pulse of run-off. The best time to fish, however, is whenever you get the chance. Before and after work is an excellent bet, but midday may be just as good if the pressure has dropped off a bit.

As long as minimum water quality is met, 8 to 10 inches of visibility, the water is fishable. Clear water dictates the "fine and far off" approach with small lures, baits, or flies. Colored water may give better results with bright, even fluorescent, colors.

If the fish are in the stream, water temperatures are not overly influential. Trout can be taken with anchor ice in the stream or with temperatures approaching 50 degrees F. In other words, the best conditions are the ones you encounter. After all, you can't be there yesterday when they were really hitting!

To take spawning rainbows consistently, you must have at least minimum water quality. You must fish right on the bottom in good holding water, preferably using eggs or their imitations You must use sensitive tackle, and you must be persistent. Have faith in your equipment. Be adaptable and observant. Follow these "simple" guidelines, and you will be able to catch trout along with the experts.

12/Deepwater Trolling Techniques

by Nelson Wertman

In the following pages I will talk about the various techniques used in deep water trolling, most of which are easily adaptable to any body of water. Since I fish for lake trout, salmon, rainbows and brown trout, these trolling techniques are primarily for these species, but can also be used successfully for pike and bass.

Tackle

I will first deal with tackle and lures. Some of this equipment is specialized and therefore sometimes difficult to find. At the end of the chapter is a list of tackle dealers who may be able to help you. It is best to buy locally, but if you are unable to find what you need nearby, this list will be of help.

RODS

The thermocline rod (which was developed for salt water trolling) is a 6 to 7 foot rod of medium light to heavy action. If you plan to use monofilament line, you can save yourself some money by getting away with regular guides. I do, however, recommend a roller top. If you use wire line, you will need a rod with all roller guides. The action of the rod remains a matter of personal choice. Just keep in mind that the heavier the rod the less action you can expect. Brogdon and National both make thermocline rods that will serve the purpose. Garcia has a good selection of light to heavy salt water rods. Prices will vary considerably, depending on the type and brand, from $10 to $30. The price difference is based on whether the rod comes with regular guides, aluminum oxide or roller guides.

When fishing leaded line or using weight to get to the desired depth, the rods mentioned above can be used, but I prefer a 7 foot rod of medium to heavy action. Although spinning rods are more popular, spinning reels are not recommended for leaded line. A couple of suggestions would be the Garcia 2142 or 2656, or the Berkeley Buccaneer B90 in the 7 foot model. If you are using leaded line, the Brogdon 7 foot solid glass rod will do just fine. The Shakespeare BWS 595, a 7 foot rod, is plenty rugged for this type of fishing. Some of the above rods will also do well for those of you who are going to use Les Davis' Deep Six, and the Pink Lady by Luhr Jensen. With this type of trolling device don't use the lighter action spinning rods; they just don't have the backbone for it. The heavier action spinning rods and trolling rods are more suitable.

Downrigger rods are another story. They are also called Steelhead rods. Generally 7 to 9 foot rods in the light to medium action are preferred. I like the 8 to 9 footers in the 1/8 to 3/8 ounce lure range, and the same length in the 1/2 to 1 ounce range. They are light enough for smaller fish yet have enough guts for larger fish. Locating some of the rods may be a bit of a problem, but they are available. Fenwick and Wright-McGill build one that will do the job. Both are available with spinning guides or standard casting rod guides.

After you become more and more familiar with rods, you'll find yourself in the same situation I did. You can't quite find what you're looking for or the action you want. This problem can be solved easily enough by having a rod custom-made to your specifications, or building one yourself. Refer to

the end of the chapter for names and addresses where rod
supplies and custom rods can be purchased.

REELS

For the thermocline rod a much heavier reel is used.
Recommendations would be the Penn super mariner 49M or the
Olympic DS No. 3 with a built in digital line counter. Penn makes
several reels that will work well for either wire, leaded or
monofilament line. Also take a look at Garcia's line of trolling
reels. I have used these and they have served me well.

For downriggers, most any spinning reel will work, but
without a doubt the best reel I know of is the level wind. The
Penn 9MF or the Penn 209MF are good choices. Penn has a very
large selection of reels. For those of you who are into bass
fishing and have the bass level wind casting reels, the level wind
reels do a fair job. Their biggest drawback is their lack of line
capacity. One of my reels is a Garcia 5000D which works very
well. I've caught 2 pound rainbows and salmon over 30 pounds
and have had no problems with it. If you decide to use the bass
reels, I would suggest you purchase the extra large handles that
are available. Since the grips are larger and made out of rubber,
they are much easier to control than the smaller ones. You'll
really appreciate them when you get a fighter on your hands.
The cost of the replacement handle runs somewhere around $3.
Most of the Penn reels have extra large handles so replacements
usually aren't necessary. When purchasing such a reel keep in
mind the type of fish you'll be going after. If you are catching
30 pound salmon and have a light action reel that holds only 100
yards of line, you could very easily get into trouble. Salmon are
well known for their long runs and a reel with small line capacity
isn't the one to have. The Penn 209MF holds about 350 yards of
20 pound test line which is just fine for salmon fishing.

If you're into spinning reels, most any of them will do
when it comes to downriggers, but stay away from discount store
specials and stick to name brands. I have two Ryobi's, the 3000
and GX-20, both of which work just fine with the downriggers,

but I do like the level winds over anything else. I am not going to
go into every reel on the market in detail; any tackle store will be
more than happy to give you details on anything you are interested
in.

LINES

If using a thermocline rig, I suggest you make a decision
as to what kind of line you are going to use: wire, monofilament,
or dacron. If you are using wire line, the Penn 49M works very
well. Usually 200 yards of 30 to 40 pound test is correct.
Williams Duro-Lus or Mason stainless steel stranded wire will do
very nicely, and Fenwick 7-strand stainless steel wire is becoming
popular. The prices vary from about $6 to $12.

When using monofilament line for thermocline fishing, it
should be at least 30 pound test. The leader material is usually 15
to 20 pound test. Any good quality line will work. One of my
favorites is gold Damyl, it's a good quality line at a reasonable
price. Berkley's Trilene and Dupont Stren are also very good.
Dacron trolling line by Gudebrod or Cortland will also do very
nicely.

If you decide to use the thermocline rigs, you'll hear much
discussion about wire line and monofilament. I have used both
and can't really find anything bad to say about either one. Wire
does cut through water better and will run deeper than
monofilament. You can make up your own mind.

When selecting a monofilament line for running out of
downriggers, you will get a lot of advice on how heavy the line
should be. Many people suggest using at least 20 pound test. My
personal selection is from about 8 to 15 pound test leaning very
strongly toward even lighter lines. I am very partial to 4 and 6
pound test although they really aren't recommended for
downrigger use. If you want to try the lighter lines, I would
recommend that you go to a Luhr Jensen line release. I will
describe it later on.

I generally run 10, 12 and 15 pound test lines on my level
wind reels and 6, 8 and 10 on my spinning reels. On my Garcia

5000D I have 12 pound test line and have caught fish of all sizes without any problems. I grant you that 20 pound test line gives you a feeling of security when fighting a 30 pound salmon but 12 and 15 will also get the job done. Your odds of getting a strike increase when you are using the lighter lines. The heavier lines are bigger in diameter and this thickness will be magnified in the water. The lighter lines have smaller diameters and therefore magnify less. Anything that will increase your odds is well worth trying. Try different lines and make your own conclusions.

LURES

There are hundreds of lures, all designed to catch fish and some to catch fisherman. Let's talk about the ones that catch fish.

When fishing the thermocline rigs, about 90 percent of the time you will be using a flutter spoon. This is an extremely thin, lightweight spoon that is anywhere from 2 to 4 inches long. Most have single hooks which I prefer over the treble hooks. They come in such a vast array of colors that listing them all would be impossible. Some of the better known spoons (my favorites) are as follows: Luhr Jensen, Andy Reekers, Suttons, Quick-strike, Daredevle, and Millers. They come plain, hammered, striped, colored, dotted, taped, and anything else you can possibly imagine.

Luhr Jensen has a large selection of excellent lures with single hooks. The construction is good throughout. One of my favorites, when you can find it, is the 44 series in the gold and silver finish. The prism tape lures are also good, especially in silver, green and blue. Luhr Jensen makes many lures in spinning size as well which come in a variety of color choices.

Andy Reekers is another good trolling spoon for most any game fish, but primarily for salmon, steelhead and lake trout. They are slightly heavier than some of the usual flutter spoons but work very well in any type of situation.

Sutton makes an excellent flutter spoon primarily in a silver finish, either plain or hammered. They are silver plated, and

Some of the quick strike lures that are available. From left to right No. 31, No. 11 (silver), No. 11 (gold), No. 35 and No. 88.

therefore a little expensive, but well worth the money. You won't find these in the discount stores.

Quick-strike lures are quite difficult to find but worth the search. They make one in particular that is my favorite for landlocked salmon and rainbows, a small gold colored lure No. 11, of 2 inch length, great on cloudy days. Their other selections are good but come in silver only. The one distinguishing feature of a Quick-strike is its unusual surface design that gives great light reflection. It is good for almost any variety of fish.

Daredevle is probably best known for its famous red and white spoon, but they do make an excellent flutter spoon that should not be overlooked with colors ranging from silver to two-tones, including fluorescents.

Miller makes a good selection of lures in many sizes, a real must for the tackle box. Their color selection is pretty much

limited to silver but a little prismilite tape can change that easily
enough. A couple of my favorites are the flutter-lite No. 2, and
the trouter No. 3. I've caught my fair share of rainbows and
browns on these two and wouldn't be without them.

Another lure I use frequently is the Flash-King Wobbler in
the 1/4 and 3/8 ounce size which comes in nickel, fluorescent red,
blue and silver. After you remove this lure from its package, bend
it in the middle until you have it arched; then run the lure in the
water to check the action and bend it again if necessary. To prove
this, take one of these lures straight from the package and run it
alongside the boat. Then take another, follow the bending
directions, and use it in the water. You'll soon see the difference.
There are many brown trout in our freezer because of this lure.

I've mentioned these lures primarily for the thermocline
rigs, but they are used for most every type of trolling. As for you
spin fishermen, they are a big "no," unless you add weight. The
flutter spoons work very well behind most any type of trolling
rig, from thermocline to Pink Ladys and downriggers.

The following are some of my favorite lures to run from
downriggers and Pink Ladys: flutter spoons, Little Cleos, Little
Jewels, Flash-Kings, Flatfish, J-plug, Fire-plug, Rapala's, Heddon
Tadpolly, Mepps spoon and Hot Shot. I mention these because
they are fairly easy to find and most any fishing tackle store
carries at least some of them.

Equipment

THE RIGHT BOAT

It would be really nice to own a 20-25 foot boat but we
have to look at things from a practical standpoint. You can get as
much money tied up in a 20 foot fishing boat as you can in a
house boat or small cabin cruiser. The boat itself in actuality isn't
important, good boating sense is. Know what kind of water your
boat is capable of handling. The fishing we are talking about can

be done out of a 12 foot aluminum boat or a 25 foot fishing machine. It's not any more difficult to mount a couple of downriggers on a 12 foot boat than it is on a 25 foot boat. My own boat is only a 14 footer, but as long as I watch the weather conditions I can fish anywhere the big boats can. I must admit that I would much rather have an open 18 footer so that I could move around in it and take on some rougher water.

I strongly recommend a vee hull over a tri-hull. It takes rough water better and you have more control at slower trolling speeds.

If you will be trailering your boat a lot, make your trailer selection carefully. A good trailer can really make a difference when loading and unloading your boat. The best trailer I ever used was an Easy-Loader. The name really fits.

Since the price of C.B.'s have come down considerably, it wouldn't be a bad idea to install one in your boat. A quick call will bring aid from another fisherman or from the Coast Guard which monitors the marine channel. Most fishermen use channel 13 so you can keep in touch.

Probably small motors ranging from 6 to 35 horse power are the best. They are cheaper in price and cheaper to run, since they use less gasoline. On the other hand, big outboards are now built so they can run at trolling speed.

Buy a large ice chest if you have room in your boat, some plastic trash bags and a heavy instrument to kill the trout with after you've got them in the boat. You don't have to fill the ice chest with ice, just enough to keep the fish cooled down.

ELECTRONIC FISHING AIDS

I strongly recommend some type of flashing or recording device. Such devices are not absolutely necessary but can save you a lot of guesswork about the depth of the water or type of bottom. But a device is no guarantee of fishing success. It's just a tool, great for locating breaks in structure, suspended fish and, of course, depth. I have marked unbelievable schools of fish on my graph and have still come home empty-handed.

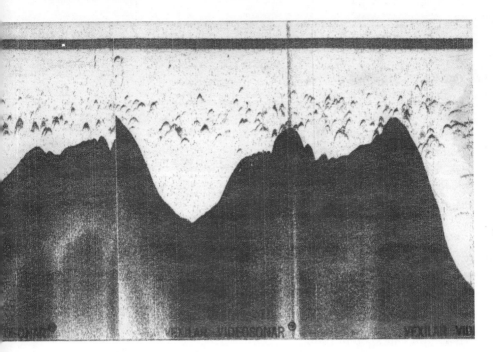

A graph printout showing a large school of smaller trout, probably rainbows or browns. Notice how closely they are holding to structure.

___

The flasher units are cheapest but be careful of bargains and unfamiliar brands. Service is also very important. Lowrance, one of the leaders in the industry, makes several good units at different prices. Lowrance also has an excellent service department which can help you if you encounter problems with your unit. Ray Jefferson, Hummingbird, Vexilor and Garcia also make good units.

The first fish locator I owned was the flasher type. It worked very well but was the devil to read on bright sunny days. I frequently had to put a jacket over the dial face just to get a reading. Some of the new flashers have beepers. You can set the beeper to go off at certain depths; for example, you are in 200 feet of water and you are fishing in depths of 120 feet. If you set the beeper to go off from 0 to 120 feet, any fish or bait fish in that range will set off the beeper. At the same time the flasher will give you their depth. This will keep you from watching the finder every second you are on the water. I used to come off the lake with little red lines flashing in front of my eyes from constantly watching the dial scale.

Lowrance makes one model that is just great for this type of fishing: model 460 will read from 0 to 60 feet, 0 to 180 feet, and 0 to 60 fathoms (360 feet). It also has the beeper. Garcia and the Hummingbird are excellent units which come in various depth ranges. If you are planning on purchasing such a unit, be careful that you don't buy one of the 0 to 30 and 0 to 60 feet depth units. They are really great for the structure bass fisherman but worthless for deep water trout fishing.

Without any reservations whatsoever my choice would be the straight line graph. They come in all shapes and sizes and in many brands. If you are working on limited funds, you can save a little money and go to a curved line graph (under $200) but I really don't like that type as well.

The Vexilar model 555 or the Lowrance model LRG 515 are two of the nicer, less expensive graphs on the market. I have worked with both these units and for my money they are excellent. The Vexilar 155D is also a good unit but be prepared to pay more for this one. The price on the graphs will vary considerably depending on where you live; it's best to shop around. Both the Vexilar 555 and the Lowrance model LRG-515 are sensitive enough to pick up the thermocline in a lake and mark dark enough so you can easily read and interpret what you see. My ten year old daughter has no problems in working and reading my Vexilar 510SR (model 555 has replaced the 510SR).

One thing you want to keep in mind when shopping for a graph is not only the price of the graph but the cost of the paper that runs though it, which is pretty expensive, as high as $7 a roll. Most graphs have adjustable speeds which will regulate the amount of paper that runs through the unit. I keep mine on the slowest speed which is about ½ inch per minute. I use the Vexilar video sonar paper and get about 12 hours per roll which is 35 feet

A selection of printout from a Vexilar graph unit. Large black area is submerged island coming up to about 40 foot depths, sharp dropoffs on either side go to greater than 200 foot depths. Crescent shaped marks are suspended trout, horizontal lines are the paths of the downriggers. Thick black line on top is the lake surface.

long. Learning to use a graph is not at all difficult; just read and follow the instructions that come with each unit carefully.

DOWNRIGGERS

Downriggers can get pretty sophisticated. There are some available with electric motors for lowering and raising the weights. Some come with digital readout for temperature changes in the water. But their basic function is the same, to get the lure to the fish zone. Riviera, Walker, Big John and Luhr Jensen all make good downriggers with prices usually starting around $35. I like all of these. You can save yourself some money on your initial purchase by buying the less sophisticated devices. The model 40 by Riviera comes with everything you need to get started except the weight but you can make that or buy one of the empty shells and fill it with buckshot. There's no depth meter on the less expensive models but as long as you can count by two's, you're in great shape. Most downriggers, including the model 40, let out two feet of cable for every revolution of the handle. Also if you're running a graph, you should be able to track the weights without any problems.

One of the smallest but most important parts of a downrigger is the release. No matter how much money you spend, none of them are much good without a smooth working release. The release that comes with the Rivieras is good but will flatten your line. Since they were first introduced there have been been some improvements. I've been using the Riviera release for some time now, and the only real complaint I've had is the line flattening. This causes a weakening of the line and ultimate breaking.

A release I have never used but have heard good reports about is the Walker, which has easy line hook-up and a stainless steel hanger. It can be used for fresh or salt water. Luhr Jensen makes one that is very smooth since it is completely adjustable for a light release or a heavy setting for larger fish. It works on a magnet and costs a little more than some others but it is well worth the investment. It will rust on the inside, but this doesn't seem to hurt its performance. For you fishermen who want to get into light line downrigger fishing, this is the one I mentioned earlier.

Once you get into downrigger fishing, there will be times when you want to run more than one rod off each unit. The release I've been using for this is the Mac-Jac line release. It's convenient because you can clip into any part of the downrigger cable that you wish and disconnect when you're finished. If you want to run another lure 10 to 20 feet above the first lure, simply clip it on the line. This release comes in two parts, the clip and the release button. Your fishing line goes through the center of the button and will move up and down the line allowing you to put out as much leader as you desire. Twist the button four to six times and then press into the metal clip. When you get a strike, the button will break away from the clip, untwist and move freely once again. Now that's the way it's supposed to work. But, if for example, you get into a school of small rainbows that don't have the striking power to pull the button free, you'll end up dragging them around until they die. I hate to see any fish killed unnecessarily, especially when they're that small.

This problem can be overcome by taking a pair of needle nose pliers and very gently working the release so that the button pulls out easier. Be careful when you do this as it breaks with hardly any effort at all. Line releases are cheap. They come two to a package and the buttons come four to a package. Prices will vary from 90 cents to $1.25.

ROD HOLDERS

There are some fine ones available but some of the prices are a little on the high side. I make my own and you can too. Buy some PVC pipe at a hardware store and cut it to the length you want. You can mount the pipe on the side of your boat or if your downriggers are mounted on a board, as mine are, drill a two inch hole just behind the downrigger and slip the pipe into the hole. The pipe works and it's cheap.

Mac-Jac makes a nice little rod holder that attaches about anyplace on a boat and at just about any angle. Riviera attaches directly to their downriggers. There are some rod holders that are PVC coated and adjustable to different vertical as well as horizontal positions. They also come in your choice of mounting bracket, side or flush mount. You can expect to pay from $8 to $15 each for them. Another rod holder that I like quite well is the Down-Easter. They come with a single clamp, a double clamp and an in-board mount. They are the fast breakaway type. When you get a strike simply grab the rod and pull straight up. The rod holder breaks away in the middle allowing the rod to be lifted out without any problems. Prices run from $5.50 to $11.

TERMOCLINE RODS

Most of us refer to a thermocline rig as simply "rigs" but some of you may have heard phrases such as "Seth Green Rig," "10, 7 and 5 leader rods" and "Thermocline rods."

This type of equipment is designed to fish an area of a lake referred to as the thermocline. The thermocline is water that is layered with each layer having a different temperature. A lake may have a surface temperature of 75 degrees but this doesn't mean the water temperature is 75 degrees all the way to the bottom. The surface may be 75 degrees but just a few feet under, the temperature may change 5 to 10 degrees. As you go deeper, the temperature will change again a number of times until you reach bottom. You can easily have four or five changes before you you reach bottom, and to make things even more complicated, the thermocline can change from day to day, depending on wave action, currents, wind direction and time of year.

When fishing the rigs, you will usually be in water depths in excess of 150 feet. The thermocline rod is set up to locate the preferred comfort zone for lake trout, a range of 45 to 52 degrees F.

Let's put together a serviceable rig. First, use a medium action salt water trolling rod of 6 to 7 feet. Many fishermen will argue about what line works best with this system, but I have found they all do a good job. If using steel line, be sure the rod is equipped with roller guides. If using monofilament or dacron, roller guides aren't necessary but a roller top is recommended. The reel should be one of the heavier ones made by Penn or Garcia. A good one would be Penn's 49M.

You'll want at least 200 yards of good quality line. Take some 15 or 20 pound test line and make some leaders after you decide on the length you want. The lengths are usually 12, 15 and 20 feet. Cut the leaders in the lengths you have decided upon and set them aside.

The next item for the rig is beaded swivel chains. These come in various sizes. I use No.'s 61 and 101 which come in packages of three and four. They are not too expensive. Next are the wire connectors. This is simply 2 inch wire leaders with push-pull spring clips. They are inexpensive and shouldn't run you more than 10 to 15 cents apiece. Grab yourself a bunch as they will rust and you'll want to replace them when necessary. As long as you're in the store pick up some 20, 24 and 32 ounce lead sinkers. Also some three-way swivels and, of course, snap swivels. The snap swivels should be the swivel chains or the ball bearing type. This type will help keep down line twisting while trolling. The only other item that you may want is a one gallon milk container (plastic) or the new plastic pop containers. I'll explain their use later.

The next step is to put all this together. First get about 120 yards started on the reel. Now you should know what size leader you are going to use. Let's assume that you have decided to go wit! ¹5 foot leaders. Make your first break in the main line and tie one beaded chain into the line. The improved clinch knot works best for this. Run the line through the hole in one end of the beaded chain, twist the line about five times and run the end of the line back through the loop at bottom. Bring it back through the large loop remaining and pull tight. Now tie the main line back into hole remaining on the beaded chain and use the improved clinch knot again. You'll be using this knot for all your ties. Measure off another 20 feet and cut. Again tie in another beaded chain. Continue to do this until you've got ten or fifteen

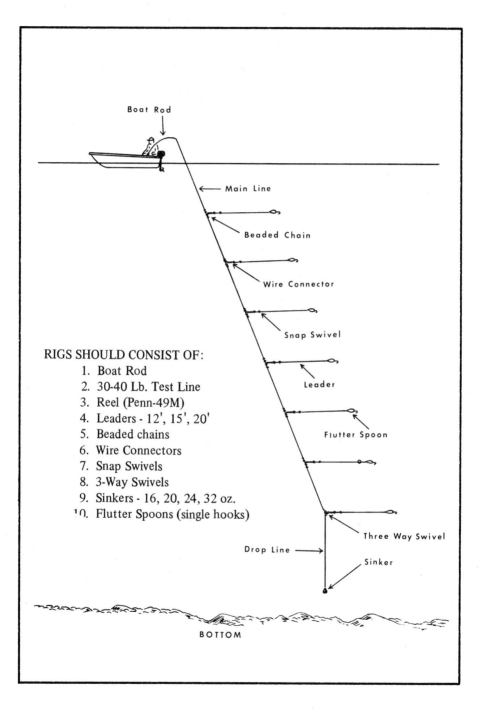

Boat Rod

Main Line

Beaded Chain

Wire Connector

Snap Swivel

RIGS SHOULD CONSIST OF:
1. Boat Rod
2. 30-40 Lb. Test Line
3. Reel (Penn-49M)
4. Leaders - 12', 15', 20'
5. Beaded chains
6. Wire Connectors
7. Snap Swivels
8. 3-Way Swivels
9. Sinkers - 16, 20, 24, 32 oz.
10. Flutter Spoons (single hooks)

Leader

Flutter Spoon

Three Way Swivel

Drop Line

Sinker

BOTTOM

tied in. After you have made your last break in the line, tie on your last beaded chain. Measure another 20 feet, and cut the line and tie a three-way swivel on the bottom. Take some of your leader material and cut off about 18 inches and tie a large snap swivel on one end and a 32 ounce sinker on the other. You'll find yourself using the 32 ounce sinkers more than any of the others.

Since you've already measured out your leaders, tie a chain or ball bearing snap swivel on one end only. Then attach a wire leader to the snap swivel. At the other end of the leader tie your lure. You can use a snap swivel for this also but I prefer to tie directly. Don't forget to use the improved clinch knot for this also.

The leaders and spoons are easy to store by getting a piece of styrofoam and wrapping the leader around the styrofoam and then imbedding the hooks right into it. This keeps the hooks secure. Depending on the size of the styrofoam, you can keep about 10 leaders on each piece. There are fishing leader spools of polyethylene available, but they are rather expensive for what they are. The come in 4 and 6 inch sizes and run between 75 and 90 cents each. They hold one leader with a spoon. Since your rigs will run anywhere from 5 to seven leaders, you can get quite a bit tied up in leader spools.

Putting one of these rigs together isn't really as complicated as it sounds. Refer to the diagram and it will give you a much clearer picture.

Another piece of equipment that I should mention is a deep water trolling device called the Pink Lady or Deep Six which comes in three sizes depending on the depth you want to fish. Size 000 has a maximum depth of 50 feet, 001 will go to about 85 feet, and the 002 will reach 120 feet. It's a very easy device to use—just read the directions on the back of the package. These diving planes put considerable strain on a rod. Be sure to get a good stout rod in the 7 foot range. Keep in mind that you can build your equipment up as you go. You can get started by using hand lines and 32 ounce weights.

Trolling Techniques

THERMOCLINING

The type of trolling I will be discussing is normally in large lakes from 20 to 200 feet deep, containing lake trout, rainbow trout, landlocked salmon, brown trout and, where applicable, coho and chinook salmon. You can also try this technique for pike and bass suspended or on deep water structure.

We should start out by talking about thermoclining. In all honesty this is not my favorite way to fish but catch fish it does. If you don't mind the lack of a real fight, this technique puts fish on the table.

To begin with, it really makes no difference how many leaders you run as long as you stay within your local laws. New York State allows 15 hook points per rod. In other states, I strongly urge you to check with the Conservation Department. I'd hate to see you spend a hundred dollars or more rigging your rod, and spend the first days of the fishing season in jail.

Start out by using three to five leaders until you get the feel of it and then you can go to seven or even ten. Many people start out with five and never go any further. If you're planning on running seven, have at least 150 feet of water under you, more if you can get it.

You can run these rigs almost any time of year, but usually it's best to start in late June and go through July, August and part of September. If you're using these rigs in late winter into spring, I would suggest running two rigs of seven leaders, one on top and the other deep. Keep them scattered until you locate fish. If the school isn't scattered all over the place at different depths, you can adjust the other rig to be in their strike zone. If they don't seem to fit into any particular pattern, keep your rigs scattered and watch your graph or flasher carefully. No matter how many articles you've read about trout being on top in the spring, it ain't necessarily so. In the early spring I've found them just about everywhere from the surface to more than 150 feet below. Spring fishing can be very unpredictable—one day the trout will be on top and the next day 120 feet under. Trout usually stay in water temperatures best suited for them, going out of these comfort zones to feed but eventually going back. Water temperatures are constantly changing due to air temperature, wave action, currents and wind direction.

Watch your trolling speed in the spring and winter, especially when after lake trout; usually the slower the better since they aren't the most aggressive fish in the world. Also fish aren't as active in winter and early spring as they are when the water starts to warm.

Lakers are famous for following lures so be alert. Don't be afraid to change trolling speeds and gun your engine once in a while, making the lures look like bait fish trying to escape. Kick the engine into neutral and let the spoons flutter toward the bottom, then put it back in gear and gun it again. Any of these movements can provoke a strike.

If you have never fished a lake before, most of the marinas that sell bait and tackle and rent boats will be more than happy to point you in the right direction.

As the water warms, lake trout will move out into deeper water and by July and August most of the fishing is done out in the middle of the lake in the thermocline. Your tactics don't really change all that much. The main difference is you'll be fishing deeper. Again, until you locate the fish, run your rigs so that you are covering as much water as possible.

In the summer we usually run seven and sometimes ten leaders. As you recall, the beaded swivel chains were set at 15 to 20 foot intervals and anywhere from ten to fifteen were used. For example, let's say there are two of you fishing and you're going to run four rigs with five leaders each. Until the fish are located, I would run one rig close to the top. After you put the last leader on, run the rig down to the next beaded chain. Take one of the plastic jugs I mentioned earlier, attach a large snap swivel to the jug and attach the jug to the beaded chain. The jug will keep the rig from going any deeper. Run about 50 feet of line off the reel and let the jug drift back of the boat. Lock the reel from the free spool. Then adjust the drag so that the reel

A fine pair of chinook salmon caught using downriggers and graph unit.

clicks every so often. When a strike does occur, the drag will sound off. Set the next rig out the same way but this time after the last leader is out, drop down not one, but two or three more beaded chains. Fasten the jug on and set the rod in its holder. Go back to the first rod and again let out additional line. Now allow the second rod to drop back to the position the first rod was in. Continue to do the same thing with the other two rods, each one at a different depth and a different distance behind the boat. You'll be covering a lot of different depths and the rigs will be spaced far enough apart so if you take your turns nice and easy, very slowly, you shouldn't run into a lot of trouble. You've got the whole lake to turn around in.

Once you have located the fish, don't be foolish and catch one fish and keep trolling straight down the lake. If you are marking fish on the graph or flasher, steer the boat in a large circle and stay on the fish. If your jugs are spaced properly and your turns are easy, don't worry about getting tangled. Just tangle one of these rigs once and it won't take long to learn how not to.

Remember that currents can easily change the action of your lures without you being aware of it. Once in a while take one of your lines in your fingers and pull and let drift back. If you repeat this process, you can usually feel the current. It's rather hard to describe but it's like something pulling back at you from the other end. If you're trolling against the current, it's best to slow your boat down a bit to compensate. The lures can change their action to the point where they go into a frantic spin instead of a gentle rocking action. The same holds true when trolling with a current, but this time the spoons won't have enough action. In situations like this increase your speed slightly. If there's some good wave action, try running your boat in between the waves. The rocking motion of the boat can be just enough to give the lures that little something extra that will turn the trout on.

One of the things I can't stress enough is to watch those rods. Many times a lake trout will strike, and, if hooked, won't fight, but will follow. Sometimes the only clue you will have is the rod tip will have one or two sharp raps, and that's all you'll ever see. I know several fishermen who have small bells on the ends of the rods. It's really not that bad of an idea, — it works.

Once you have a strike and the fish is on, don't rush the rod or try to set the hook. You've got plenty of time and generally they hook themselves. By all means keep the boat moving. When you start to bring the fish in, take it nice and easy. Don't pump the rod, just a steady, easy retrieve. If you feel the fish pumping or starting to make a run, ease off, and the drag will go into action. Once the fish settles back down, begin your retrieve again. The most critical time is when your first leader appears. From here on in, be on your toes. If the fish isn't on the first leader, have your fishing partner remove the leaders by simply pushing the spring back and removing the wire leader from the beaded chain. Keep that leader out of the way. Put it back on the leader spool or up in the front of the boat. Continue retrieving slowly removing your leaders until you reach the leader with the fish on. At this point there are a couple of ways of bringing him in. One is to remove the leader and bring him to the boat by hand; or very carefully raise the rod tip, and carefully set the rod towards the front of the boat, or hand it to your partner and have him hold the rod while you bring the fish to net. You'll make out a lot better by keeping the net out of the water until the very last minute. If the net is in the water at the time you're bringing the fish in, he may see the net and take off again. Most of the time he'll come alongside the boat quietly. Make a quick pass with the net, get him in the boat, administer a sharp blow to the head with a piece of pipe, remove the hook, put the fish in one of the plastic bags, and throw him in the ice chest.

One of my biggest complaints with the rigs is that when fighting a really nice rainbow or landlocked salmon on such a stiff rod, the hooks can tear out because rainbows and landlocks are usually very hard fighters. A thermocline rod doesn't have the give of a spinning rod or a good downrigger rod and you just don't have the control. It's times like these that you wish you had a nice 8 or 9 foot downrigger rod with a level wind reel, anything so long as you had more control.

I probably don't talk about the rigs favorably. I prefer other methods, but I do use them, and they sure catch fish.

TROLLING DEVICES

If you are just getting started in deep water trolling and don't want to spend a lot of money, purchase a Pink Lady or a Deep Six. These are simple and inexpensive, but since they are diving devices that force your lure down, they require the use of a heavy rod.

You'll find a level wind reel is excellent for this kind of trolling. I prefer monofilament line from 12 to 17 pound test.

The biggest problem you'll face with these devices is depth control. A good flasher will help here in at least telling you how deep the water is.

If you use a level wind reel you can measure the amount of line that comes off the reel for every cycle of the line guide. Simply start out with the line guide all the way over to the left or

right and pull line out until the guide has traveled once across the
reel spool. Not every reel will be the same but my 5000D
measures 8 feet for each line guide pass. Using this method you
will know how much line to let out to reach a certain depth.

Lower your Pink Lady into the water and start letting out
line with the boat moving at trolling speed. Count the number of
times the line guide moves back and forth. Once the device
touches bottom, stop the reel and you know how much line it
takes to get to that depth.

I usually use flutter spoons when trolling with these
devices. Any lure can be used, but keep in mind that the heavier
the lure the more they tend to sink below the device.

When using any of these trolling devices, you will notice a
very heavy pulling action on the rod. When a strike occurs, the
device will trip and plane back to the surface as you fight the fish.

DOWNRIGGERS

One of my favorite ways of trolling is with the downrigger
which is very easy to operate. The brand you buy makes little
difference as they all work basically the same. Most fishermen
start out with one, but once you start catching fish with it, it
won't be long before you'll have one on the other side of the boat
and then if your boat is big enough you'll find yourself considering
a couple of long arm models for the forward section of your boat.

The downrigger can be fished effectively in a number of
ways but let's start simple and go from there. The downrigger is
designed primarily to operate with one and two rods, the line
release coming off the weight or just above it.

You should decide first what type of rod and reel you're
going to use. Here again, I strongly recommend a level wind reel,
but a spinning reel will also work. The rod is generally an 8 to 9
footer with light to medium action. One of my favorites is a 9
footer with a light action, capable of handling any situation and
just about any size fish. I caught a 32 pound salmon with an 8
foot downrigger rod in the 1/8 to 3/8 ounce range, 12 pound test
line, a Garcia 5000D level wind casting reel, and a fluorescent

green J-plug. Not exactly a perfect outfit, but the salmon is in the freezer. The only real complaint I had was that the rod should have been heavier with a Penn 209M which holds 350 yards of 20 pound monofilament line. When you're using a reel that only holds about 190 yards of 10 pound test, you can get a little shaky in the knees. These salmon are known for their long sizzling runs. There has been more than one time when I saw the bottom of my spool staring back at me. But the 5000D stood the strain well and for everyday use for lake trout and rainbows it's just great.

One of the questions I hear all the time is, "How much line should I run out behind the downrigger?" To be perfectly honest, the only time I have found it really critical is when fishing for salmon and brown trout. Both of these fish spook easily and the more line you have away from the boat the better off you are. Generally 90 to 110 feet for browns and 100 to 120 feet for salmon. These are the distances that work best for me. For lake

---

The author with a 32 pound chinook caught on an 8 foot downrigger rod, 12 pound test line and J plug.

trout I usually run about 90 feet, but I've been successful with as little as 40 feet of line out.

When fishing rainbows, I prefer to use a shorter leader, about 10 to 20 feet. This never seems to bother the fish. Rainbows aren't too particular or, for that matter, too bright.

I use flutter spoons. I don't have any real favorites, but I do prefer some over others. The Sutton spoons are hard to beat, but they are expensive. The only time I use them is when I'm fishing deep water and not following bottom contours or some rocky point. Every time you hang one of these on bottom, you can kiss about $2.50 goodbye. If I locate some lake trout in 50 feet of water over a rocky ledge, I use my cheaper flutter spoons or go to a Flash-King Wobbler in either a 1/4 or 3/8 ounce and most times I run one off one downrigger and one off the other. Many times a trout will go for the larger spoons, and, also, the reverse can happen. If you should hang one of these on the bottom you're not out too much.

If you're trolling close to bottom with your downriggers, I can't put enough importance on having a good flasher unit or a graph. Downrigger weights can be expensive, and losing a few of these could easily pay for a good flasher. The more expensive downriggers have drags on them, but I wouldn't want to depend on them.

Trolling with downriggers really isn't any different than trolling other systems. I've run them as little as 2 feet deep and as much as 120 feet below the surface. Let's assume you are working an area well known for lake trout. The body of water begins with shallow water of about 20 feet but slopes fast to 50 feet and then drops off to 150. There are a number of ways to work this area, but let's go the way that calls for the least amount of work. In the spring and fall we usually run like this: one downrigger running just off bottom, usually 2 to 4 feet, and the next 6 to 10 feet off bottom. We almost always run at least one top water line, usually two. Once in a while it isn't a bad idea to run two downriggers at varied depths, one Pink Lady and a top water line. Using this system you are covering all the water from surface to bottom. Remember it's spring, and those fish are likely to be anywhere. The area we are covering is about 1/2 to 3/4ths of a mile long. We start out by trolling the 20 foot depths and if no fish contact is made, swing the boat around and begin working back, but this time we move the boat into deeper water, say 25 to 30 feet and repeat the procedure. If still no contact is made, continue working back and forth each time in deeper water. Be sure to adjust your downriggers for these depths. Remember we are attempting to locate the fish which may be on bottom, suspended off bottom, or cruising the surface. If no contact is made by the time you reach the dropoff, take great pains to stay on the dropoff from 50 to 150 foot depth. Work this area back and forth thoroughly. If still no contact is made, move out over the dropoff and run the downriggers and boat so you are running parallel to the cliff. Have your downriggers set at least 20 feet

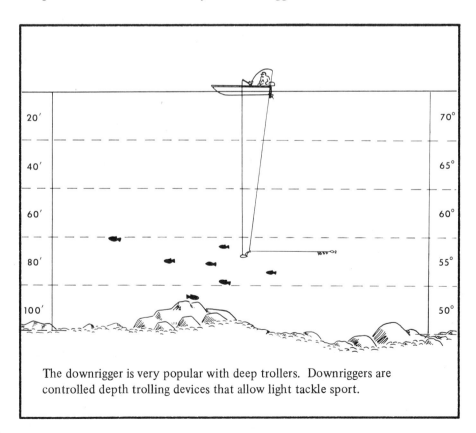

The downrigger is very popular with deep trollers. Downriggers are controlled depth trolling devices that allow light tackle sport.

apart. You are working one set of lures so they are running just below the dropoff and the other so it runs just below the first. Stay on the dropoff. On every pass, adjust your downriggers by several feet until fish contact is made. Then adjust the other downrigger for the same depth. If you locate a fish, don't do what I see so many do. They catch a fish, boat it, admire it and troll right on down the lake and AWAY from the fish. Chances are good that if you caught one fish in the area, you can catch more. Turn the boat around and go back through. The odds of catching another one in the same area are excellent.

You can also troll this same area working from shore out towards the dropoff. This works quite well but is more work as you're constantly changing downrigger depths, a two man operation.

No matter which pattern you decide upon, if fish contact is not made, have another spot in the back of your mind and be prepared to move on. Don't spend your whole fishing day in one area unless you're catching fish. Come back a little later in the day. By that time the trout may have moved in.

If you're using a graph or flasher and you're marking fish but not getting any strikes, stay in the area but change lures and don't be afraid to vary your trolling speeds and directions. Try kicking the engine in neutral, allowing the spoons to flutter towards bottom; then kick back into gear, even speeding up a bit at the same time. If you can't get them turned on, move on to the next location.

Another way of fishing the downriggers is to set up your rods similar to the thermocline rigs except you use only two or no more than three leaders. Use about 12 or 15 leaders and tie your spoons on the end. Use the same wire leader releases as on the thermocline rigs. Actually, you are converting your downrigger rods into small thermocline rigs. Be sure you use a beaded chain small enough to pass through the line guide of your reel; or remove the line guide altogether and use your fingers to guide the line evenly across the spool. Only the bottom leader will be hooked into the release; therefore, it is important that you put a pretty good bend into the rod. Generally, if a strike occurs on the top leader or the second leader, the line will not release. Your first indication will be an irregular bobbing and jumping of the rod, and usually the downrigger itself. You'll have to release the bottom leader with a sharp pull upwards. Play the fish as you normally would; just be sure your fishing partner gets the remaining downriggers out of the way, including any other rods you may have out. Remove your leaders just as you would if you were fishing with the thermocline rigs. This really isn't a bad way to fish and it's a lot of fun since the rods are lighter. Use the same trolling patterns as we discussed, but pay attention to your flasher or graph. I can't emphasize enough the importance of knowing where those lures are at all times. If you locate fish in 60 feet of water, it will do no good if your lures are in 40 feet. Don't guess—know!

If you want to use more than one rod off each downrigger, there is really no problem, so long as you have the right equipment. Run your first leader off the bottom with your regular release. Then decide where you want the next one to be. You can run it anywhere from 10 feet above the first on up. I generally run them 15 or 20 feet apart. If running two downriggers, it is a good idea to space them as follows: the first downrigger, run your lure out behind the weight, the depth depending on what you are fishing for. Then about 10 or 15 feet above the weight slip in a MacJac release. If the MacJac's are new, be sure you adjust them because if you don't you can expect problems. Do the same with the other downrigger and be sure the spacing stays the same. It's not important to the fish that the spacing is the same, it just makes it easier for you. This system is again used when looking for fish. If your first downrigger is dropped to 80 feet, the lures will be running at 80 and 65 feet. On the other side drop it to 50 feet and the lures will be running at 50 feet and 35 feet. Using this system and running each of the leaders 15 feet apart, you are covering water from 35 to 80 feet. Naturally, you can separate your leaders at any distance you wish. After you have made fish contact, you can readjust your downriggers to the depth where fish have been located. This is where a graph is nice as it will track your weights and you can tell at a glance if you're above or below the fish.

Another good way to fish deep under water structure is by using copper or stainless steel wire line. The setup isn't too complicated consisting of a three-way swivel twisted to the end of the copper or the stainless line. Use about an 18 inch drop line with about a 32 ounce sinker. Running off the three-way swivel is a flutter spoon and you can run a 12, 15 or 20 foot leader. About 20 feet above the first leader, it wouldn't hurt to splice in a beaded chain and run another leader. This way you will be able to find some of those suspended trout off the bottom. This type of rig can be run off the usual medium action trolling rod and reel similar to the thermocline rods, but you will have a better feel of the bottom if you use the cheapest rod around—your fingers. The line is generally spooled on a automatic reel which can be attached somewhere on the boat. As the line is being pulled from the reel, it will automatically wind the main spring and when pulling the line back to the boat it will rewind the line back onto the reel. Other reels can be used that are a whole lot cheaper but the automatics are nice to have. These reels look very much like a giant automatic fly reel and cost a whole lot more, running around $45.

When fishing with this type of rig you have contact with the line directly, thereby being able to feel the bottom and any changes in the bottom. Keep your weight just off bottom. Every so often release enough line to feel the bottom and locate where you are. Once bottom is located, pull just enough line to pick the weight off it. Here again if using a flasher or graph, keep alert enough to be able to spot any changes. In this way you'll be able to make the necessary changes in the positioning of your lures to follow the contour. Use the same trolling patterns as previously mentioned. It's a good way to fish and you won't have a lot of money tied up in equipment. One of my favorite ways to fish this rig for lake trout is to use the same setup as above except the bottom leader is about 60 feet long and on the end is tied a black Twin Minnow which works just off bottom. In the spring of the year, especially May and early June, it can be fantastic.

The trolling techniques we have talked about are easy enough to learn. Just be patient. Don't expect to go out the first time and knock'em dead.

The above systems were introduced primarily for lake trout, rainbow trout, brown trout, landlocked salmon, coho salmon and chinook salmon. These fish can be located in fairly shallow water in early spring and fall. But as the water warms, these fish will move out to the water temperatures that they find most comfortable.

In the summertime when boats move out into really deep water, bottom structure fishing ceases. You're not really fishing structure, but fishing sanctuary. Sanctuary is where fish live most of the time, their comfort zone. As summer approaches and waters begin to warm, fish move back out to deep water and suspend in the layers of water most comfortable for them. Your trolling techniques aren't really any different: you'll just be working deeper water and usually more of it. Troll up and down the lake, back and forth between the two shorelines. Use an expanding figure eight trolling pattern as you go, covering more water each time. Once you locate fish, put the boat into a large circle and keep working the same area repeatedly. Vary your speed, work the waves, do everything possible to induce a strike.

Probably one of the hardest things to get used to is trolling in the middle of a lake that is 2 to 3 miles across and 400 or more feet deep, and catching rainbows, lake trout or landlocked salmon in as little as 35 to 150 feet under the boat. It never ceases to amaze me. But after you've done it a few times, the terms thermocline and sanctuary really start to make sense. All this mass confusion begins to come together. The next thing you know you'll be spending your summers in the middle of a lake trolling back and forth enjoying the fresh air and the break from the every day hustle and bustle. All it takes is one bragging-size fish and you'll become a believer, another one addicted to deep water trolling.

WHERE TO BUY SUPPLIES

As I promised at the beginning of the chapter, here is a list of some of the fishing tackle stores where the equipment I mentioned can be found.

* CANANDAIGUA FISHING TACKLE CO., INC., 113-119 South Main Street, Canandaigua, New York 14424, (716) 394-4706. Carries a large variety of tackle of all sorts, an excellent selection of flutter spoons, deep water equipment, sonars and graphs. Discount prices.

* CABELA'S, 812 13th Avenue, Sidney, Nebraska 69162, (308) 254-5505. Has a good selection of reels of all types, rods, some deep water equipment, sonars and graphs.

* SHOFF'S TACKLE SUPPLY, P.O. Box 1227, Kent, Washington 98031, (206) 852-4760. Carries rod building components and fly tying materials.

* ORCHARD TRADING, 1308 S. Jefferson, Hastings, Michigan 49058, (616) 948-8684. Has a good selection of flutter spoons, reels, rods and sonar equipment.

* BULLARD INTERNATIONAL, 10139 Shoreview Road, Dallas, Texas 75238, (214) 341-3509. Carries an excellent selection of rod building components for both fresh and salt water rods, salt water lures and leaders, downriggers, and fresh and salt water reels.

* DALE CLEMENS CUSTOM TACKLE, Route 2, Box 860, Wescosville, Pennsylvania 18106, (215) 395-5119. Has an excellent selection of rod building components for both fresh and salt water rods; and two of the best books ever published on rod building available.

FISHERMAN'S FRIEND, Waterloo-Geneva Road, Waterloo, New York 13165, (315) 539-3847. One of the better places for rod and reel repair; carries some flutter spoons and is one of the few places that has Quick-Strike spoons.

THE COMPLEAT ANGLER, INC., 305 Taughannock Blvd., Ithaca, New York 14850, (607) 272-5251. Some rod components are available; has a fair selection of trout and salmon lures and an excellent selection of bass lures and spinner baits.

NELSON WERTMAN, RD 2, 6187 Poplar Beach, Romulus, New York 14541, (607) 869-5867. Has custom rods of all types, both fresh and salt water. Rods are available in semi-custom, custom and full custom.

R. NEAL CUSTOM RODS, Payne Road, Penn Yan, New York 14527, (315) 536-3698. Carries custom made rods of all types, both fresh and salt water; some rod components available.

* These stores offer catalogs.

About the Authors

BILL BUTLER

Bill Butler is a Bass Pro. He is a veteran on the professional BASS tournament trail and has enjoyed tremendous success on northern natural lakes as well as southern man-made reservoirs. In addition, he is a representative for several major fishing tackle companies. However, his fishing is not limited to pro BASS tournaments where numbers of fish caught are important. His true love is fishing for individual trophy sized largemouth or smallmouth bass, as well as northern pike and muskies. He currently lives in Virginia, but he fishes all types of water from southern impoundments to Canadian lakes and rivers.

GORDON L. EGGLESTON

Gordon is an assistant professor of physical education at Ithaca College.

Born and brought up on a farm near Cooperstown, New York, his fishing exploits began at age ten and have included fishing northern New York and Canada for walleyes and northern pike as well as fly fishing for trout and salmon throughout the Northeast.

A versatile and highly skilled angler, Gordon, frequently called The Eagle, has taken over 50 northerns 36 inches or longer, 14 of which were trophy fish, 40 inches or more in length. His in-depth records and photos of his many fishing trips would impress the most serious anglers.

An avid outdoorsman, he has instructed physical education majors in archery, wilderness canoe camping, survival camping, fly fishing and fly tying. He has also authored publications dealing with these subjects. He is also a commercial artist, fish taxidermist and fly tier.

RONALD A. HOWARD, JR.

Ron is an extension associate responsible for youth programming in Cornell University's Department of Natural Resources.

He grew up in the hills of northwestern Pennsylvania, where he started fishing for trout at age five. After spending 6 years in Texas attending college, he came to Ithaca, New York in the fall of 1967 to work on a doctorate in ecology and animal behavior.

A professional fly tier and a fan of light tackle, he has pioneered the use of ultra-light spinning tackle for spring run rainbow trout in the Finger Lakes region. In recent years he has been an innovative member of the small but growing group of flyfishing rainbow anglers.

An expert, versatile angler, Ron is one of the most skilled trout fishermen in an area famed for good fishing and good fishermen.

J. MICHAEL KIMBALL

Michael Kimball, a real estate developer who makes his home in Ithaca, New York, has fished extensively throughout the Eastern and Western United States and Canada, the Carribean, Mexico and many European countries. He has been fly fishing for close to twenty-five years and has been a nymph specialist almost exclusively for over fifteen of those years.

While still in his early twenties, he taught fly fishing and fly tying, and has acted as a guide and instructor for the Federation of Fly Fishermen conclaves. He has done extensive graduate work at Cornell University in Fisheries Biology and Aquatic Ecology. He earned a reputation through his work on the advisory board of the American League of Anglers, and is also a

member of the Theodore Gordon Fly fishers and the Federation
of Fly Fishermen. He has contributed to and been featured in
numerous outdoor magazines and books. Recently his methods
of fishing and tying the nymph received special recognition in
Flyfisherman magazine. Presently he is working on a book about
nymph fishing.

TODD SWAINBANK

Todd is a Bass Pro, having competed successfully against
New York's finest bass anglers. In addition he is a professional
fishing guide, operating out of The Compleat Angler, a Bass Pro
Shop in Ithaca, New York.

A Cornell University Environmental Conservation
graduate, Todd is The Outdoor Writer for the Grapevine Press,
and a member of the New York State Outdoor Writers'
Association.

A versatile and highly skilled angler, he is at home pursuing
a variety of game fish throughout the East using artificial lures
only. His specialties are fly fishing for trout and salmon and
jigging for smallmouth bass.

NELSON WERTMAN

The dictionary defines the word expert as "a person who
knows a great deal about some special thing." Nelson Wertman
knows a great deal about deepwater trolling for trout and
salmon. What he has learned and the success he's had come from
many hours on the water practicing a variety of trolling
techniques.

When he moved to the Finger Lakes region of New York
State, Nelson was introduced to deepwater trolling through the
use of a thrmocline rod. Seeking ways to take deep trout on
lighter tackle, it wasn't long before he started using downriggers.
Nelson does his trolling from a small 14 foot boat and uses two
inexpensive downriggers and a vexilar graph unit.

When Nelson Wertman isn't fishing, he is a Prudential
Insurance agent.

Glossary

Appetite Moods: Fish, like people, aren't hungry all the time. They have different feeding habits just as we do. In a *positive mood,* fish are actively feeding and will pursue and strike most lures. At such times even unskilled anglers making sloppy casts with poorly chosen lures will catch some fish. In a *neutral mood,* fish are not actively feeding but will succumb to the proper presentation with the right lure. In a *negative mood,* fish aren't interested in feeding at all but can still be caught if the presentation can prompt an "impulse" strike.

Big Boy: Generally used in denoting large, trophy size fish. However, one should always realize that in all freshwater fish species the largest members are nearly always the females.

Breakoff: The loss of a fish due to breakage of the leader tippet.

Cover: Those certain spots, either man-made or natural, most often near shorelines, where bass and other fish spend considerable time semi-concealed. Examples are boat docks, flooded or blown down trees and weed beds.

Crankbait: A lure that usually floats at rest but dives to varying depths when "cranked" in. Most crankbaits imitate crayfish or baitfish.

Dead Float: A form of fly presentation whereby the fly is allowed to drift along on a slack line with the flow of the stream's current and is affected in its movements only by such current.

Deep Water: A relative term depending on the water depth available and the species of fish sought. For smallmouth bass in the gin clear, super deep Finger Lakes, depths greater than 20 feet can be called deep water.

Depth and Speed Control: Two of the controls an angler has over his lure that most often govern success or failure in catching fish.

Depth Sounder: An electronic "sonar" device that enables anglers to spot schools of fish and underwater structure.

Developing a Good Touch: The acquired sensitivity of an angler to know *exactly* what his lure is doing every second. A good touch is demanded in situations that call for an accurate presentation and in those techniques such as jigging, fluttering spinnerbaits and plastic worm fishing that require intense visual concentration. There are many *good* fishermen that don't possess a good touch, but there are no *great* fishermen without it.

Dry Fly: Imitation of the wide range of both adult aquatic and terrestrial insects which are fished either atop or within the surface film.

Dubbed: Most nymphs and many dry flies are tied using the under hair of certain animals. The long hairs (guard hairs) are removed and the under fur (dubbing) is formed around the tying thread to form a yarn for body wrapping and is then teased with a needle to offer a more natural buggy appearance.

Eliminating Water: The process of fishing areas *correctly*, such that if they produce no fish, eliminating them from further fishing consideration at the moment.

Establishing a Pattern: In a body of water fish are *not* randomly and equally distributed throughout. Fish will concentrate in areas that offer them food, cover protection, good spawning sites, suitable amounts of dissolved oxygen and suitable temperatures. Finding concentrations of fish and determining the most effective techniques to catch them is establishing a pattern.

Feeder Streams: Small tributary headwater streams which are generally spring fed.

Flutter Fishing: The technique of casting a spoon, jig or spinnerbait and allowing the lure to flutter down toward the bottom. A strike on such a free falling lure can be *extremely* subtle and line watching is necessary to detect strikes. Many species of fish can be caught as the lure sinks without imparting any other action to it.

Fly Book: A folding single or multi-leafed case used to store wet flies, streamers/bucktails or nymphs. The cover is of waterproof material and the leaves and/or lining is generally of either clipped sheepskin or thick flannel.

Hatch: A swarming of a particular mayfly variety as an emergence from nymphal stage to adult (dun) stage takes place from the surface film.

Heavy Wire: A fly fishing and fly tying term for the larger diameter fish hooks often used in tying and fishing nymphs and streamers.

Jigging: A broad term describing perhaps the single most effective lure technique for consistently taking smallmouth bass. Jigging can range from the most subtle "Do Nothing" technique made famous by Charlie Brewer, to the rapid and powerful rod movements used to fish spoons and bucktails in deep water.

Jigging Spoon: A short heavy spoon designed to sink quickly and be used to fish in deep water or under tough situations like high winds or heavy current. Examples are the Bomber Slab Spoon, Mannolure and Hopkins Shorty.

Leader Link: A plastic device for quickly and easily connecting the leader butt to the end of a fly line by passing the end of each through opposite end holes and out through the open center, forming a knot in each and pulling tight. The device is made in either plain white or fluorescent orange (as a strike indicator) and floats when fished.

Leader Planing: Because of the extreme difference in diameter and density between a sinking line and its attached leader, the line will sink faster than the leader. Therefore, the longer the leader, the higher it (and the attached fly) will plane. A short leader attached to a sinking line will help maintain a more proper line-to-fly level during both the float and the retrieve.

Line the Boat: To pull and maneuver a boat upstream along the edge of rapids or fast, shallow waters through the use of a rope.

Line Watching: The combination of intense visual concentration teamed with a high visibility monofilament line that is required to identify the often gentle ticks of a softly striking fish. Line watching is an absolute *must* for serious jig, spinnerbait and plastic worm fishing.

Matched Tackle: Tackle that is not only matched to the situation but also to the person using it. As in any endeavor, getting the best equipment one can afford is an investment in enjoyment.

Mend the Line: To reposition the bow in a line, caused by a current's flow, to a reverse bow in order to prevent the line from dragging the fly either down, across or under the surface in an unnatural manner.

Nymph: Imitation of the larval and pupal stages of the various mayfly species or of certain crustaceans (*e.g.,* freshwater shrimp or scuds, sow bugs, *etc.*) which are either tied weighted or tied unweighted but fished weighted *via* fine split shot attached to the leader tippet except for the Floating Nymph which is tied and fished unweighted in or barely beneath the surface film in imitation of the emerging stage of the mayfly.

Operculum: The bony covering protecting the gills of fishes.

Pelagic: A term referring to some saltwater fishes' preference for the open seas, also used in discussing the movements of freshwater trout and salmon in large lakes.

Pink Lady: A deep trolling device that forces a lure down to great depths. When a fish is hooked it will plane back toward the surface as the fish is fought.

Plastic Grubs: A family of plastic baits such as Mister Twisters Meeny Worm, Bass Pro Shops Spring Grub and Manns Stingray Grub that when fished on lead head jigs or used as trailers on spinnerbaits produce excellent results on bass.

Presentation: The method or act of casting or working a fly.

Rainbow Feeders: Lake run rainbow trout will frequent the lower reaches of an inlet stream for a brief time to feed. Such an occurrence may take place either during the spring or fall when water conditions (rising and colored water) prompt such runs.

Reading the Water: Observing an area of water to be fished in light of weather conditions (bright, cloudy, calm, windy, warm, cold, *etc.*), water conditions (temperature, clear, colored, calm, choppy, high, low, *etc.*), structure and obstacles (man-made, natural, in stream, above stream, along stream, *etc.*), aquatic life (type fish, their degree of activity, abundance and types of food source, *etc.*) and the interaction of all five.

Redd: A shallow depression dug in a stream bottom for spawning by salmon and trout.

Riffs (Riffles): Shallow, rapid current passing over an incline of rock and stone resulting in a choppy or bouncing stream flow.

Riprap: The large stones placed in and around riverbanks, marinas, highways and bridges to prevent erosion. These spots make excellent homes for crayfish and baitfish and can be game fish magnets.

Rise: The surfacing of a trout or salmon to take an insect, other food source or an angler's imitation of either. Such rises may range all the way from a subtle bulge producing a slight V-shaped mark on the surface to that spectacular full body leap to either take on the way up, on the way down, or in some instances, to take a free flying insect from above the water's surface.

Searching Pattern: Flies of no specific insect imitation which are designed to entice a trout to rise, *e.g.,* Attractor and Variant flies.

Selective Trout: Those trout which are extremely particular in their feeding habits. Such fish are generally native rather than hatchery trout and are difficult to entice into taking an artificial imitation of its food source.

Slick: A glassy-smooth section of current located at the tail end of a rapids or riffs where the current widens or forms a pool.

Spinnerbait: A single hook, safety pin style spinner that enjoys a nationwide reputation for consistently catching bass and other game fish. These lures are remarkably snagless and weedless in the hands of an expert and can be fished in many ways.

Streamer/Bucktail: Imitation of various minnows, trout fry, sculpins and crayfish tied either weighted or unweighted and using either rooster neck hackle wing material (streamers) or animal hair wing material (bucktails).

Stripping Basket: An open-top container worn in front of the angler and supported by belt or cord around the waist. Such a container is utilized to catch and hold stripped line and thus prevent it from being allowed to float into obstructions or to become knotted by the stream's flow.

Structure: The changes in the lake or river bottom that distinguish one spot from another. Most often the changes include changes in depth and or bottom composition. It has been said that "You can have structure without fish, but you can't have fish without structure." The importance of relating structure to fish cannot be over emphasized.

Suspended Fish: A wide variety of fish spend considerable time suspended at mid-depths between the surface and the bottom. It takes no more effort for a fish to hover suspended 20 feet down in 40 feet of water than it does to lie just off the bottom. Suspended fish often relate to a specific structure situation or a preferred temperature and oxygen comfort zone.

Suspending Lure: A neutral buoyancy crankbait that holds its present level when stopped in its retrieve before continuing.

Team Fishing: Two or more anglers working together using a systematic approach to eliminating as many variables as possible in determining the *best* lure choice, size, color, retrieve speed, depth and technique for the fishing conditions they face.

Technique Fishing: Those specialized aspects of fishing that require a high degree of skill in mastering. Examples are jigging, skittering, flutter fishing, trolling, *etc.*

Thermocline: A condition on some lakes where water will stratify according to different temperatures.

1X, 2X and 3X Tippet: Standard tippet material maximum stress strength for these sizes are, 1X = 5 1/2 pounds, 2X = 4 1/2 pounds and 3X = 3.8 pounds.

Trout Unlimited: A nationwide non-profit organization dedicated to the improvement of this country's trout and salmon fishing and habitat.

Twister Tail: Refer to Plastic Grubs.

Water Color: The presence of turbidity caused by numerous factors such as wind, waves, rain, erosion, pollution or vegetation that affect the clarity of the water.

Wading Staff: A metal or wood walking stick used to maintain balance while while either crossing or moving about within a heavy current stream.

Weighted Line: A fly line designed to sink rather than float. Such lines may be either 1) floating lines with the last 8 or 10 feet being of a fast sinking density (*e.g.*, Orvis Sinking Tip Line), 2) sinking lines with prime density in the forward taper (*e.g.*, Scientific Angler Wet Cel), or 3) weighted shooting head lines with an epoxy connection to a light, generally monofilament, running line (*e.g.*, Cortland Rocket Taper).

Wet Fly: Imitation of a drowned insect and fished just beneath the surface.

Wind Knot: A knot in the leader (generally the tippet section) caused by a combination of faulty casting mechanics and air current whereby the end section of leader loops on itself so as to allow the fly to pass through the loop and thus cause a knot to form. Such a knot tends to weaken the strength of a leader at this point so as to increase the chance of breakage through stress caused in hooking and/or playing (fighting) a fish.